THE PRICE OF OIL

Corporate Responsibility and Human Rights Violations in Nigeria's Oil Producing Communities

Human Rights Watch
New York · Washington · London · Brussels

Printed in the United States of America.

ISBN: 156432-225-4
Library of Congress Catalog Card Number: 99-60123

Addresses for Human Rights Watch
350 Fifth Avenue, 34th Floor, New York, NY 10118-3299
Tel: (212) 290-4700, Fax: (212) 736-1300, E-mail: hrwnyc@hrw.org

1522 K Street, N.W., #910, Washington, DC 20005-1202
Tel: (202) 371-6592, Fax: (202) 371-0124, E-mail: hrwdc@hrw.org

33 Islington High Street, N1 9LH London, UK
Tel: (171) 713-1995, Fax: (171) 713-1800, E-mail: hrwatchuk@gn.apc.org

15 Rue Van Campenhout, 1000 Brussels, Belgium
Tel: (2) 732-2009, Fax: (2) 732-0471, E-mail: hrwatcheu@gn.apc.org

Web Site Address: http://www.hrw.org

Listserv address: To subscribe to the list, send an e-mail message to majordomo@igc.apc.org with "subscribe hrw-news" in the body of the message (leave the subject line blank).

Human Rights Watch is dedicated to
protecting the human rights of people around the world.

We stand with victims and activists to prevent
discrimination, to uphold political freedom, to protect people from inhumane
conduct in wartime, and to bring offenders to justice.

We investigate and expose
human rights violations and hold abusers accountable.

We challenge governments and those who hold power to end abusive practices
and respect international human rights law.

We enlist the public and the international
community to support the cause of human rights for all.

HUMAN RIGHTS WATCH

Human Rights Watch conducts regular, systematic investigations of human rights abuses in some seventy countries around the world. Our reputation for timely, reliable disclosures has made us an essential source of information for those concerned with human rights. We address the human rights practices of governments of all political stripes, of all geopolitical alignments, and of all ethnic and religious persuasions. Human Rights Watch defends freedom of thought and expression, due process and equal protection of the law, and a vigorous civil society; we document and denounce murders, disappearances, torture, arbitrary imprisonment, discrimination, and other abuses of internationally recognized human rights. Our goal is to hold governments accountable if they transgress the rights of their people.

Human Rights Watch began in 1978 with the founding of its Europe and Central Asia division (then known as Helsinki Watch). Today, it also includes divisions covering Africa, the Americas, Asia, and the Middle East. In addition, it includes three thematic divisions on arms, children's rights, and women's rights. It maintains offices in New York, Washington, Los Angeles, London, Brussels, Moscow, Dushanbe, Rio de Janeiro, and Hong Kong. Human Rights Watch is an independent, nongovernmental organization, supported by contributions from private individuals and foundations worldwide. It accepts no government funds, directly or indirectly.

The staff includes Kenneth Roth, executive director; Michele Alexander, development director; Reed Brody, advocacy director; Carroll Bogert, communications director;Cynthia Brown,program director; Barbara Guglielmo, finance and administration director; Jeri Laber special advisor; Lotte Leicht, Brussels office director; Patrick Minges, publications director; Susan Osnos, associate director; Jemera Rone, counsel; Wilder Tayler, general counsel; and Joanna Weschler, United Nations representative. Jonathan Fanton is the chair of the board. Robert L. Bernstein is the founding chair.

The regional directors of Human Rights Watch are Peter Takirambudde, Africa; José Miguel Vivanco, Americas; Sidney Jones, Asia; Holly Cartner, Europe and Central Asia; and Hanny Megally, Middle East and North Africa. The thematic division directors are Joost R. Hiltermann, arms; Lois Whitman, children's; and Regan Ralph, women's.

ACKNOWLEDGMENTS

This report was written by Bronwen Manby, researcher in the Africa Division of Human Rights Watch, based on research in the Niger Delta in July 1997, subsequent correspondence with the major oil companies operating in the region, and information provided by Nigerian human rights and environmental activists. The report was edited by Peter Takirambudde, executive director of the Africa Division; Mike McClintock, deputy program director; and Wilder Tayler, general counsel. Elizabeth Thapliyal, Associate in the Africa Division, prepared the report for production.

Human Rights Watch would like to thank its NGO partners who contributed to the report by assisting our research and providing additional information. In particular, we wish to thank the committed and courageous activists of Environmental Rights Action, without whom the report could not have been written. We would also like to thank all those who agreed to meet with us and be interviewed for the report, especially the many residents of oil producing communities of the Niger Delta.

TABLE OF CONTENTS

I. SUMMARY

This report is an exploration of human rights violations related to oil exploration and production in the Niger Delta, and of the role and responsibilities of the major multinational oil companies in respect of those violations. The Niger Delta has for some years been the site of major confrontations between the people who live there and the Nigerian government security forces, resulting in extra-judicial executions, arbitrary detentions, and draconian restrictions on the rights to freedom of expression, association, and assembly. These violations of civil and political rights have been committed principally in response to protests about the activities of the multinational companies that produce Nigeria's oil. Although the June 1998 death of former head of state Gen. Sani Abacha and his succession by Gen. Abdulsalami Abubakar has brought a significant relaxation in the unprecedented repression General Abacha inflicted on the Nigerian people, and General Abubakar appears committed to ensuring the installation of an elected civilian government in May 1999, human rights abuses in the oil producing communities continue and the basic situation in the delta remains unchanged. As this report went to press, the fatal shooting by security forces of tens of youths demonstrating for the oil companies to withdraw from Nigeria was reported, and the deployment of large numbers of soldiers and navy to the delta to suppress such protests.

Since the death of Abacha, there has been a surge in incidents in which protesters have occupied flow stations and closed production or taken oil workers hostage. In the context of increasing threats to the safety of their workers and of damage to their property, oil companies legitimately require security for their personnel and property; but equally there is an even greater need for companies to ensure that such protection does not result in further human rights abuses. The oil companies share a responsibility to oppose human rights violations by government forces in the areas in which they operate, in addition to preventing abuses by their own employees or contractors. Companies have a duty to avoid both complicity in and advantage from human rights abuses, and a company that fails to speak out when authorities responding to corporate requests for security protection commit human rights abuses will be complicit in those abuses.

Human Rights Watch traveled to the Niger Delta in 1997 to investigate human rights violations in connection with the suppression of protest at oil company activities. We found repeated incidents in which people were brutalized for attempting to raise grievances with the companies; in some cases security forces threatened, beat, and jailed members of community delegations even before they presented their cases. Such abuses often occurred on or adjacent to company property, or in the immediate aftermath of meetings between company officials and individual claimants or community representatives. Many local people seemed to be the object of repression simply for putting forth an interpretation of a compensation agreement, or for seeking effective compensation for land ruined or livelihood lost.

We subsequently corresponded with the five multinationals with the largest share of Nigerian production, asking them to comment on our findings about particular incidents at their facilities, as well as their approach to human rights and community relations in general and their relationships with the Nigerian authorities in respect of security and other issues. This correspondence has continued during 1998. The most ample responses were received from Shell, a Dutch-British company, which has faced the most high profile international focus on its responsibilities in Nigeria. Responses on several cases were also received from Chevron and general information was provided by Mobil: both companies have faced pressure in the U.S., where they are based, concerning corporate responsibility in Nigeria. Elf, headquartered in France, answered most of our questions, though it avoided some, without giving much detail or taking the opportunity to provide background information on its operations; while Agip, an Italian state-owned company, provided an uninformative two page general response to our inquiries and failed to answer many questions. The difficulty that Human Rights Watch, a well known international organization with access to the press worldwide, has had in getting several of the oil companies to pay attention to its concerns appears to be representative of their response to local communities.

In many cases, even where they did respond in connection with particular incidents, companies denied knowledge of government attacks on individuals protesting company action or inaction, or sought to justify security force measures as appropriate responses to threats to company personnel or property. Most of the companies cited in the report failed publicly to criticize security force abuses related to their operations. There were also cases in which witnesses reported that company staff directly threatened, or were present when security force officers threatened communities with retaliation if there were disruption to oil production.

The Role and Responsibilities of the International Oil Companies

The multinational oil companies operating in Nigeria face a difficult political and economic environment, both nationally and at the level of the oil producing communities where their facilities are located. Successive governments have misspent the oil wealth which the oil companies have helped to unlock, salting it away in foreign bank accounts rather than investing in education, health, and other social investment, and mismanaging the national economy to the point of collapse. At the same time, the government has in the past failed to fund its share of the joint ventures operated by the multinationals, and has played the different oil companies against each other so that it has not been easy—even for Shell, the industry giant—to insist that the government contribute towards the investment needed to keep the industry functioning. At the community level, the companies are faced with increasing protests directed at oil company activities and the lack of development in the delta; these have included incidents of hostage-taking, closures of flow stations, sabotage, and intimidation of staff. While the political environment has improved for the oil majors with the death of General Abacha and the succession to the presidency of Gen. Abdulsalami Abubakar, it is unclear what the position will be with the scheduled inauguration of a civilian government in June 1999, and unlikely that relations between the multinationals and the Nigerian government, military or civilian, will ever be entirely smooth.

Acknowledging the difficult context of oil operations in Nigeria does not, however, absolve the oil companies from a share of responsibility for the human rights abuses taking place in the Niger Delta: whether by action or omission they play a role.

In countries characterized by severe human rights violations, like Nigeria, corporations often justify their presence by arguing that their operations will enhance respect for rights, but then adopt no substantive measures to achieve that end. Corporations doing business in these states take on a special obligation to implement proactive steps to promote respect for rights and to ensure that they do not become complicit in violations. The dominant position of the oil companies in Nigeria brings with it a special responsibility in this regard to monitor and promote respect for human rights. Given the overwhelming role of oil in the Nigerian national economy, the policies and practices of the oil companies are important factors in the decision making of the Nigerian government. Because the oil companies are operating joint ventures with the government they have constant opportunities to influence government policy, including with respect to the provision of security for the oil facilities and other issues in the oil producing regions. All the oil companies operating in Nigeria share this responsibility to promote respect for human rights.

In addition to these general responsibilities, the oil companies operating in Nigeria have specific responsibilities in respect of the human rights violations that take place in connection with their operations. These responsibilities must be seen against the context of oil production in Nigeria and the fact that the security provided to keep the oil flowing benefits both the Nigerian government and the oil companies, since disputes which threaten production affect the revenue of both.

Many of the cases investigated by Human Rights Watch which have led to security force abuses concern claims that oil companies have not abided by environmental standards or provided compensation in accordance with the law for damage resulting from oil exploration and production. Other cases concern claims that the oil multinationals have not provided compensation which community members believe to be due to the traditional landholders, although the realities of the Nigerian legal system make it difficult to establish or enforce such an obligation. Often, the Nigerian government effectively entrusts the oil companies themselves to provide the facts on such matters as land claims and valuation, environmental impact assessments, agreed terms of compensation for property and labor, assessment of sabotage, and damage claims. Most negotiations for compensation are bilateral, between the community affected and the oil company concerned, although government structures may play a nominal monitoring role. The process of valuation, negotiation, and payment is therefore in practice controlled almost entirely by the company. The affected communities are in an unequal bargaining position, largely obliged to accept whatever compensation is offered by the companies in such situations. Although there are independent lawyers and environmental groups attempting to monitor oil company compliance with the law and assist the oil communities in pressing their claims, their activities have in the past been seriously hindered by security force harassment, office raids, detentions, and other repressive measures.

Oil companies are legitimately concerned to prevent damage to their facilities and to the environment and to protect their personnel. Security arrangements between the oil companies and the Nigerian government are inevitable, as are internal oil company provisions for security responses in the event of incidents of hostage taking, sabotage, or intimidation. At the same time, the companies emphasize their commitment to avoid violent confrontations between community members and security forces, while underlining a legal obligation to inform the Nigerian authorities when there is a threat to oil production.

However, Human Rights Watch is concerned at the level of secrecy that surrounds the arrangements relating to security for oil installations: not one of the oil companies with which we corresponded responded to our requests to be given access to the parts of the Memorandum of Understanding or Joint Operations Agreement with the Nigerian government governing security, nor to internal guidelines relating to protection of their facilities. Given the abuses that have been committed by the Nigerian security forces in protecting oil installations, most notoriously in Ogoni, it is all the more important that there be transparency in these arrangements and clear commitments from the oil companies to monitor security force performance related to their operations, take steps to prevent abuses, and publicly protest violations that do occur. Yet none of the oil companies publish regular, comprehensive reports of allegations of environmental damage, sabotage, claims for compensation, protest actions, or police or military action carried out on or near their facilities. Often, based on Human Rights Watch's correspondence, the companies claim to be unaware that arrests, detentions and beatings have taken place in the vicinity of their facilities, despite assertions that they are concerned to maintain good relations with the communities where they operate.

Human Rights Watch believes that the oil companies have responsibilities to monitor security force activity in the oil producing region in detail and to take all possible steps to ensure that human rights violations are not committed. These responsibilities are reinforced when the company has itself called for security force intervention, especially by the military or by notoriously abusive forces such as the Mobile Police, or if the company has made payments to the security forces in return for protection. In particular, Human Rights Watch recommends that:

- Companies should include in written agreements with the Nigerian government relating to the regulation of the oil industry, especially any agreements relating specifically to security, provisions requiring state security forces operating in the area of company operations to conform to the human rights obligations the government has assumed under the International Covenant on Civil and Political Rights, the African Charter on Human and Peoples' Rights and other international human rights and humanitarian norms.
- Companies should make public the provisions of their security agreements with state entities and private organizations.
- Companies should insist on screening security force members assigned for their protection, to ensure that no member of the military or police credibly implicated in past human rights abuses is engaged in protecting oil facilities. Companies should similarly screen security staff in their direct employment.
- Companies should investigate abuses that do occur, and make public and private protests to the authorities where excessive force is used, or where arbitrary detentions or other abuses take place. Companies should publish details of such incidents in their annual reports both in Nigeria and in the country of their head office.
- Companies should publicly and privately call on the Nigerian authorities to institute disciplinary or criminal proceedings, as appropriate, against those responsible for abuses and to compensate the victims. Companies should monitor the status of such investigations and press for resolution of the cases, publicly condemning undue delay.

- Companies should adopt internal guidelines surrounding the provision of security for their facilities, emphasizing the need to ensure respect for human rights, and should take disciplinary action against any employee that does not follow such guidelines.

The following sections summarise the background to human rights abuses in the delta, and give examples of particular incidents in which companies have failed to take these steps.

The Oil Industry and the Oil Producing Communities

Nigeria is the largest oil producer in Africa, and the fifth largest in the Organization of Petroleum Exporting Countries (OPEC). The discovery of oil has transformed Nigeria's political economy, and oil has for the past two decades provided approximately 90 percent of foreign exchange earnings, and 80 percent of federal revenue. Nigeria also has huge reserves of natural gas, yet to be fully exploited. Yet, instead of turning Nigeria into one of the most prosperous states on the African continent, these natural resources have enriched a small minority while the vast majority have become increasingly impoverished: with a per capita gross national product of only U.S.$260 a year, Nigeria is one of the poorest countries in the world. At the same time, the struggle among the elite to gain access to the profits of the oil boom has been a factor in the rule of successive military governments: since independence in 1960, Nigeria has enjoyed only ten years of civilian rule, though the current military regime has committed itself to leave office in May 1999. While minority ethnic groups in Nigeria's multi-ethnic federation have successfully demanded that new states and local government units be carved out to fulfil their hopes of receiving some benefit from the oil money and to compensate for the damage done by oil production, the Nigerian federation has in practice, paradoxically, become ever more centralized and power and money has been concentrated in the hands of fewer and fewer people. Politics has become an exercise in organized corruption; a corruption perhaps most spectacularly demonstrated around the oil industry itself, where large commissions and percentage cuts of contracts have enabled individual soldiers and politicians to amass huge fortunes.

The first discovery of commercial quantities of oil in Nigeria was in 1956; today, the country produces approximately two million barrels per day (bpd) of crude oil. Estimates of Nigeria's oil reserves vary from sixteen to twenty-two billion barrels, mostly found in small fields in the coastal areas of the Niger Delta. According to the Nigerian constitution, all minerals, oil, and gas belong to the Nigerian federal government, which negotiates the terms of oil production with international oil companies. Most exploration and production activities in Nigeria are carried out by European and U.S. oil companies operating joint ventures in which the Nigerian National Petroleum Corporation (NNPC), the state oil company, owns 55 or 60 percent; more recent contracts relating to offshore fields have been structured rather as "production sharing contracts" in which the government is not a formal partner. Shell operates a joint venture that produces close to one half of Nigeria's crude production; Mobil, Chevron, Elf, Agip, and Texaco operate other joint ventures, and a range of international and national oil companies operate smaller concessions.

Oil production has had damaging effects on the environment of the oil producing region, though the extent of the damage is subject to dispute. The Niger Delta is one of the world's largest wetlands, and the largest in Africa: it encompasses over 20,000 square kilometers, of which perhaps 6,000 square kilometers is mangrove forest, and has the high biodiversity typical of extensive swamp and forest areas, with many unique species of plants and animals. Despite decades of oil production, there is surprisingly little good quality independent scientific data on the overall or long-term effects of hydrocarbon pollution on the Delta, yet oil-led development has clearly seriously damaged the environment and the livelihood of many of those living in the oil producing communities. The oil companies operating in Nigeria maintain that their activities are conducted to the highest environmental standards; but Nigerian environmental laws, in most respects comparable to their international equivalents, are poorly enforced.

Occasional large oil spills kill fish and agricultural crops, and pollute water, with serious effects for the communities and families affected, especially on dry land or in freshwater swamp zones where spills are contained in a small area. The long-term effect of these major pollution incidents, regular small spills, and effluent deliberately discharged to the environment is largely unevaluated. Poorly designed causeways and canals used by the oil industry affect the hydrology of the seasonally flooded freshwater swamp and the brackish water of the mangrove forest, again killing off crops, destroying fishing grounds, and damaging drinking water supplies. Compensation for such damage is inadequate, and—in the absence of a properly functioning court system—there is no effective recourse to an independent arbiter to determine the value of the damaged property. The oil companies state that many spills are caused by sabotage, and, in accordance with Nigerian law, they pay no compensation in such cases; but the determination that sabotage has occurred is largely left in their own hands, increasing the chances of injustice. At the same time, in an area of Nigeria where there is great pressure on cultivable and habitable land, land is expropriated for oil production under laws which allow no effective due process protections for landholders and only inadequate compensation for the loss of livelihood of those affected. Although the amount of land used for oil production is small, by comparison with the total area of the Niger Delta, the effect on individual landholders can be devastating. The Niger Delta clearly faces many environmental problems that are not the direct responsibility of the oil industry, but these distinctions are irrelevant to those who have their land confiscated or polluted, without receiving compensation to the value of the benefit lost.

While the people of the Niger Delta have faced the adverse effects of oil extraction, they have in general also failed to gain from the oil wealth. The people living in the oil producing communities largely belong to ethnic groups other than the three major groups in Nigeria (Hausa-Fulani, Yoruba, and Igbo), and speak a diverse range of languages and dialects; the largest of these groups are the Ijaw, who collectively form Nigeria's fourth largest ethnic group. Since the creation of the Nigerian state by the British, the peoples of the delta have complained of marginalization by the regional and federal governments who have ruled their affairs. Despite the vast wealth produced from the oil found under the delta, the region remains poorer than the national average; and though in the north of Nigeria poverty is more extreme, the divisions between rich and poor are more obvious in the areas where gas flares light up the night sky.

Nevertheless, oil production itself and oil-based industrial expansion have transformed the local economy, and some in the oil producing communities have benefitted greatly from oil production. Those with full time employment in the oil industry are paid high wages for skilled work, but they are a well-paid minority surrounded by a mass of un- or underemployed; most do not come from the oil producing communities in any event. Contractors to the oil industry, often traditional leaders or those with close links to the military administrations of the oil producing states, also potentially make large amounts of money, often increased by the widescale corruption surrounding the award of contracts for construction and other oil industry projects—from which those in the oil companies in charge of the choice of contractor also benefit. Development spending by the oil companies has also brought schools, clinics, and other infrastructure to remote parts of the country that might otherwise be far more marginalized by the Nigerian government; but many of these projects are inappropriate for the needs of the communities where they are sited, and others are incomplete or shoddily carried out. Although a minority of politicians, traditional leaders and contractors have become rich on the spoils of oil, and hence support the oil industry's activities, the great majority of people from the minority ethnic groups of the oil producing areas have remained impoverished; at the same time, the potential benefits of links to the oil industry have exacerbated conflicts within and among the oil producing communities.

Protest and Repression in the Oil Producing Communities

Anger at the inequities attributed to the oil economy has led increasing numbers of people from the communities in the oil regions to protest the exploitation of what they see as "their" oil—though the constitution provides that all oil is owned by the federal government—without benefit to them or compensation for the damage done to their land and livelihoods. These protests, mostly disorganized and localized, hit the international news headlines during the early 1990s, when the Movement for the Survival of the Ogoni People (MOSOP), led by well-known author Ken Saro-Wiwa, successfully mobilized tens of thousands of Ogonis, an ethnic group of just half a million people occupying a small part of the oil producing region, to protest at the policies of the federal government in relation to the oil wealth, and at the activities of Shell, the oil company that produces almost half of Nigeria's oil. In 1993, Shell was forced to close its production in Ogoni following mass protests at its facilities, citing intimidation of its staff, and the flowstations there remain closed until today, though active pipelines still cross the region. MOSOP's protests provoked a violent and repressive response from the federal government, for which any threat to oil production is a threat to the entire existing political system. Thousands of Ogonis were detained or beaten by the Rivers State Internal Security Task Force, a military body specifically created to suppress the protests organized by MOSOP, and hundreds were summarily executed over a period of several years. In 1994, Ken Saro-Wiwa and several others were arrested in connection with the murder of four traditional leaders in Ogoni. On November 10, 1995, Saro-Wiwa and eight other MOSOP activists were hanged by the military government for those murders, after a trial before a tribunal which blatantly violated international standards of due process and produced no credible evidence that he or the others were involved in the killings for which they were convicted.

Since 1995, no organization has emerged with the cohesion and dynamism of MOSOP, yet protests aimed at oil production take place on a regular basis, and the memory of Ken Saro-Wiwa is respected across the delta. The great majority of these protests are not organized by well-known leadership figures or by recognized political groupings, but by local community members. Many of these protests are never reported, even in the Nigerian national press: only when there is a threat to oil production is reporting guaranteed. Community members demand compensation for use of their land or for oil spills or other environmental damage, employment in oil industry projects, or development projects for their villages.

Many protests are aimed at the government as well as the oil companies and relate to claims for a greater part of the revenue derived from oil to be spent in the oil producing region. Sometimes these demands are made by individuals or families in respect of their own land, sometimes youths who feel excluded from the political system and the benefits of oil wealth organize together and successfully halt production at flow stations in their areas, or prevent construction work going ahead, until the international oil companies have satisfied their demands, or part of them. Sometimes these demands are made by individuals or families in respect of their own land. In other cases, youths who feel excluded from the political system and the benefits of oil wealth join together and successfully halt production at flow stations in their areas, or prevent construction work going ahead, until the international oil companies have satisfied their demands, or part of them. On some occasions there has been damage to property, theft, or intimidation of oil company or contractor staff. Sabotage of oil pipelines does occur, though its extent is disputed between the companies and the communities. Incidents of hostage-taking have recently increased, with some of these cases involving attempts to extort money from the oil companies.

In the face of the threat to oil production caused by some of these protests, the Nigerian government has created a number of special task forces handling security in the oil producing areas, of which the most notorious and brutal is the Rivers State Internal Security Task Force, created in response to the Ogoni crisis. Like many other states, those in the delta have also created anti-crime task forces: Operation Flush in Rivers State and Operation Salvage in Bayelsa state have been active in the oil regions. The paramilitary Mobile Police, deployed throughout Nigeria, are also active in the delta; and on occasion, the navy is used to maintain order in the riverine areas. From their side, the oil companies operating in Nigeria hire "supernumerary police," recruited and trained by the Nigerian police force, but paid for by the oil companies. They are supposed to operate only within the perimeter fence of oil facilities. Some of these police are armed, though Shell states that most working on its behalf are not; some operate in plain clothes. In addition, the oil companies state that they hire private firms for routine security provision at entrance barriers and other duties at their premises; and local "guards" hired from among landholders across whose land pipelines run or where other facilities are built.

Nigeria's new head of state, Gen. Abdulsalami Abubakar, has greatly reduced the repression enforced by his predecessor, Gen. Sani Abacha, who died in June 1998, releasing many political prisoners and relaxing restrictions on freedom of expression, assembly and association throughout Nigeria. The government has withdrawn the Internal Security Task Force from Ogoni. Many Ogoni exiles have been able to return, and MOSOP has been able to hold rallies once again. Nevertheless, the response of the security forces to threats to oil production continues to be heavy handed, and in the oil regions human and environmental rights activists report little change. On December 30, 1998, soldiers shot dead at least seven youths protesting in Yenagoa, the capital of Bayelsa State; the following morning, eight others were reported killed, and over the following days a crackdown continued that was still ongoing as this report went to press.

In virtually every community, there have been occasions on which the paramilitary Mobile Police, the regular police, or the army, have beaten, detained, or even killed those involved in protests, peaceful or otherwise, or individuals who have called for compensation for oil damage, whether youths, women, children, or traditional leaders. In some cases, members of the community are beaten or detained indiscriminately, irrespective of their role in any protest. Under the government of General Abacha, activists from human and environmental organizations, especially from political movements attempting to organize resistance to oil company abuses, faced regular harassment from the authorities. While this situation has eased in recent months, the decrees are still in force that allow detention without trial and establish special tribunals to try cases of "civil disturbances" or sabotage without due process protections.

Human Rights Watch investigated a number of cases of protest against oil company activity that have taken place since the 1995 trial and execution of Ken Saro-Wiwa and his eight codefendants, during a one-month visit to the Niger Delta during July 1997 and in subsequent research. The cases we investigated can be grouped under two broad thematic headings. On the one hand, there are those incidents where community members have claimed that operations of oil companies have damaged the material interests of the peoples of the areas in which they operate and have not compensated fully for that damage. The incidents involve disputes over legal obligations to provide compensation for claims of damage, for encroachment on community land or waters, or for access rights, though claims are often couched in terms of community rights to a "fair share" of the oil wealth derived from their land. Accordingly, community members have made demands for compensation for oil company activities, whether in the form of cash payments following spillages or land expropriation, development projects in communities close to oil installations, or employment of local community members as casual laborers when work is being carried out in the vicinity. On the other, there are cases of harassment and apparently untargeted assaults upon community members that are a general consequence of the deployment of security personnel to provide protection for oil operations.

In the worst cases, people have been killed by the paramilitary Mobile Police or other security responding to threats to oil production. In May 1998, two youths were killed on Chevron's Parabe Platform, off Ondo State, by members of the security forces transported to the platform by Chevron to remove two hundred protesters who had closed down production. The protesters had demanded compensation for environmental damage caused by canals cut for Chevron which opened local waterways to the sea. Frequently, protesters are beaten and arbitrarily detained, for periods ranging from hours to weeks or months; sometimes individuals are detained who simply go to oil company or contractors' premises asking for compensation for works being carried out. In one case in 1997, landholders interviewed by Human Rights Watch had been detained overnight and released without charge following a spill on their land which Elf alleged had been caused by sabotage. They had apparently been held on suspicion that they had caused the sabotage despite the lack of evidence to this effect and the uncompensated damage caused to their crops. Following a major Mobil oil spill in January 1998, up to three hundred people who demanded compensation were reportedly detained; in July, further protests over damage done by the spill and delays in compensation payments led to disturbances in which eleven people were reportedly shot dead by police. As this report went to press, the fatal shooting of tens of Ijaw youths calling for the oil companies to withdraw from Nigeria was reported, together with the deployment of thousands of troops to the Niger Delta region.

The Role of Shell in the Ogoni Crisis

The role of Shell in Nigeria has received by far the most attention internationally, for three reasons: first, because it is the biggest oil producer in Nigeria with the longest history, dominating the industry for as long as oil has been produced and in the early days enjoying a monopoly and a privileged relationship with government; secondly, because Shell's facilities are largely onshore, in or near inhabited areas and thus exposed to community protests; and thirdly, because it formed the main target of the campaign by MOSOP, which accused the company of complicity in what it alleged was the genocide of the Ogoni people.

During the height of the Ogoni crisis, allegations of Shell collaboration with the military were regularly made, even after the company ceased production from its flow stations in Ogoni in January 1993. A document alleged to be a leaked government memorandum from 1994 implicated Shell in planned "wasting operations" by the Rivers State Internal Security Task Force, stating that the oil companies should pay the costs of the operations. The head of the Task Force several times publicly claimed to be acting so that Shell's oil production could resume. Former Ogoni members of the Shell police have claimed that they were involved in deliberately creating conflict between different groups of people, and in intimidating and harassing protesters during the height of the MOSOP protests in 1993 and 1994; Ogoni detainees have also alleged that they were detained and beaten by Shell police during the same period. Nigerian environmental and human rights activists in the delta also allege that Shell (and other companies) continue to make payments of field allowances to soldiers deployed to its facilities.

Shell has denied all such allegations, and distanced itself from statements by government or security officials calling for repressive responses to protests, while stating that the company had repeatedly expressed its concerns "over the violence and heavy handedness both sides on the Ogoni issue have displayed from time to time." Shell also denied any collusion with the authorities. However, Shell has since admitted having made direct payments to the Nigerian security forces, on at least one occasion in 1993, under duress. Under great public pressure, both inside and outside Nigeria, to intervene on behalf of the accused during the trial and following the conviction of the "Ogoni Nine," Shell wrote to Gen. Abacha pleading for commutation of the death sentences against Ken Saro-Wiwa and his co-accused on humanitarian grounds, but did not make any comment on the unfairness of their trial.

Shell states that its production in Ogoni remains closed, but that it has made attempts to open negotiations with the communities involved in order to resume production, and to undertake development projects aimed at resolving some of the problems faced by the Ogoni. Community members, on the other hand, reported that, while it was still deployed, the Rivers State Internal Security Task Force forced individuals to sign statements "inviting" Shell to return. Shell has also stated at various times over the last few years that it has opened negotiations with MOSOP representatives, though spokespeople for MOSOP have denied this, and challenged Shell's statements that its presence in Ogoni is limited to provision of social programs and attempts to arrange a reconciliation with the Ogoni people, claiming that Shell staff have on occasion entered Ogoni with security force protection to work on pipelines. MOSOP remains opposed to the reopening of Shell's production in Ogoni, stating that the company should "clean up or clear out" by Ogoni Day, January 4, 2000.

Attempts to Import Weapons

During 1996, newspaper investigations revealed that Shell had recently been in negotiation for the import of arms for use by the Nigerian police. In January 1996, in response to these allegations, Shell stated that it had in the past imported side arms on behalf of the Nigerian police force, for use by the "supernumerary police" who are on attachment to Shell and guard the company's facilities (and other oil company facilities) against general crime. The last purchase of weapons by Shell was said to be of 107 hand guns for its supernumerary police, fifteen years before. But court papers filed in Lagos in July 1995 and reported in the British press in February 1996 revealed that Shell had as late as February 1995 been negotiating for the purchase of weapons for the Nigerian police. Shell acknowledged that it had conducted these negotiations but stated that none of the purchases had been concluded. However, the company stated to Human Rights Watch that it "cannot give an undertaking not to provide weapons in the future, as, due to the deteriorating security situation in Nigeria, we may want to see the weapons currently used by the Police who protect Shell people and property upgraded."

Threats to Community Members

During its investigation of the situation in the delta during July 1997, Human Rights Watch heard disturbing allegations of three separate meetings, two in connection with the same matter, at which eyewitnesses interviewed by Human Rights Watch alleged that Shell staff, or military authorities in the presence of Shell staff had directly threatened community members, using the situation in Ogoni as an example. Two of these meetings had occurred only days before Human Rights Watch interviewed the people present; the third dated back two years, to the period of Ken Saro-Wiwa's trial. In another case, a youth was assaulted by Mobile Police at Elf's Obite gas project, and then threatened by a manager with C&C Construction, a contractor working at the project owned by the Lebanese Chagoury family, which was close to General Abacha. When he refused to withdraw a legal complaint he brought for the assault, despite recommendations that he should "learn the lessons from the Saro-Wiwa trial," armed men from the State Security Service came to look for him, and he fled several days later to Togo. Since returning to Nigeria several months later, he has been detained several times.

Oil Company Failure to Monitor or Protest Abuses

The most serious case in which an oil company is directly implicated in security force abuses continues to be the incident at Umuechem in 1990, where a Shell manager made a written and explicit request for protection from the Mobile Police (a notoriously abusive force), leading to the killing of eighty unarmed civilians and the destruction of hundreds of homes. Shell states that it has learned from the "regrettable and tragic" incident at Umuechem, so that it would now never call for Mobile Police protection and emphasizes the need for restraint to the Nigerian authorities. Nevertheless, in several of the incidents investigated by Human Rights Watch, oil companies, including Shell, or their contractors, called for security force protection in the face of protests from youths, taking no steps to ensure that such protection was provided in a non-abusive way and making no protests when violations occurred.

In July 1997, youths from Edagberi, Rivers State, for example, were detained overnight following a written complaint to the local police station by Alcon Engineering, a contractor to Shell. While it is claimed by Shell that the youths concerned had been engaged in the intimidation of its contractor, and therefore that security force intervention was appropriate, no safeguards were sought to ensure that such intervention was made in a non-abusive manner. Similarly, at Yenezue-Gene, Rivers State, where Shell faces community hostility caused by the construction of a causeway to its Gbaran oil field which had devastated a forest area of great economic importance to local residents, soldiers present at the site had harassed local community members during 1996 and 1997. Shell stated to Human Rights Watch that its contractors had called for police (though not army) assistance, "due to community hostilities." Shell did not report, in response to Human Rights Watch inquiries, that any guarantees had been sought for the good behavior of these police; the company was also unaware of reports of abusive behavior by security forces that community members stated had been made to local Shell personnel.

In an August 1995 incident at Iko, Akwa Ibom State, a community where a defective flare (used to burn off gas released at a well-head) had caused significant damage, Shell's contractor Western Geophysical stated that it had requested naval assistance to recover boats taken by youths who wanted to obtain benefits from the contractor, including employment. Following the naval intervention, Mobile Police came to the village and assaulted numerous villagers, beating to death a teacher who had acted as an interpreter in negotiations between Western Geophysical and the community. Shell has stated to Human Rights Watch that it does not call for military protection, but justified calling the navy in this case due to the terrain; it stated that the Mobile Police had been called by the navy and not by Shell or its contractor. In its detailed response Shell did not report that the company or its contractor had made any attempt to protest the Mobile Police action, simply reporting that "this incident is unrelated to Western's seismic activities."

In May 1998, when Chevron's Parabe platform was occupied by approximately 200 youths and production shut down, Chevron acknowledged that it had called for navy intervention, and that the company had flown the navy and Mobile Police to the platform. Despite the serious result of this action, including the shooting dead of two protesters whom it admitted were unarmed, Chevron did not indicate, in response to inquiries from Human Rights Watch, that any attempt had been made to prevent abusive actions by the security forces in advance of the confrontation. Nor did it state that concern had been expressed to the authorities over the incident or that any steps would be taken to avoid similar incidents in future. Chevron's response concerning an earlier case involving a Chevron facility in which a youth was killed by Mobile Police in July 1997 at Opuama, Bayelsa State, similarly included nothing to indicate that it had raised human rights concerns with the authorities over the incident.

Calling for security force protection increases the responsibility of the oil company to ensure that intervention does not result in human rights violations; but even if the security forces have acted on their behalf without a specific company request for assistance companies cannot be indifferent to resulting abuse. Yet in the great majority of cases the oil companies do not report any attempt to monitor or protest human rights violations by the security forces against those who have raised concerns about environmental problems, requested financial compensation or employment, protested oil company activity, or threatened oil production. In a handful of high-profile cases of detention, one or two oil companies have, under consumer pressure in Europe and the U.S., made public statements, but the great majority go unremarked. In none of the cases of abuse researched by Human Rights Watch which had not reached the international press did any of the oil companies indicate that they had registered concern with the authorities. In the cases reviewed, it was generally only after the behavior of the Nigerian authorities had embarrassed the oil companies on the international stage that action of any kind ensued on behalf of those who were abused by the security forces. In other cases, the oil companies said they were ignorant of arrests or beatings that had occurred, although some concerned quite major incidents at their facilities.

Shell, for example, denied knowledge of detentions that took place following major disturbances during June and July 1995 at Egbema, Imo State, during which Mobile Police carried out indiscriminate beatings and arrested more than thirty people, detaining them for several weeks without trial, before releasing them on bail charged with sabotage. Instead, Shell stated that the disputes at that time had been "amicably settled," through negotiations between the community and the military administration. Elf denied to Human Rights Watch that it knew of the beating and detention of an activist at its Obite gas project in October 1998. Agip, when asked about the case of a youth beaten to death by security guards at its Clough Creek flow station, near Egbemo-Angalabiri, did not even respond to community representations nor to inquiries from Human Rights Watch. When several hundred people were arrested following demonstrations over a January 12, 1998 spill from an offshore pipeline near its Qua Iboe terminal, Mobil did publicly distance itself from the arrests, but did not indicate that any protests had been made to the authorities, stating to reporters in Lagos: "It is a security issue. It is nothing to do with Mobil at all."

Shell's Internal Review Since 1995

Since the international focus on its Nigerian holdings in 1995, the Royal Dutch/Shell group has undertaken a major review of its attitude toward communities and issues of human rights and sustainable development. No other oil company operating in Nigeria has, so far as Human Rights Watch is aware, announced any similar review of its policies and practices as a they relate to human rights violations committed in connection with oil company operations. While we welcome this introspection, the test of its effectiveness in changing Shell's practice can only be gauged by its performance on the ground in countries like Nigeria. It is too soon to tell whether this performance will be changed.

Conclusion

There can be no solution to the simmering conflict in the oil producing areas of the delta until its people gain the right to participate in their own governance and until the protection of the rule of law is extended to their communities. The injustices facing the peoples of the delta are in many ways the same as those facing all Nigerians after decades of rule by successive military regimes, yet in the oil producing regions the suppression of political activity, the lack of legal redress for damage to the environment and the resulting loss of livelihood, and the sheer ubiquity of human rights abuses by the region's security forces have generated greater protest, in turn generating greater repression. While the death of General Abacha and the succession of General Abubakar has recently improved respect for human rights and fundamental freedoms in Nigeria, the situation in the delta remains fundamentally unchanged—as the recent escalation of protest actions has demonstrated.

The first responsibility for resolving these injustices lies with the Nigerian government. Yet the multinational oil companies operating in Nigeria cannot avoid their own share of responsibility. It is not enough simply to say that the political environment in Nigeria is as difficult for the oil companies as it is for anyone else, and that the oil industry does not have the power to alter government policy towards the oil regions: the oil companies in many respects contribute towards the discontent in the delta and to conflict within and between communities that results in repressive government responses. The oil companies must take all steps to ensure that oil production does not continue at the cost of their host communities simply because of the threat or actual use of force against those who protest their activities. There is an ever-growing likelihood that, unless corrective action is taken, protest in the oil areas will become violent in an organized and concerted way, with consequent reprisals and an ever-worsening security situation that will harm all those with interests in the delta region, whether residents or companies.

II. RECOMMENDATIONS

To the Nigerian Government

- Ensure that the ethnic groups resident in the oil producing areas are able to make their voices heard within Nigeria's political system.
- Respect the rights of those in the oil producing communities to freedom of expression, association and assembly.
- Cease harassment of individuals and organizations that engage in research into oil industry compliance with environmental and other international and industry standards, and of activists seeking to hold oil operators and their contractors to these standards.
- Immediately and unconditionally release—or release on bail, charge with legally recognizable criminal offenses and try promptly before a regular court respecting international standards of due process—all individuals who are arbitrarily detained or imprisoned, and repeal decrees enabling detention without charge, including Decree No. 2 of 1984.
- Ensure that conditions of detention and imprisonment are in full compliance with international standards and obey all court orders for individuals held in custody to be released, produced before court, allowed visitors, given access to lawyers or doctors of their choice, removed to hospital when a prison or personal doctor recommends, or permitted reading material.
- Restore the independence of the judiciary by instituting appointment and removal procedures that do not involve the executive, giving the judiciary and courts adequate financial resources and autonomy, repealing decrees that oust the jurisdiction of the courts to consider executive acts, and obeying court orders.
- Allow members of the Movement for the Survival of the Ogoni People (MOSOP) and of other organizations formed to challenge the operations of the oil industry in Nigeria to organize, meet and express their views, in accordance with international standards.
- Allow freedom of association and protection of the right to organize in accordance with Convention 87 of the International Labor Organization (ILO), and repeal decrees restricting these rights.
- Appoint an independent judicial inquiry into the actions of the security forces in the oil producing areas, make public the findings of the inquiry, and bring to trial those alleged to be responsible for human rights abuses.
- Appoint an independent judicial inquiry into the situation in Ogoni, including the role of Shell staff and contractors, as well as the security forces, in past

human rights violations, and bring to trial those alleged to be responsible for human rights abuses.

- Set up a process for paying compensation to the relatives of the Ogoni activists executed on November 10, 1995, in accordance with the recommendations of the fact-finding mission of the U.N. secretary-general and the U.N. special rapporteur on the situation of human rights in Nigeria.
- Establish a committee composed of representatives of minority communities in the oil producing regions (including the Ogoni) for the purpose of examining the situation of these communities and providing redress for rights that have been violated, in accordance with the recommendations of the fact-finding mission of the U.N. secretary-general, the U.N. Committee on Economic, Social and Cultural Rights, and the U.N. special rapporteur on the situation of human rights in Nigeria.
- Undertake a review of laws affecting the relations of oil companies with the communities in which they operate, including the Land Use Act, the Petroleum Production and Distribution (Anti-Sabotage) Act, the Petroleum Decree and its subsidiary legislation, and other laws regulating payment of compensation for damage to livelihoods caused by oil operations, with a view to ensuring that those adversely affected are adequately compensated and protected by due process of law.
- Take the necessary legislative or other steps to require all oil companies operating in Nigeria.
- To publish all details relating to security arrangements for the protection of oil facilities and to ensure that all security staff employed by the company, including "supernumerary police" seconded from the Nigerian police force, are trained in human rights standards. Establish effective monitoring systems to ensure that these standards are followed and that criminal proceedings, if appropriate, are instituted where they are violated.
- To publish all documents relating to payments, gifts or contracts in relation to operations in the oil producing communities, including payments of compensation for oil spillages.
- To carry out a "human rights impact assessment," identifying in particular problems related to security provision and conflict resolution, in addition to the already required "environmental impact assessment," to develop plans to avoid the problems identified by such assessments, and to cancel the project if they cannot be avoided.
- To ensure the widest possible consultation of the people who will be affected by oil installations in their planning, and the greatest possible transparency in

what is planned, so that oil operations have the consent of those who will suffer their negative consequences.

To the International Oil Companies Operating in Nigeria

- Develop guidelines on making or maintaining investments in or withdrawing from countries where there is a pattern of ongoing and systematic violation of human rights.
- Adopt explicit company policies in support of human rights; establish procedures to ensure that company activities do not result in human rights abuses; and publish annual reports to shareholders on the company's activities in Nigeria, including information on the nature and extent of the company's relations with the Nigerian government and measures taken to prevent human rights abuses by the Nigerian security forces in the oil producing areas.
- Jointly establish a committee of the Oil Producers Trade Section of the Lagos Chamber of Commerce which will monitor the human rights situation in the oil producing communities and make public and private protests to the Nigerian government when violations occur.
- In addition, as individual companies, appoint specific high ranking corporate officials responsible for monitoring in detail respect for human rights in the oil producing communities, publicly and privately call on the Nigerian government to restrain the use of armed force in oil producing areas, condemn human rights abuses by Nigerian security forces in the areas where the companies are operating, both in general and in specific cases, and make clear that activities undertaken in defense of oil company installations must be in accordance with international human rights principles.
- Include in written agreements with the Nigerian government relating to the regulation of the oil industry, especially any agreements relating specifically to security, provisions requiring state security forces operating in the area of company operations to conform to the human rights obligations the government has assumed under the International Covenant on Civil and Political Rights, the African Charter on Human and Peoples' Rights and other international human rights and humanitarian norms.
- Make public the provisions of security agreements with state entities and private organizations.
- Insist on screening security force members assigned for their protection, to ensure that no member of the military or police credibly implicated in past human rights abuses is engaged in protecting oil facilities. Companies should similarly screen security staff in their direct employment.

- Ensure that all security staff employed by or assigned to the company, including "supernumerary police" seconded from the Nigerian police force, are trained in human rights standards, providing the same training to all those within the company authorized to have contact with the Nigerian authorities in connection with security threats to oil installations.
- Investigate all reported abuses, and make public and private protests to the authorities where excessive force is used, or where arbitrary detentions or other abuses take place. Publish details of reported incidents and the findings of internal investigations in their annual reports both in Nigeria and in the country of their head office.
- Publicly and privately call on the Nigerian authorities to institute disciplinary or criminal proceedings, as appropriate, against those responsible for abuses and to compensate the victims. Companies should monitor the status of such investigations and press for resolution of the cases, publicly condemning undue delay.
- Adopt internal guidelines surrounding the provision of security for their facilities, emphasizing the need to ensure respect for human rights, and establish effective monitoring systems to ensure that these guidelines are followed and that disciplinary proceedings are instituted where they are violated.
- When new facilities or investments are planned, carry out a "human rights impact assessment," identifying in particular problems related to security provision and conflict resolution, in addition to the legally required "environmental impact assessment," and develop plans to avoid the problems identified by such assessments. If they cannot be avoided, cancel the project.
- Ensure the widest possible consultation of the people who will be affected by oil installations in their planning, and the greatest possible transparency in what is planned, to ensure that oil operations have the consent of those who will suffer their negative consequences.
- In the case of Shell, publicly and privately call for and cooperate with an independent judicial inquiry into the situation in Ogoni, including the role of Shell staff and contractors, as well as the security forces, in past human rights violations.
- Publicly and privately call on the Nigerian government to establish an independent judicial inquiry into the actions of the security forces in the oil producing areas, including security specifically posted to oil installations, and to bring to trial those alleged to be responsible for violent abuses, and fully cooperate with such an inquiry and prosecutions.

- Publicly and privately call on the Nigerian government to allow freedom of assembly, association and expression, in particular with respect to grievances directed against the oil industry and in accordance with ILO Convention 87, and protest particular cases where these rights are not respected.
- Publicly and privately call on the Nigerian government to release unconditionally all those detained for exercising their rights to freedom of expression, assembly and association, especially in the oil producing communities, and to ensure fair and prompt trials before independent tribunals for all those charged with criminal offences.
- Make public all documents relating to payments, gifts or contracts relating to operations in the oil producing communities, including payments of compensation for oil spillages.
- Ensure that oil operations are carried out in accordance with all local environmental legislation in force in Nigeria, or with international standards if they are higher.
- Support the development of civil society in Nigeria by cooperating with nongovernmental organizations for human rights and environmental research and advocacy, and with universities and institutes engaged in academic research and policy development in these areas.
- Provide access to company facilities, officials, and documentation relevant to the protection and promotion of human rights, to personnel of domestic and international nongovernmental human rights and environmental organizations.
- Review programs of community assistance to ensure that development projects are planned by people who are professionally trained, that all members of communities can participate in devising development plans—and not only elites who already have good relations with the oil industry, and that projects genuinely address the needs of the people in those communities. Consider establishing independent, professionally administered bodies for the implementation of development projects.
- Develop and publicize policies to provide compensation to victims of human rights abuse committed by the Nigerian security forces or oil company private security either at oil company facilities or in connection with protests at oil company activity. Consider establishing independently and professionally administered funds for this purpose.
- Arrange independently funded verification, by national and international nongovernmental organizations and other appropriate bodies, of compliance by the company with international human rights and environmental standards.

To the International Community

- Maintain existing sanctions in place until an elected civilian government is installed in Nigeria, following a transition program that complies with international standards, set clear benchmarks that must be observed to satisfy those standards, and make clear that additional sanctions may be implemented (including the restoration of visa restrictions against members of the government and security forces and other measures), both multilaterally and bilaterally, if such a program is not successfully completed.
- Develop U.N. guidelines on the conduct of multinational companies, including oil companies, as regards human rights and other international standards, based on the draft U.N. Code of Conduct on Transnational Corporations, the ILO Tripartite Declaration of Principles Concerning Multinational Enterprises and Social Policy, and other appropriate standards.
- Re-establish within the U.N. system a commission on transnational corporations with a mandate to examine the human rights implications of activities by multinational companies.
- Support the efforts of Nigerian individuals and nongovernmental organizations who are monitoring and protesting violations of environmental and human rights standards in the oil producing communities, by channeling development assistance to them and by raising concerns surrounding these issues publicly and privately with the Nigerian government and the multinational oil companies directly.
- Take steps to coordinate action by different international actors to monitor and promote respect for human rights in Nigeria, including the U.N., Commonwealth, OAU, E.U., U.S., individual E.U. member states and other countries.

III. OIL AND NATURAL GAS IN NIGERIA

Crude Oil

The first discovery of commercial quantities of oil in Nigeria was in 1956 at Oloibiri, about ninety kilometers west of Port Harcourt in what is now Bayelsa State; other discoveries soon followed and exports began in 1958, although significant quantities only began to flow from 1965, with the completion of a terminal on Bonny Island, on the Atlantic coast, and pipelines to feed the terminal. Following a drop in production due to the civil war of 1967 to 1970, output rose rapidly from 1970, and by 1974 oil revenues constituted over 80 percent of total federal revenues and over 90 percent of export earnings, figures which have remained similar since then. In 1980, when oil export revenues peaked at U.S.$24.9 billion, external indebtedness had reached U.S.$9 billion, oil accounted for 27 percent of Gross Domestic Product (GDP), about 80 percent of government revenues and expenditures, and 96 percent of total export receipts.[1] Today, the petroleum sector comprises more than 40 percent of GDP, continuing to provide more than 95 percent of exports.[2]

Estimates of Nigeria's oil reserves range from 16 billion to 22 billion barrels.[3] Most of this oil is found in small fields in the coastal areas of the Niger Delta (according to the Ministry of Petroleum Resources, there are 159 oil fields, producing from 1,481 wells).[4] As a result, there is a need for a developed network of pipelines between the fields, as well as for constant exploration to augment existing oil reserves. Nigerian crude is classified as "light" and "sweet," with a low sulphur content, similar in quality to North Sea varieties, and its price is linked to the price for Brent. Average operational costs in Nigeria are around U.S.$2.50 a barrel, higher than the Persian Gulf, but lower than the Gulf of Mexico and the North Sea; other local expenses, including the payment of kickbacks to government officials and other corruption, are estimated to push costs up by another U.S.$1.00

---

[1] Sarah Ahmed Khan, *Nigeria: The Political Economy of Oil* (Oxford: Oxford University Press, 1994), p.189; Tom Forrest, *Politics and Economic Development in Nigeria* (Boulder, Colorado: Westview Press, 1995), p.133.

[2] *Nigeria: Selected Issues and Statistical Appendix,* IMF Staff Country Report No.98/78 (Washington DC: International Monetary Fund, August 1998), pp.6 to 11.

[3] U.S. Energy Information Administration (U.S. EIA), "Nigeria Country Analysis Brief," December 1997.

[4] Environmental Resources Managers Ltd, *Niger Delta Environmental Survey Final Report Phase I; Volume I: Environmental and Socio-Economic Characteristics* (Lagos: Niger Delta Environmental Survey, September 1997), p.195.

a barrel.[5] Nigerian crude oil production averaged 2.21 million barrels per day (bpd) for the first nine months of 1997, half a million barrels per day above the country's 1.865 million bpd quota set by the Organization of Petroleum Exporting Countries (OPEC). Nigeria's quota rose to 2.042 million bpd in 1998 as a result of the OPEC meeting of November 1997; but, with the collapse of the oil price early in the year, Nigeria promised to cut back production by 125,000 bpd from April 1998, in line with an OPEC agreement attempting to halt the downward trend in prices.[6] In July 1998, the oil multinationals operating in Nigeria were given an order to cut a further 100,000 bpd, in accordance with another OPEC ruling.[7] Nonetheless, output of 2.3 million bpd was reported in March 1998, and Minister of Petroleum Resources Dan Etete was said to have set a target of 3 million bpd by 2002 and 4 million bpd by 2010.[8] This oil is exported mainly to the U.S. and Western Europe. Nigeria is the fifth largest supplier of crude to the U.S., sending an average of 699,000 bpd during the first nine months of 1997, or approximately 30 percent of its output.[9]

The Structure of Oil Company Agreements with the Nigerian Government

According to the Nigerian constitution, all minerals, oil, and gas in Nigeria belong to the federal government.[10] Nigeria did not have sufficient indigenous

---

[5] Jonathan Bearman, "Squandered Inheritance," *Financial Times* (London), June 7, 1998.

[6] U.S. EIA, "Nigeria Country Analysis Brief"; Reuters, March 31, 1998.

[7] Radio Nigeria (government radio), July 3, 1998, as reported by the BBC Summary of World Broadcasts (SWB), July 7, 1998.

[8] Bearman, "Squandered Inheritance"; "Minister on Oil Situation, Processing Oil Abroad," Lagos NTA Television Network May 19, 1998 as reported by the U.S. Foreign Broadcast Information Service (FBIS), May 20, 1998.

[9] U.S. EIA, "Nigeria Country Analysis Brief."

[10] Article 40(3) of the 1979 constitution, Article 42(3) of the 1989 constitution, and Article 47(3) of the draft 1995 constitution (echoing similar provisions in previous Nigerian constitutions, and the situation prior to independence) each provide that: "the entire property in and control of all minerals, mineral oils and natural gas in, under or upon any land in Nigeria or in under or upon the territorial waters and the Exclusive Economic Zone of Nigeria shall vest in the Government of the Federation and shall be managed in such matter as may be prescribed by the National Assembly." The 1979 constitution, which was drafted during the process of the first military handover to civilian rule, was suspended by the military coup of 1984. The 1989 constitution was drafted in the course of a subsequent transition program, implemented by Gen. Ibrahim Babangida. It was brought into force by the Constitution of the Federal Republic of

expertise at the time oil was discovered to develop the oil reserves itself, and in all likelihood still does not. In this context, the federal government negotiates the terms of oil production with international oil companies, and takes a proportion of the revenue generated. Since independence in 1960, and in concert with the resolutions of the Organization of Petroleum Exporting Countries (OPEC),[11] the government has steadily increased both its control over and the degree of competition within Nigerian oil production.

From 1914, the date of the Colonial Mineral Ordinance, the first oil related legislation in the new colonial state of Nigeria, the grant of licenses for oil production was restricted to British companies and individuals. In 1937, the Shell D'Arcy company, jointly owned by Shell and by British Petroleum (B.P.), was given exclusive exploration and production rights in the whole of Nigeria. This monopoly was maintained until 1955, when the concession area was reduced and Mobil entered the field for the first time. In 1960, Nigeria gained independence from Britain; by 1962, Shell's concession areas had been further reduced, to the most promising areas, and other companies also began exploration. By the mid-1960s, Gulf Oil (now Chevron), Elf, and Agip were all involved in production. In 1959, still under colonial rule, the Petroleum Profits Tax Ordinance introduced a fifty-fifty profit share between the oil companies and the government; in 1967, the government imposed OPEC terms on the companies operating in Nigeria, ensuring that much greater royalties were paid.[12] The 1968 Companies Decree forced all companies operating in Nigeria to become Nigerian corporations; the 1969 Petroleum Decree further increased state control of the industry, and remains the basis for the regulatory system in operation today. The 1970s saw partial nationalization of the industry, as the Nigerian government took an equity stake in

---

Nigeria (Promulgation) Decree No.12 of 1992 and was suspended by the Constitution (Suspension and Modification) Decree No.107 of 1993, which restored the 1979 constitution in general, while suspending certain guarantees set out in the bill of rights. The draft 1995 constitution was prepared by a constitutional conference meeting in 1994 and 1995 as part of the discredited transition program of General Abacha. It was finally published by General Abubakar in September 1998, and a committee appointed to receive public submissions and make recommendations as to its amendment and adoption. The committee was given until December 31, 1998 to report to the government on its recommendations, and ultimately recommended the readoption of the 1979 constitution with a number of amendments.

[11] Nigeria first attended an OPEC conference as an observer in 1964, and joined the organization in 1971. Khan, *Nigeria*, pp.16-18.

[12] Scott R. Pearson, *Petroleum and the Nigerian Economy* (Stanford: University of California Press, 1970), pp.24-26.

the oil industry, raising its participation in most companies from 35 percent in 1971, to 55 percent in 1974, and 60 percent in 1979.[13]

The main onshore exploration and production activities undertaken today by foreign oil companies in Nigeria are in joint ventures with the Nigerian National Petroleum Corporation (NNPC), the state oil company.[14] The distribution of shares in a joint venture determines the division of investment in all capital projects carried out by the operating company, including exploration, drilling, construction, or environmental improvements; the participating shareholders also jointly own the reserves still in the ground. The multinational companies operate these joint ventures, and take all day-to-day decisions in their management.

The six joint ventures involving foreign owned oil companies are operated by the following companies:[15]

- Shell Petroleum Development Company of Nigeria Limited (SPDC): A joint venture operated by Shell accounts for more than forty percent of Nigeria's total oil production (899,000 barrels per day (bpd) in 1997) from more than eighty oil fields. The joint venture is composed of NNPC (55 percent), Shell (30 percent), Elf (10 percent) and Agip (5 percent) and operates largely onshore on dry land or in the mangrove swamp.[16]

---

[13] Khan, *Nigeria*, pp.16-18, and 69. The actual dates on which the government acquired an equity share varied in the case of each company. See below for a description of the regulatory regime.

[14] The NNPC was created by Decree No. 33 of 1977, as a successor to the Nigerian National Oil Company, itself created in 1971 as the first major effort to "indigenize" the oil industry, in response to the OPEC call for member states to participate more actively in oil operations. NNPC is responsible for production, transportation, refining, and marketing of oil and petroleum products. In 1986, the Petroleum Inspectorate, responsible for regulation and policy formulation, was detached from NNPC and given instead to the Department of Petroleum Resources; while preferable to the previous situation, in which NNPC regulated itself, the inspectorate still lacks independence. NNPC became a "commercial and autonomous" entity in 1992, though it remains state owned. Khan, *Nigeria*, pp.22-28.

[15] Information from U.S. EIA, "Nigeria Analysis Country Brief," except where otherwise indicated.

[16] Figure for bpd from Tony Imevbore, Paul Driver, and Chris Geerling, "Environmental Objectives Discussion Document" prepared by SPDC for its April 1998 "Stakeholders Environmental Workshop" held in Port Harcourt, section 1.2.a. In 1973, the government first acquired a 35 percent stake in the Shell-B.P. Petroleum Development Company of Nigeria, Ltd, jointly owned by Shell and British Petroleum

- Chevron Nigeria Limited (CNL): A joint venture between NNPC (60 percent) and Chevron (40 percent) has in the past been the second largest producer (approximately 400,000 bpd), with fields located in the Warri region west of the Niger river and offshore in shallow water. It is reported to aim to increase production to 600,000 bpd.[17]
- Mobil Producing Nigeria Unlimited (MPNU): A joint venture between NNPC (60 percent) and Mobil (40 percent) operates in shallow water off Akwa Ibom state in the southeastern delta and averaged production of 632,000 bpd in 1997, making it the second largest producer, as against 543,000 bpd in 1996. Mobil also holds a 50 percent interest in a Production Sharing Contract for a deep water block further offshore, and is reported to plan to increase output to 900,000 bpd by 2000.[18] Oil industry sources indicate that Mobil is likely to overtake Shell as the largest producer in Nigeria within the next five years, if current trends continue.
- Nigerian Agip Oil Company Limited (NAOC): A joint venture operated by Agip and owned by NNPC (60 percent), Agip (20 percent) and Phillips

---

(B.P.) and operated by Shell. This share was raised to 55 percent in 1974, and 60 percent in July 1979. In August 1979, B.P.'s assets in Nigeria were nationalized (for which compensation of U.S.$125 million was paid), following the "Kulu incident" when a B.P. chartered tanker with connections to South Africa unloaded at Bonny, and the company was suspected of breaking the oil embargo against South Africa. NNPC's share in the joint venture (of which the operating company was renamed the Shell Petroleum Development Company of Nigeria, Ltd) thus rose to 80 percent, and was reduced again to 60 percent only in 1989, when Shell's share rose to 30 percent, and Elf and Agip each acquired a 5 percent holding. In 1993, Shell's share decreased to 55 percent, and Elf increased its holding to 10 percent. Khan, *Nigeria*, pp.69-71; for further detail on the structure of Shell's business operations in Nigeria see also Jedrzej Georg Frynas, "Political instability and business: Focus on Shell in Nigeria," *Third World Quarterly* vol.19, no.3, pp.447-468. "Shell" is used here to refer to the Royal Dutch/Shell Group of companies, of which the two ultimate holding companies are the U.K.-based Shell Transport and Trading PLC (40 percent) and the Netherlands-based Royal Dutch Petroleum Company (60 percent). Elsewhere, "Shell" will be used to refer either to the group of companies or to SPDC; similarly for the other international oil companies listed below.

[17] Bearman, "Squandered Inheritance."

[18] Matthew Tostevin, "Nigerian Mobil Says More Funding Needed," Reuters, December 18, 1997; "International Close Up: Africa," on the Mobil website, at http://www.mobil.com, as of March 4, 1998; Bearman, "Squandered Inheritance."

Petroleum (20 percent) produces 150,000 bpd mostly from small onshore fields.

- Elf Petroleum Nigeria Limited (EPNL): A joint venture between NNPC (60 percent) and Elf (40 percent) produced approximately 125,000 bpd during 1997, both on and offshore. Elf and Mobil are in dispute over operational control of an offshore field with a production capacity of 90,000 bpd.
- Texaco Overseas Petroleum Company of Nigeria Unlimited (TOPCON): A joint venture operated by Texaco and owned by NNPC (60 percent), Texaco (20 percent) and Chevron (20 percent) currently produces about 60,000 bpd from five offshore fields.

Under the terms of the more-or-less standard Memorandum of Understanding (MOU) between each oil company and the Nigerian federal government, the operating company in a joint venture receives a fixed sum per barrel provided the price of oil per barrel remains within certain margins. The risk and benefit of oil price fluctuations thus largely accrue to the government. For example, provided the oil price remains between U.S.$12.50 and U.S.$23 a barrel, the Shell joint venture pays U.S.$3 per barrel to be distributed to the private shareholders according to their shareholding and to provide future investment, U.S.$2 goes to notional operating costs, and the remainder is paid to the government.[19] The last MOU was negotiated between the government and the oil companies in 1991, for five years. Although due for renewal, no new MOU has been agreed. In addition, each joint venture has a Joint Operating Agreement (JOA) with NNPC, which governs the administrative arrangements between the partners.

Aside from the partners in the six main joint ventures, other foreign oil companies involved in Nigeria include B.P, Statoil, Total, Pan Ocean, British Gas, Tenneco, Deminex, and Sun Oil.

In recent years, the Nigerian government has also endeavored to increase indigenous participation in the oil industry. Over twenty local firms have been awarded oil mining leases, allowing them to produce, and the government has issued new guidelines for the development of "marginal fields" which favor local companies, threatening to review the license arrangements of NNPC's joint venture partners and reallocate to indigenous operators marginal fields in blocks previously granted to the oil majors. In August 1996, the Petroleum (Amendment) Decree provided that any holder of an oil mining lease may farm out any marginal field within its area, with the consent of the head of state, and also that the head of state

[19] SPDC, "Nigeria Brief: Harnessing Gas," Lagos, August 1996.

may compulsorily farm out a marginal field where it has been left unexploited for ten or more years.[20] Although this threat has not been carried out, due to legal and commercial objections from some of the partners, notably Shell, who claim that such fields are unexploited because of funding difficulties caused by NNPC, former Minister of Petroleum Resources Dan Etete looked set to move forward with the proposal.[21] If the new government does implement the decree, abandoned or underexploited fields will be recovered from joint venture partners and production rights re-allocated. Foreign firms may participate as technical partners, but they will be limited to a maximum of 40 percent equity.[22] Some deals of this type have gone through on a voluntary basis: in May 1997 it was reported that Nigerian African Petroleum had taken on U.S. company Huffco (founded by a former U.S. ambassador, Roy Huffington) as a technical partner in a deal to acquire marginal acreage from Chevron.[23]

Disagreements between the oil companies and the Nigerian government over the level of funding budgeted by the government for the joint ventures with NNPC have dominated the politics of the upstream (exploration and production) sector in recent years. Funding to the NNPC from the Finance Ministry was below budgeted levels throughout the period during which General Abacha was head of state, and consequently exploration and other investment in the joint ventures has been greatly reduced. In the budget for the coming year announced in early January 1998, the U.S.$2.5 billion allocated to the six joint ventures was again more than U.S.$1 billion below the amount requested by the international oil companies. By April 1998, the oil companies were reported to be considering borrowing on the international capital markets to make up the shortfall.[24]

Although the cuts affected all the six main joint venture partners, they were not, reportedly, at a uniform across-the-board rate, leaving the oil companies fighting over the distribution of the money that has been allocated and exacerbating the usual rivalry for political goodwill with the key players in the military government. In this regard, Mobil and Chevron were active in the U.S., lobbying to fight off threats of oil sanctions against Nigeria; Shell believes it suffered as a

[20] The Department of Petroleum Resources published "Guidelines for Farm-out and Operations of Marginal Fields" in September 1996.

[21] *Energy Compass*, (London) vol.9, no.3, January 17, 1998.

[22] U.S. EIA, "Nigeria Country Analysis Brief." The main domestic companies are Dubri Oil, Pan Ocean, Consolidated Petroleum, Yinka Folawiyo Petroleum, Amni International, Atlas Petroleum, Cavendish Petroleum, and Express Oil and Gas.

[23] *Energy Compass*, vol.8, no.21, May 23, 1997.

[24] *Energy Compass*, vol.9, no.15, April 10, 1998.

result of the more assertive stand of the U.K. Labour Party government against the Nigerian military; while Elf, with the support of the French government (which regularly flouted European Union visa restrictions for members of the Nigerian government coming to France for discussions with oil companies and argued for those sanctions to be lifted) and apparently in an effort to curry favor with the Nigerian government, drilled a well in an offshore area over which Nigeria has a territorial dispute with Equatorial Guinea, and which is already being explored on behalf of Equatorial Guinea by Mobil.[25]

One of the consequences of the perpetual financial wrangles between the Finance Ministry, NNPC, and the oil companies has been a shift to production sharing contracts (PSCs). Under a PSC the operator covers all exploration and development costs and pays tax and royalties to the government only when it starts to produce; the contractor has title to oil produced, but not to oil in the ground. Since PSCs entail no capital expenditure from the state oil company there is less risk of political interference to the foreign investor. New prospecting licences and mining leases granted in the deep water fields off the Nigerian coast have been on these terms, and the oil companies have been pushing for the onshore joint ventures to be converted, freeing them from the annual budget struggle.

Following the death of Gen. Sani Abacha, Gen. Abdulsalami Abubakar, the new head of state, announced that "as a first step" he had immediately paid a quarterly amount of U.S.$630 million in line with outstanding "cash call" obligations to the joint venture partners (though no commitment was made that underpayment for the first quarter of 1998 would be redressed), and that the government was "currently reviewing an alternative funding mechanism for the joint venture operations with a view to permanently eliminating the cash call problem."[26] The speech was welcomed by the oil majors, and negotiations for a new structure are continuing. The fall in the oil price, however, meant that, at U.S.2 billion, the cash call contributions announced in the January 1999 budget speech were again well below those requested by the oil companies, and arrears remained unpaid.

Natural Gas

In addition to its oil wealth, Nigeria has an estimated 104.7 trillion cubic feet (tcf) of proven natural gas reserves, the tenth largest reserves in the world; reserves

---

[25] Interviews with oil industry sources 1997 and 1998; *Energy Compass*, vol.8, no.49, December 5, 1997.

[26] Reuters, July 21, 1998.

may in fact be as high as 300 tcf.[27] Plans to exploit this gas by liquefying it and shipping it to gas markets in Europe and the U.S. date back at least thirty years.

In November 1995, in a move heavily criticized by human rights groups, including Human Rights Watch, since it was in the immediate wake of the internationally condemned executions of Ken Saro-Wiwa and eight other Ogoni activists, a project to construct a U.S.$3-4 billion liquefied natural gas (LNG) facility on Bonny Island was finally announced. When completed, planned for 1999, it will be able to process 5.2 million metric tonnes per year (mmt/y) of LNG. Nigeria LNG Ltd, which is developing the project, is a consortium jointly owned by NNPC (49 percent), Shell (25.6 percent), Elf (15 percent), and Agip (10.4 percent). It is planned that "non-associated" gas, from gas reserves, will be used to supply the facility initially, but "associated" gas, produced as a by-product of oil extraction, will comprise 65 percent of supply by 2010.[28] Nigeria LNG Ltd has been subject to disagreements among its partners. In June 1997, oil minister Etete dissolved the board of directors of the company and accused Shell of using its position as technical adviser to the project "to subject other shareholders to its whims and caprices."[29] The project does, however, appear to be moving forward: by May 1998, all but 5 percent of its projected production had been sold, and there were new plans to add 50 percent to its capacity.[30]

In July 1998, a liquefied natural gas plant jointly owned by Mobil (51 percent) and NNPC (49 percent) came on stream, producing 50,000 bpd. Also based at Bonny, the facility collects associated gas from Mobil's Oso field.[31]

In addition, there are plans to build a West African gas pipeline to transport Nigerian gas to Ghana, Togo, and Benin. In October 1998, Chevron, responsible for the project, succeeded in signing up its first potential customer, a twenty-year commitment from a Ghanaian power-plant run by Virginia-based KMR Power.[32]

---

[27] U.S. EIA, "Nigeria Country Analysis Brief."

[28] Ibid.

[29] Robert Corzine, "Shell is Accused in Nigeria Gas Row," *Financial Times* (London), June 13, 1997; Felix Onuah, "Nigeria's Etete Blasts Shell Over LNG Project," Reuters, June 12, 1997.

[30] *Energy Compass*, vol.9, no.22, May 29, 1998.

[31] "Abubakar Commissions Offshore Gas Project," AFP, November 20, 1998; Dulue Mbachu, "Mobil Natural Gas Project Questioned," IPS, April 1, 1996.

[32] *Energy Compass*, vol.9, no.42, October 23, 1998.

The Downstream Sector

Exploration and production is referred to in the oil industry as the "upstream" sector; processing of crude oil into the various petroleum products is the "downstream" sector. Nigeria has refineries in Kaduna (in the "middle belt" of the country, outside the oil producing area), in Warri (Delta State), and two in Port Harcourt (Rivers State), with a nominal total capacity of 445,000 bpd. However, chronic lack of maintenance means that the refineries rarely if ever operate at this level, usually coming in at around 200,000 bpd or less: in December 1997, for example, crude oil allocation to the refineries was cut to 150,000 bpd, as a result of the poor state of equipment in the plants.[33] In November 1998, a breakdown of the fluid catalytic cracker at the 125,000 bpd Warri refinery left the country without a single operational catalytic cracker, needed to separate different petroleum products from crude.[34] The older refinery in Port Harcourt has been out of regular production since 1989; the new refinery was commissioned in 1989 and has a nominal capacity of 150,000 bpd. There are also petrochemicals plants at Eleme, on the edge of Ogoniland, near Port Harcourt, and two in Ekpan, Warri.[35]

If all the refineries are working, output of gasoline should be thirteen million liters a day; instead it was in July 1997, for example, less than five million liters a day. Domestic demand was estimated at the same time to be around eighteen million liters a day.[36] The Nigerian government was for a large part of 1997 in negotiation with French oil company Total to carry out "turnaround maintenance" at the 110,000 bpd Kaduna refinery at a cost of U.S.$240 million, a deal favored by finance minister Anthony Ani, though oil minister Etete claimed that it could be done at a cost of U.S.$170 million by NNPC.[37] In May 1998, it was reported

[33] Reuters, December 12, 1997.

[34] *Energy Compass*, vol.9, no.45, November 6, 1998.

[35] Environmental Resources Managers Ltd, *Niger Delta Environmental Survey Final Report Phase I, Volume I*, p.199.

[36] *Energy Compass*, vol.8, no.31, July 31, 1997.

[37] Allocation of funds for maintenance at the refineries was the subject of a struggle between finance minister Anthony Ani and petroleum minister Dan Etete under General Abacha's regime. Ani refused to release funds unless NNPC and the Ministry of Petroleum Resources provided him with a satisfactory explanation of expenditure since 1994, which he alleged should have been adequate to carry out the required repairs. Officials in NNPC and the oil ministry, however, stated that the funds were not in fact transferred from the Finance Ministry, as alleged. The joint external auditors of NNPC, Peat Marwick, Ani, Ogunde & Co (of which former Minister Ani is, extraordinarily, one partner) and Makhtari Dangan and Co, have yet to complete their audit of the 1993 and 1994 accounts, and so the issue remained unresolved. *Energy Compass*, vol.8, no.31,

that Total had finally started work on the project and hoped to have the refinery back in production by July, subject to funding.[38] In mid-August, it was hoped it would resume production "in the next few weeks"; in November, the refinery was still out of commission.[39] In September 1998, NNPC appointed Shell as technical adviser for the turnaround maintenance of the Port Harcourt refinery complex.[40]

The price of gasoline (petrol) on the forecourts of Nigeria's gas stations was fixed at ₦11 (eleven naira; U.S.12¢) per liter from November 1994 (when it was raised from ₦3.25 (U.S.4¢)) until December 1998, when it was raised to ₦25 (U.S.28¢).[41] Previous attempts to reduce the level of subsidy in recent years, prompted by negotiations with the IMF for structural adjustment lending beginning in 1986, or otherwise, have led to street riots, strikes and security clamp-downs on several occasions, most recently in 1992. Following negotiations with the union umbrella organization the Nigerian Labour Congress over a threat to strike, the government announced that it would review the increase, and on January 7, 1999, the price was reduced again to ₦20.[42] Nevertheless, on January 4, five were shot dead in riots in Lagos over the fuel price rise. During fuel shortages unofficial

---

July 31, 1997; *Energy Compass*, vol.8, no.46, November 14, 1997; James Jukwey, "Oil-Rich Nigeria has no Answer to Fuel Scarcity," Reuters, June 20, 1997; "The Oil Hostage," *Africa Confidential* (London), August 29, 1997.

[38] "Business confidence hits rock bottom," *Africa Analysis* (London), May 15, 1998.

[39] "Nigeria's Ruling Council Ends Meeting on Fuel, Security," Lagos NTA TV Network, August 14, 1998, as reported by FBIS, August 15, 1998; *Energy Compass*, vol.9, no.45, November 6, 1998.

[40] *Energy Compass*, vol.9, no.39, September 25, 1998.

[41] AFP, December 21, 1998. Revenue from the sale of domestic petroleum products is paid into the Petroleum Trust Fund (PTF), which subsequently disburses the funds. With the price at ₦11, ₦2.00 (U.S.2¢) went to NNPC as notional payment for refining, storing and distributing products (although the true cost of refining was estimated at ₦5.67 (U.S.6¢) in early 1988); ₦2.40 (U.S.3¢) to the federal government as compensation for the cost of the crude; and ₦5.30 (U.S.6¢) to the Petroleum Special Trust Fund (PSTF) for the implementation of various projects in health, education, and infrastructure. The marketers deducted ₦1.30 (U.S.1¢) per liter directly from the pump price prior to transfering the balance to the PTF. Dalhatu Bayero, "The Politics of Oil," *West Africa* (London), February 2 to 8, 1998; IMF, *Nigeria: Selected Issues and Statistical Appendix*, p.52. In 1993, with the price at ₦3.25, the level of the annual subsidy to the domestic petroleum product market was estimated at 17 percent of oil export earnings. Khan, *Nigeria*, pp.127-128. Throughout this report, an exchange rate of ₦90 to one U.S. dollar has been used, the rate current in late December 1998.

[42] Lagos NTA TV Network Network December 29, 1998, as reported by FBIS, December 30, 1998; *Nigeria Today*, January 8,1999.

gasoline prices can rise many times: during a shortage in April 1997, for example, a fifty-liter can was selling for ₦4,000 (U.S.$44), more than seven times the usual price; in July 1998, a liter was going for ₦400 (U.S.$4.44) on the black market.[43]

Nigeria's perennial shortages of fuel and other refined petroleum products have owed perhaps as much to corruption as to refining shortfalls. Allocations of refined products to political favorites by the president's office have often been sold in neighboring countries, where prices have been up to fifteen times higher—in 1993 some oil industry sources estimated that up to 100,000 bpd were being smuggled into Benin, Cameroon and Niger.[44] The Abacha government itself identified hoarding and smuggling as major causes of fuel shortage, and threatened those alleged to be involved with trial before the Miscellaneous Offences Tribunal.[45] The right to import gasoline also allows spectacular profits to be made: although expensive for the country, individual oil trading companies and their political sponsors have made lucrative deals based on crude-for-refined swaps or cash deals; the government budgeted U.S.$600 million for import of fuel between January and September 1998.[46] Large up-front payments for the right to such deals are common: in mid 1997, for example, Swiss trader Glencore was said to have paid a sum of several million dollars for a contract to supply thirty-three cargoes of petroleum products.[47] At the same time it was estimated that NNPC had overpaid by about U.S.$20 million since late 1995 for deliveries of Saudi Arab Light oil to the Kaduna refinery, as a result of "high-level interference in structuring the deal," which was based on swaps for Nigerian oil.[48] Hence, although fuel shortages are usually precipitated by refinery breakdowns, they can also be generated or exacerbated by profit-seeking among government officials.

In October 1997, while the Kaduna refinery was completely closed down and the usual technical problems reduced output from Port Harcourt and Warri, a

---

[43] James Jukwey, "Nigeria Fuel Crisis Caused by Greed, Watchdog Says," Reuters, April 9, 1997; *Nigeria Today* (London-based e-mail news service), July 14, 1998.

[44] Khan, *Nigeria*, pp.127-128.

[45] Opposition radio reporting the acting director of defense information, Col. Godwin Ugbo, following a meeting of the "states task force on petroleum products." Radio Kudirat Nigeria, June 6, 1997, as reported by BBC SWB, June 17, 1997; see also "Meeting on Fuel Crisis Ends, Measures Taken," Lagos Radio Nigeria Network, as reported by FBIS, May 14, 1998.

[46] James Rupert, "The Collapse of Nigeria: Oil but no Fuel," *Washington Post*, March 31, 1998.

[47] *Energy Compass*, vol.8, no.27, July 3, 1997.

[48] *Energy Compass*, vol.8, no.24, June 12, 1997.

twenty-cargo import program was awarded to Swiss-based trading firm Glencore, supplied by German refiner Wintershall AG. This fuel was found by the Nigerian Federal Environmental Protection Agency (FEPA) to have been contaminated with a high level of pyrolysis gasoline, that could be hazardous to human health. Residents of traffic-choked Lagos complained of nausea and respiratory problems.[49] Fuel shortages persisted through 1998, and in March 1998—at which time only one of Nigeria's refineries was working, producing only 70,000 bpd and forcing a closedown of much of Nigerian industry—further contracts were awarded to Wintershall and Glencore for import of thirty 30,000 tonne cargoes of petroleum products.[50] Commissions on these contracts were reported to have averaged U.S.$14 to $15 a tonne. The Wintershall contracts were canceled by General Abubakar on Abacha's death, and contracts for import of fuel given to the major oil companies instead: following their cancellation officials of the state-owned Pipelines and Products Marketing Company (PPMC) estimated that Nigeria had overpaid by about U.S.$10 per tonne and stated that the government would not pay for the fuel, which in any event did not comply with specifications.[51] Abubakar also announced that payments in hard currency for fuel supplies would no longer require presidential approval, while funds would be released for the rehabilitation of the refineries. Shell, Elf, Agip, and Mobil were contracted to import a total of forty cargoes of petroleum products, producing huge savings over the Glencore/Wintershall contracts.[52] Within a few months, however, this new regime had broken down, and the oil traders were back in business, including Glencore as well as several involved in the business under the government of Gen. Ibrahim Babangida, reportedly at the same inflated prices.[53] The fuel shortage remained as severe as ever at the end of the year.

The ongoing fuel crisis had tragic effects on Saturday October 17, 1998, when more than one thousand people were burned to death by an explosion at a ruptured NNPC petroleum products pipeline at Jesse, near Warri, Delta State. Those killed were collecting fuel from the pipeline—fuel unavailable from the proper sources. It was not clear whether the leak had been deliberately created to tap the fuel or was due to mechanical failure, although the government immediately claimed it was due to sabotage and that consequently there was no question of compensation.

---

[49] Reuters, October 8, 1997.

[50] *Energy Compass*, vol.9, no.11, March 13, 1998.

[51] Reuters, August 13, 1998.

[52] Reuters, July 21, 1997 and July 23, 1997; *Energy Compass*, vol.9, no.34, August 21, 1998.

[53] "As bad as it gets," *Africa Confidential*, vol.39, no.25, December 18, 1998.

The government appointed a panel from within NNPC to investigate the causes of the disaster, but resisted calls for an independent inquiry.[54]

[54] Adekunbe Ero and Adegbenro Adebanjo, "Horror in the Delta," *Tell* (Lagos), November 2, 1998; Janet Mba-Afolabi, "Jesse Town tragedy," *Newswatch* (Lagos), November 2, 1998.

IV. OIL WEALTH AND THE NIGERIAN CONSTITUTION

Conflict in the Niger Delta is directly related to the debates, ongoing since before independence, about the structure of the Nigerian polity. It can be assumed that there would have been disputes as to the relationship between center and periphery in Nigeria in any economic circumstances, given the complexity of the country and the lack of established nationwide democratic institutions at independence. Yet the addition of oil production and oil wealth to the difficulties already posed by the problem of ruling a country of at least 250 ethnic groups, each with its separate traditions of government, has greatly increased the potential for conflict and the stakes at play in that conflict. The following section attempts to give some idea of the way in which the Nigerian federal system has developed and how it has been shaped by the influx of oil wealth. At the heart of discontent among the oil producing communities is an acute sense that the wealth derived from their land is siphoned off by the federal government and never returned: the seemingly dry debates on revenue allocation formulae are central to the cycle of protest and repression.

State Creation and Revenue Allocation

The history of Nigeria since independence has been dominated by attempts to restructure the federation into a form acceptable to all the various peoples it houses. The trend has been towards increasing fragmentation of state structures, as the federal government has sought to appease the demands of the different minority groups by the creation of new states and local government areas. This fragmentation of government has been, paradoxically, paralleled by increasing centralization in practice, as individual states have become less and less viable without federal financial support and oil revenues have supplanted all others as the foundation of the Nigerian economy.

The boundaries of the territory now known as Nigeria were first defined in 1907. Nigeria itself was brought for the first time under one government in 1914 by the amalgamation of two British colonial protectorates. Although the country was in theory ruled as a single unit, in practice the northern and southern parts of the country were administered by the British as distinct entities with little attempt at coordination. The policy of "indirect rule" strengthened, centralized, and reduced the flexibility of existing structures of authority, especially in the north, where powerful emirates formed the basis of local government. In 1939 the colonial government divided the Southern Protectorate into the Eastern and Western Protectorates, but the three units were still administered without any central political focus or representative institution. Only in 1954 did Nigeria became a true federation with a central government, including a Federal House of Representatives (responsible for foreign relations, defense, the police, overall aspects of trade and finance policy, and major transport and communications issues), and three constituent components with a large degree of autonomy in all other matters: the Northern, Western, and Eastern Regions. At the same time, elected regional houses of assembly were created for the Eastern and Western Regions with independent legislative powers, the British governor retaining only limited responsibilities; the North, however, at the request of its own house of assembly, only gained self-rule in 1959, one year before independence.[55]

At independence, the Western Region was the richest, as a result of the presence of the capital and port of Lagos, cocoa production, and much of the industrial development in Nigeria, as well as early access to education. The Eastern Region, economically dependent on palm oil production, already suffered substantial population pressure on the available land and depended on food imports. The Northern Region was larger in population and area than the other regions combined, but was also the poorest and least educated.[56] In each of these three regions, a majority ethnic group constituted about two-thirds of the population, the Hausa-Fulani in the north, the Yoruba in the west, and the Igbo in the east; the remaining third being made up of various minority groups. In the absence of an indigenous or even colonial tradition of political unity, ethnic loyalties became the dominant force in political organization; as a consequence, the minority groups, of which there may be 250 or more in Nigeria, were in practice politically subordinated to their larger neighbors.

---

[55] At the time the British first proclaimed a protectorate over northern Nigeria, the traditional rulers in the area, the emirs, were promised that there would be no interference in matters of religion. Missionary activities were therefore disallowed. As a consequence, the northern region was in the main excluded from European education, largely provided by the missionaries in southern Nigeria. Colonial administration in the north therefore came to be dominated, in the posts filled by Nigerians, by southerners. For this and related reasons, the Northern Peoples' Congress (NPC), which held the majority of seats in the Northern Region House of Assembly, at one point wanted independence to be delayed until sufficient northerners could be trained to fill government positions previously held by expatriates or southerners. In 1957, however, the NPC decided to ask for self-government for the Northern Region in 1959 and to join with other parties in pressing for independence in 1960. *Report of the Commission Appointed to Enquire into the Fears of Minorities and the Means of Allaying Them* (London: HMSO, July 1958; hereafter "Willink Commission Report"), Chapter 1, paragraph 12.

[56] Forrest, *Politics and Economic Development in Nigeria*, p.21.

During the debates in the constitutional conference that was established in 1953 to decide the form of the future independent state, these minority groups expressed fears as to their domination by the majority Hausa-Fulani, Yoruba, and Igbo in each region. The British government appointed a commission of inquiry to investigate these fears and advise on safeguards to be included in the constitution to address them. This commission, known as the Willink Commission, after its chair, Henry Willink, reported in 1958. The Willink Commission considered and rejected demands for the creation of new states, but recommended certain other administrative arrangements to allay the fears of minorities, in the form of constitutional guarantees of certain rights, regional advisory councils for "minority areas," and a federal board to consider the specific problems of the riverine areas of the Niger Delta.[57]

The tripartite structure of colonial rule was thus inherited by the new government at independence in 1960, reflecting and reinforcing the political dominance of Nigeria's three major ethnic groups. Although the Willink Commission had rejected the option, minority groups remained convinced that the creation of new states in which they would be majorities would improve their political and economic status. These demands became impossible to resist by those playing ethnic politics at federal level. As early as 1963 a new constitution was adopted and the Western Region was divided into two, with the creation of the Mid-West Region, giving autonomous status to the two administrative districts where Yorubas were not in a majority.

The first military coup of January 1966, in which northern Prime Minister Sir Abubakar Tafawa Balewa was killed and which brought Maj.-Gen. Johnson Aguiyi-Ironsi, an Igbo, to power saw a brief and disastrous attempt to create a

[57] The Willink Commission considered each region of Nigeria (Northern, Western and Eastern) and the demands for state creation from minorities. In each case, it rejected the idea of new states on the grounds that: "it is seldom possible to draw a clean boundary which does not create a fresh minority: the proposed state had in each case become very small by the time it had been pared down to an area in which it was possible to assert with confidence that it was desired.... [Furthermore] The powers left to the Regions by the decision of 1953 are considerable, and ... we do not regard it as realistic to suppose that any of the Regions will forgo the powers they now have.... [A] new state created today would have to compete with the existing Regions, and the cost in overheads, not only financial but in resources—particularly of trained minds, would be high. This consideration, when combined with the difficulty of finding a clean boundary, was in each particular case to our minds decisive." Willink Commission Report, Chapter 14, paragraph 3.

unified state, with the abolition of the federal system. The immediate reaction from the north, threatened by the southern dominance that would result from centralized government on a unified basis, resulted in a July counter-coup staged by junior northern army officers, which brought Lt.-Col. (later Gen.) Yakubu Gowon to power at federal level. In May 1967, Gowon announced that the four regions would be abolished and replaced by a new federal system based on twelve states, which sought to address the concerns of minority groups and thus increase their support for the federation, while at the same time breaking down the powers of the regions. The Igbos' loss of central political power was thus exacerbated by the creation in the Niger Delta of Rivers State, which cut off the Igbo heartland from direct access to the sea and gave control of Port Harcourt, an important port at the beginning of its oil boom where there were substantial Igbo commercial interests, to a new state government. Shortly after the announcement of the new state system, in May 1967, the secession of Biafra was declared by the military governor of the former Eastern Region, Lt.-Col. Odumegwu Ojukwu. The civil war of 1967 to 1970, lost by the secessionists, increased the strength of federal government and the centralization of power.

The creation of the twelve state system, which came into effect in April 1968, began an (as yet) endless process of alteration to the system of revenue allocation in the federation between central and state governments and among the states. Increasingly, states contributed their revenues to a Distributable Pool Account (DPA) at federal level, shared out on the basis of population, need and other criteria, while the "derivation principle," by which revenues were spent in the geographical area from which they were derived, was downgraded. Federal expenditure came to dominate state expenditure: whereas during the First Republic federal and regional expenditure were about equal, by 1975/76 the federal share of expenditure was approximately 70 percent and the states came increasingly to depend on transfers from the center for their revenue.[58] During this same period, revenues from the oil industry, derived largely from the south eastern states, surged: many of the adjustments to revenue allocation were attempts to counteract the unbalanced situation the oil wealth created.

In 1967, when the new states were created, mining rents and royalties were split 15 percent to the federal government, 35 percent to the DPA, and 50 percent on a derivation basis. Obvious imbalances between states led to the review of the system, and in 1970 (backdated to 1969) the shares of mining rents and royalties became 5 percent to the federal government, 50 percent to the DPA, and 45 percent

---

[58] Forrest, *Politics and Economic Development in Nigeria*, pp.50-51.

to the state of derivation. From 1971, the federal government introduced a distinction between onshore and offshore rents and royalties, taking 100 percent of offshore revenue itself. In 1975, with the arrival of massively increased oil revenues following the OPEC price rise of 1973, the share of onshore revenue paid to the state of origin was reduced to 20 percent, while the federal government was to pay its entire share of on and offshore revenue into the DPA. In 1979, the derivation principle was dropped altogether in favor of a Special Account for mineral producing areas.[59]

The influx of cash placed strong pressures on the government to increase public expenditure in line with increased revenue: total federal expenditure increased by a massive 100 percent in 1974, and doubled again the next year.[60] In contrast to expenditure from taxation receipts, this bonanza from "rental" income brought no political pressures for accountability in the use of public funds; rather, it brought greater demands for money to be spent on patronage without thought as to its best allocation. Following a pattern common to many states dependent on extractive industries for their revenue, the non-oil sector of the economy in Nigeria, including agriculture, was neglected and steadily declined: Nigeria shifted from being an exporter of agricultural products to being a major importer of food. States became increasingly dependent on federal allocations, financial discipline and accounting deteriorated rapidly, and levels of imports and expenditure reached unsustainable levels. In the context of the weak political institutions of a newly independent and deeply divided state, there was little chance that any economic

[59] S. Egite Oyovbaire, "The Politics of Revenue Allocation," in K. Panter-Brick (ed.), *Soldiers and Oil* (London: Frank Cass, 1978); Forrest, *Politics and Economic Development in Nigeria*, p.53.

[60] Forrest, *Politics and Economic Development in Nigeria*, p.133.

control could be exercised.[61] Politics instead revolved around the "distributive" concerns generated by expenditure of the oil wealth.

In July 1975, Gowon was overthrown by a fresh and bloodless coup, which installed the six-month administration of Gen. Murtala Mohammed, before he was killed in an abortive coup attempt and succeeded by his deputy, Lt.-Gen. Olusegun Obasanjo. In February 1976, the Murtala Mohammed government increased the number of states to nineteen, adding four in the north, two in the south west, and one in the south east. In 1979, the Obasanjo regime handed over power to the civilian government of Alhaji Shehu Shagari, following a lengthy process of constitutional debate, first in a constitution drafting committee established in 1977 and subsequently in a constituent assembly which took over the process in 1978. The 1979 constitution provided for an executive president, on the U.S. model (by comparison with the parliamentary system of the First Republic), and introduced, for the first time in an explicit way, the concept of the "federal character" of the government, by which was meant the requirement that "there shall be no predominance of persons from a few States or from a few ethnic or other sectional groups in [the federal] government or in any of its agencies."[62] The president was required to appoint at least one minister from each state, and this effectively ethnically-based principle of office-sharing was duplicated at other levels of government.

The period of civilian rule saw a loss of power from the federal government to the states. In particular, states demanded and eventually received a greater share in allocation of revenues. The formula in operation in 1979, giving the federal

---

[61] See, for example, Terry Lynn Karl, *The Paradox of Plenty: Oil Booms and Petro-States* (Berkeley: University of California Press, 1997), pp.206-208. Nigeria, it is argued, had an extreme case of "Dutch disease [named by economists after Dutch elm disease], a process whereby new discoveries or favorable price changes in one sector of the economy—for example, petroleum—cause distress in other areas—for example, agriculture or manufacturing.... Persistent Dutch Disease provokes a rapid, even distorted, growth of services, transportation, and other nontradeables while simultaneously discouraging industrialization and agriculture—a process that policy makers seem incapable of counteracting." Ibid., p.5. As Karl notes, "Oil is the most important internationally traded commodity as measured by volume and monetary value. The significance of its role leads to a relatively inelastic demand, which, when combined with the small number and large size of resource owners, the high entry costs into the industry, and the difficulties inherent in energy substitution, produces extraordinary rents with a distinctive character: they have almost nothing to do with the productive processes of the domestic economy." Ibid., p.48.

[62] Section 14(3) of the 1979 constitution.

government 76 percent of shared revenues, the states 21 percent, and elected local governments (a new uniform tier of government) 3 percent, was rejected. After much political debate and conflict, a new formula finally came into effect in 1982, giving the federal government 55 percent, states 30.5 percent, local governments 10 percent, and—in a concession to the demands of the oil rich states since the derivation principle had been abolished in 1979—4.5 percent to be split three ways for the benefit of the oil producing communities (1 percent to respond to the ecological problems caused by oil production, 2 percent to go into the accounts of the mineral-producing states on a derivation principle, and 1.5 percent directly for the development of mineral-producing areas).[63] All revenue from offshore production went to the federal government. The debate around revenue allocation from the center itself generated campaigns for the creation of new states (and new local government areas), as local politicians sought to benefit from the patronage that resulted from distributing revenue at state level.

At the same time, financial controls on government spending declined yet further. The government took no steps to guard against future revenue falls by investing abroad or creating an oil stabilization fund. Currency appreciation and domestic inflation made local industries uncompetitive internationally and boosted imports, leading to balance of payments difficulties during oil-induced recessions in 1978-79 and from 1981 until the early 1990s. Expenditure rapidly outpaced income, and, with oil price slumps in the early 1980s, external debt more than doubled from 1980 to 1985. The oil price fell from around U.S.$32 per barrel in 1981 to approximately U.S.$13 per barrel in 1986, and Nigeria's gross national product (GNP) fell from a high of U.S.$99,539 million in 1980 to a low of U.S.$24,341 million in 1987. In the same year, the ratio of debt to GNP reached 112.8 percent.[64]

This boom and bust cycle contributed to political instability: in January 1984, military officers again put an end to civilian rule, and installed a fresh military regime under Maj.-Gen. Mohammadu Buhari, which immediately launched a "war against indiscipline," cracking down on dissent, and, supposedly, corruption, with a barrage of decrees. Buhari in turn was overthrown by Gen. Ibrahim Babangida in August 1985, who early on promised a return to civilian rule. As the transition program was repeatedly extended, and with it the competition for future revenue

---

[63] Allocation of Revenue Act No. 1 of 1982; see Forrest, *Politics and Economic Development in Nigeria*, p.83.

[64] Karl, *Paradox of Plenty*, Tables A-14 and A-15, based on World Bank *World Debt Tables*.

share and agitation for more states, Babangida raised the number of states by two, to twenty-one, in 1989 and by another nine, to thirty, in 1991. Local governments were also strengthened, and their share of revenue allocation increased from 10 to 15 and then 20 percent, with payments to be made directly from the federal government, and not via states.

In 1992, in the context of Babangida's transition program, the government established the Oil Mineral Producing Areas Development Commission (OMPADEC) "to address the difficulties and sufferings of inhabitants of the Oil Producing Areas of Nigeria," and the share of federal revenue allocated specifically to oil and mineral producing communities was doubled from 1.5 to 3 percent.[65] In February 1996, the senior management of OMPADEC was fired, amid allegations of corruption and mismanagement, and a sole administrator appointed. The commission was still allocated ₦2.042 billion (U.S.$22.68 million) in 1996 (according to General Abacha's 1997 budget speech), but at the time of Abacha's death in June 1998 was moribund and threatened with closure.[66] In addition, the government inaugurated the board of a new Petroleum Special Trust Fund (PSTF) in March 1995, established by decree the previous November, with a mandate to use revenue from increases in the prices of petroleum products to "identify key projects in all parts of the federation so as to bring about equitable development to all our communities."[67] The PSTF, which did not begin full-scale operations until

---

[65] Decree 23 of 1992. Oil Mineral Producing Areas Development Commission, "Policy Briefing: The Dawn of a New Era," (OMPADEC: Port Harcourt, 1992). The commission was to "embark on physical and human development in the Oil Producing Communities, with the objective of: (a) Compensating, materially, the Communities, Local Government Areas and States which have suffered damage (ecological, environmental etc) or deprivation as a result of mineral oil prospection in their areas; (b) Open up the affected areas and effectively link them up socially and economically with the rest of the country by producing various forms of infrastructural and physical development." Ibid.

[66] Akpandem James, "Why OMPADEC May be Scrapped," *Punch* (Lagos), March 4, 1998.

[67] "General Abacha Presents 1996 Budget," Lagos NTA Television Network, February 15, 1996, as reported by BBC SWB, February 19, 1996. The price of gasoline (petrol) at the pump increased from ₦3.25 (U.S.4¢) to ₦11 (U.S.12¢) per liter in November 1994; of this, ₦5.30 (U.S.6¢) was allocated to the PSTF. The PSTF received ₦25 billion (U.S.$277 million) in 1995, ₦46 billion (U.S.$511 million) in 1996, and ₦39 billion (U.S.$433 million) in 1997 in petroleum product revenue. IMF, *Nigeria: Selected Issues and Statistical Appendix*, p.54. On December 21, 1998, the fuel price was increased to ₦25 (U.S.28¢), but the breakdown for the PSTF was not announced at the

1997, was seen by members of the southern minorities as an effort to undermine OMPADEC's allocation of oil wealth to the oil producing communities.

In June 1993, the presidential elections which were to be the culmination of the transition program were annulled, when it became clear that Moshood. K.O. Abiola, a Yoruba from the southwest, was going to win. An interim government was put in place, itself overthrown by yet another coup in November 1993, which installed General Sani Abacha in power. Babangida's transition program was aborted, to be virtually duplicated by a fresh program, announced in October 1995, to terminate on October 1, 1998.[68] The Abacha administration engaged in yet another round of inconclusive—because undemocratic and military-controlled—debates over the structure of the federation. In May 1994, elections were held for a national constitutional conference, although of 369 members, ninety-six were nominated by the head of state, and other candidates were carefully screened. The conference produced a report and draft constitution, which was presented to General Abacha in June 1995. The draft constitution was not published before the death of Abacha in June 1998, though elements of the constitutional provisions had become known; for example, that there should be a rotational presidency, so that each region of the country would be represented in turn, and that other offices should similarly represent the "federal character" of Nigeria.

The Abacha government's transition program also brought a multiplication of administrative units. A State Creation and Local Government Boundary Adjustment Committee considered requests from those groups as yet unrecognized within the federal system for their own government structures, and made recommendations to the federal government. In October 1996, General Abacha increased the number of states yet again, to thirty-six, at the same time increasing

---

time of going to press. The Petroleum (Special) Trust Fund Decree No. 25 of 1994 states that the fund shall be paid "all the monies received from the sale price of petroleum products less the marketers margin," and apply the money to projects in road and railway transportation, education, health, food supply, water supply, security services, alternative sources of energy, rural development programs and such other sectors as may be approved (Sections 1(1) and 3(1)(c)). Members of the board managing the fund hold office at the pleasure of the head of state (Sections 6(1), 7(2), and 10).

[68] See Human Rights Watch/Africa, "Permanent Transition: Current Violations of Human Rights in Nigeria," *A Human Rights Watch Short Report*, vol.8, no.3(A), September 1996, and "Transition or Travesty? Nigeria's Endless Process of Return to Civilian Rule," *A Human Rights Watch Short Report*, vol.9, no.6(A), October 1997.

the number of local government areas by 183 to 776 (including those in Abuja, the Federal Capital Territory).

In July 1998, following the death of Abacha, the new head of state Gen. Abdulsalami Abubakar announced that the Abacha transition program would be scrapped, and a new program instituted, under more open conditions, to terminate in May 1999; however, the constitution presented to Abacha in 1995 would be retained (despite the defects in the drafting process). Abubakar promised to "publish and widely circulate the draft constitution presented by the National Constitutional Conference prior to consideration and approval by the Provisional Ruling Council," and the 1995 draft constitution was finally published in September 1998.[69] A committee was appointed to receive public comments and make recommendations as to the draft constitution and report back by December 31. In its report, the committee recommended instead the adoption of the 1979 constitution, with some amendments, including adopting the provisions of the 1995 draft constitution for an increase in the revenue allocation to the oil producing regions.

The 1995 draft constitution reflects the fact that the constitutional conference could not reach a consensus on the question of future revenue allocation, although it recognized the need for greater revenue to go to the oil producing areas. It provides that:

> The President, upon the receipt of the advice from the National Revenue Mobilisation, Allocation and Fiscal Commission, shall table before the National Assembly proposals for Revenue Allocation from the Federation Account. In determining the formula, the National Assembly shall take into account allocation principles especially those of Population, Equality of States, Internal Revenue Generation, Land Mass, Terrain, as well as Population Density, provided that the principle of derivation shall be constantly reflected in any approved formula as being not less than 13 percent of the revenue accruing to the Federation Account directly from any natural resources, so however, that the figure of the allocation for derivation shall be deemed to include any amount that may be set aside for funding any special authority or agency for the development of the State or States of derivation.[70]

[69] Reuters, July 21, 1998.

[70] Section 163(2) of the draft constitution of 1995, as finally published in September 1998.

Although the allocation of 13 percent of oil revenue to the states from which it is derived would represent a marked return to earlier patterns of revenue allocation, it is not clear that the allocation would directly benefit the communities in which the oil is produced, rather than the state governments in the oil producing areas, where the money would likely be used for patronage rather than development. For the time being, however, the revenue allocation to the oil producing communities remains at 3 percent.

General Abubakar also promised that the PSTF would apply the bulk of its resources to the roads, education and water supply sectors, and that "a fully reconstituted OMPADEC will be provided with the wherewithal as provided in the Revenue Allocation Formula to enable it to discharge its obligations to the oil producing areas."[71] A panel to probe the financial transactions of OMPADEC over the past few years was established, including the role of sole administrator, Eric Opiah, and other officers.[72] General Abubakar also announced that NNPC would enjoy greater independence and authority; after dismissing General Abacha's cabinet, he failed to appoint a new minister of petroleum, instead appointing only a special adviser within the president's office, Aret Adams, a former head of NNPC. In November 1998, a new board for OMPADEC was established, headed by former chief of naval staff Air Vice Marshall Dan Princeton Omotsola.[73] General Abubakar visited the delta region November 18 to 20, 1998, and promised increased investment to improve the standard of living of the oil producing communities.[74]

The Nigerian economy currently faces further shocks as a result of the falling price of oil on the international market, reducing the pot that can be distributed among those who demand a share. The 1998 budget was based on an estimated average oil price of U.S.$17 per barrel; in February 1998, it had fallen to U.S.$13 per barrel, and remained at depressed levels for the following months, dipping below U.S.$10 per barrel at the end of the year. In his independence day speech on October 1, 1998, General Abubakar estimated the impact of the fall in the oil

---

[71] Ibid.

[72] "Abubakar Pledges Petroleum Ministry Reorganization," Lagos NTA TV, September 7, 1998, as reported by FBIS, September 9, 1998; *Vanguard* (Lagos), August 24, 1998.

[73] Reuters, November 10, 1998.

[74] "Nigeria's Abubakar Urges Patience in Oil-Producing Areas," Lagos Radio Nigeria Network, November 18, 1998, as reported by FBIS, November 19, 1998.

price to be a decrease of 20 to 25 percent in foreign exchange earnings;[75] in his January 1, 1999 budget speech, Abubakar announced that actual receipts from crude oil in 1998 had amounted to only 62 percent of budgeted revenue.[76] Moreover, the government has few reserves, having failed to use the windfall additional profits brought by the rise in oil prices during the 1990-91 Gulf crisis wisely.[77] Even during the period when oil export revenues were increasing, gross domestic product per capita decreased;[78] per capita GNP declined from around U.S.$1,100 per year in 1980 to an estimated U.S.$260 in 1995.[79] External debt was estimated by the Nigerian government to stand at U.S.$27.08 billion at the end of 1997, down from U.S.$32.58 billion at the end of 1995, though the official statistics are greeted with some skepticism in financial circles.[80] According to one analyst of the Nigerian economy: "It is clear that the resource mismanagement in Nigeria over the last thirty years has left the economy in dire financial straits and has put at risk the very industry on which it depends."[81]

The revenue allocation formulae do not tell the whole story of the distribution of the oil money. The Nigerian political economy has come to depend on a spectacular system of corruption, involving systematic kickbacks for the award of contracts, special bank accounts in the control of the presidency, allocation of oil or refined products to the politically loyal to sell for personal profit, and sweeteners

---

[75] "Abubakar on country's domestic and foreign policies," Voice of Nigeria External Service, October 1, 1998, as reported by BBC SWB, October 3, 1998.

[76] 1999 Federal Budget Address by General Abdulsalami Abubakar.

[77] Rather than setting aside any of the windfall to provide against future price falls, the government increased expenditure, which then remained at elevated levels even when oil prices and revenue fell in 1991. World Bank, *World Development Report 1997: The State in a Changing World* (Washington DC: Oxford University Press, 1997), p.49.

[78] During the period 1986 to 1992, oil export revenues increased at an average 13 percent a year, while GDP, measured in current U.S. dollars, decreased by an average 7 percent a year. Khan, *Nigeria*, p.183.

[79] Khan, *Nigeria*, Table 8.3; World Bank, *World Development Report 1997*, Table 1, based on an estimated 1995 population of 111.3 million.

[80] "President Abacha Presents 1998 Budget," Radio Nigeria, Lagos, January 5, 1998, as reported by BBC SWB, January 13, 1998; Tony Hawkins, "Foreign Debt Burden Grows," *Financial Times* (Special Survey on Nigeria), May 26, 1995. The IMF estimated that Nigeria's external public debt at the end of 1997 was U.S.$28.7 billion, based on "an amalgam of debtor and creditor data," equivalent to 75 percent of GDP, with debt obligations falling due in 1998 projected at 36 percent of exports. IMF, *Nigeria: Selected Issues and Statistical Appendix*, p.81.

[81] Khan, *Nigeria*, p.202.

for a whole range of political favors. In effect across all sectors of the economy, this system of corruption is particularly entrenched in the oil sector, its natural home. It is this corruption that ensures that the oil money is sent to private bank accounts in Zurich or the Cayman Islands rather than spent on primary health care and education in Nigeria.[82] Technical requirements of legislation theoretically regulating the oil industry are often overlooked in the case of those who toe the right political line: the "presidential allocation" was said to amount to up to 200,000 bpd, one tenth of Nigeria's production, under General Abacha, and to have been distributed for political support, including to politicians participating in Abacha's transition program. Decisions relating to oil contracts were hyper-centralized in the president's office to ensure that the benefits involved went only to political supporters.

The oil trading companies—Swiss-based Addax and Glencore, and London-based Arcadia had the largest share of the Nigerian trade under General Abacha's government—which purchase Nigerian oil for onward sale on the spot or term markets, have close links with individual political figures in the military or civilian hierarchy. Getting a share of the trade is dependent on political patronage, and substantial commissions are paid for that patronage. The death of Abacha, the consequent falling from favor of the Lebanese-born Chagoury brothers (who had influenced decisions as to the allocation of political benefits in relation to the oil industry during his period as head of state), the dismissal of oil minister Daniel Etete, and the reforms announced by Abubakar temporarily damaged the positions of some of the traders, especially Glencore. However, their fortunes appear to be recovering as previous ways of doing business, including generous commissions, have reasserted themselves.[83]

Nigeria's oil resources have also been used to buy favor in the region. In September 1997, General Abacha awarded six crude term contracts to member states of the Economic Community of West African States (ECOWAS), allowing them to sell the oil or use it, as they pleased, bringing to nine the number of

---

[82] Corruption of this type is common to similar oil-based economies, but has reached "epidemic proportions" in Nigeria. See Karl, *Paradox of Plenty*, p.208.

[83] *Energy Compass*, vol.8, no.27, July 3, 1997; Seye Kehinde, "The Big Swindle," *News* (Lagos), December 26, 1994; "Over a Barrel," *Africa Confidential* vol.36, no.6, March 15, 1995; Obed Awowede, "Plundering and Looting Unlimited," *Tell* (Lagos), August 24, 1998; *Energy Compass*, vol.9, no.39, September 25, 1998; *Energy Compass*, vol.9, no.41, October 9, 1998. In September 1998, the Chagourys were reported to have fled the country. The oil trading companies largely use Nigerian crude, whose price is linked to Brent crude from the North Sea, to position themselves in the Brent market.

neighboring governments benefitting from Nigerian largesse.[84] These contracts were terminated in September 1998 by the government of General Abubakar.[85]

Millions of dollars appropriated by General Abacha and his close associates are currently being recovered by the government of General Abubakar, and many contracts awarded by Abacha have been canceled. Such efforts are traditional on change of regime, but have yet to lead to cleaner government in the long term: a commission of inquiry headed by economist Pius Okigbo, appointed by General Abacha himself shortly after taking power in 1993, estimated that U.S.$12.2 billion in oil earnings had disappeared between 1990 and 1994, but nobody was brought to account for this theft.[86] Nigeria's politics revolve about the distribution of the oil money, whether officially (in the form of debates over revenue allocation) or unofficially (as military and civilian politicians seek favor with those in a position to reward them with opportunities to "chop" money from contracts), and as long as the oil flows it will be difficult to overcome this legacy.

---

[84] The six states were Benin, Burkina Faso, Côte d'Ivoire, Guinea, Mali, and Niger, who joined Gambia, Ghana and Togo in receiving allocations of between 10,000 and 30,000 bpd of Nigerian crude. The governments would benefit either by refining the oil, if they have refining capacity, or by selling it at a premium to west African crude traders. *Energy Compass*, vol.8, no.37, September 12, 1997.

[85] *Energy Compass*, vol.9, no.41, October 9, 1998.

[86] James Rupert, "Nigerian Oil Corruption Began at the Top," *Washington Post*, June 10, 1998.

V. THE ENVIRONMENT

The Niger Delta is one of the world's largest wetlands, and the largest in Africa: it encompasses over 20,000 square kilometers. It is a vast floodplain built up by the accumulation of centuries of silt washed down the Niger and Benue Rivers, composed of four main ecological zones—coastal barrier islands, mangroves, fresh water swamp forests, and lowland rainforests—whose boundaries vary according to the patterns of seasonal flooding. The mangrove forest of Nigeria is the third largest in the world and the largest in Africa; over 60 percent of this mangrove, or 6,000 square kilometers, is found in the Niger Delta. The freshwater swamp forests of the delta reach 11,700 square kilometers and are the most extensive in west and central Africa.[87] The Niger Delta region has the high biodiversity characteristic of extensive swamp and forest areas, with many unique species of plants and animals.

The high rainfall in southern Nigeria in the rainy season leads to regular inundation of the low, poorly drained terrain of the Niger Delta, and an ecosystem characterized by the ebb and flow of water. Over the last few decades, however, the building of dams along the Niger and Benue Rivers and their tributaries has significantly reduced sedimentation and seasonal flooding in the delta. Coupled with riverbank and coastal erosion, it is estimated that, if it continued at a constant rate, the result of diminished siltation in the delta would be the loss of about 40 percent of the inhabited land in the delta within thirty years.[88] At the same time, since the construction of the dams, large numbers of people have settled in areas previously subject to extensive flooding; yet the progressive silting of the dams themselves, due to lack of maintenance, has meant that floods have begun to return to pre-dam levels, periodically inundating newly inhabited and cultivated areas.

---

[87] Good quality independent information on the environment of the Niger Delta is surprisingly hard to come by; but see World Bank, *Defining an Environmental Strategy for the Niger Delta* (Washington DC: World Bank, May 1995); David Moffat and Olof Lindén, "Perception and Reality: Assessing Priorities for Sustainable Development in the Niger River Delta," *Ambio (A Journal of the Human Environment)*, vol. 24, no.7-8, December 1995 (Stockholm: Royal Swedish Academy of Sciences, 1995), an article based on the research carried out for the World Bank report; and Nick Ashton Jones, *The ERA Handbook to the Niger Delta: The Human Ecosystems of the Niger Delta* (London and Benin City: Environmental Rights Action, 1998).

[88] It is estimated that around 70 percent of the sediment load of the rivers has been lost as a result of the dams. Moffat and Lindén, "Perception and Reality," pp.528-9.

Nigeria's mangrove forest is still relatively intact: an estimated 5 to 10 percent has been lost as a result of settlement or oil activities.[89] Freshwater swamp forests and forests on the barrier islands at the seaward edge of the delta are threatened by commercial logging, agriculture and settlements, but are still extensive. The lowland rainforest, on the other hand, has virtually gone: the zone it previously occupied covers about 7,400 square kilometers of the Niger Delta, but most of this has been cleared for agriculture.[90]

The Framework of Nigerian Law on Oil and the Environment

The framework for oil operations in Nigeria is set by the Petroleum Act (originally Decree No. 51 of 1969). Other relevant legislation includes the Oil in Navigable Waters Act (Decree No. 34 of 1968), the Oil Pipelines Act (Decree No. 31 of 1956), the Associated Gas (Reinjection) Act of 1979, and the Petroleum (Drilling and Production) Regulations of 1969, made under the Petroleum Act. From 1988, the Federal Environmental Protection Agency Act (Decree No. 58 of 1988) vested the authority to issue standards for water, air, and land quality in a Federal Environmental Protection Agency (FEPA), and regulations made by FEPA under the decree govern environmental standards in the oil and other industries. The Department of Petroleum Resources (DPR) has also issued a set of Environmental Guidelines and Standards for the Petroleum Industry in Nigeria (1991), which overlap with and in some cases differ from those issued by FEPA. For the most part, the specific standards set are comparable to those in force in Europe or the U.S.

Nigerian law provides that "all minerals, mineral oils and natural gas" are the property of the federal government.[91] Accordingly, the Petroleum Act requires a license to be obtained from the Ministry of Petroleum Resources before any oil operation—prospecting, exploration, drilling, production, storage, refining, or transportation—is commenced. Only a Nigerian citizen or a company incorporated in Nigeria may apply for such a license. The minister of petroleum resources has general supervisory powers over oil company activities, and may revoke a license under certain conditions, including if the operator fails to comply with "good oil

---

[89] Moffat and Lindén, "Perception and Reality," p.530.

[90] Ibid.

[91] Article 40(3) of the 1979 constitution; Article 42(3) of the 1989 constitution; Article 47(3) draft 1995 constitution. See above, footnote 10. The Petroleum Act also provides in section 1 that "The entire ownership and control of all petroleum in, under or upon any lands to which this section applies [i.e. land in Nigeria, under the territorial waters of Nigeria or forming part of the continental shelf] shall be vested in the state."

field practice."[92] Good oil field practice is not defined in the decree, but the Mineral Oils (Safety) Regulations of 1963, promulgated under the Mineral Oils Act (the predecessor to Petroleum Act), state that good oil field practice "shall be considered to be adequately covered by the appropriate current Institute of Petroleum Safety Codes, the American Petroleum Institute Codes, or the American Society of Mechanical Engineers Codes," thus effectively binding oil companies to respect international standards in their operations in Nigeria.[93] Licensees are responsible for all the actions of independent contractors carrying out work on their behalf.[94]

Oil companies are obliged to "adopt all practicable precautions including the provision of up-to-date equipment" to prevent pollution, and must take "prompt steps to control and, if possible, end it," if pollution does occur.[95] They must maintain all installations in good repair and condition in order to prevent "the escape or avoidable waste of petroleum" and to cause "as little damage as possible to the surface of the relevant area and to the trees, crops, buildings, structures and other properties thereon."[96] Oil companies are also required to comply with all local planning laws; they may not enter on any area held to be sacred or destroy any thing which is an object of veneration; and they must allow local inhabitants to have access, at their own risk, to roads constructed in their operating areas.[97] Specific rules relating to compensation in the event of infringement of these and other requirements are described below.

The Environmental Impact Assessment Act (Decree No. 86 of 1992) requires an environmental impact assessment (EIA) to be carried out "where the extent, nature or location of a proposed project or activity is such that it is likely to significantly affect the environment."[98] The public and private sector are enjoined

---

[92] Petroleum Act, Cap. 350, *Laws of the Federation of Nigeria*, Schedule 1, section, 24(1).

[93] Mineral Oils (Safety) Regulations, Regulation 7.

[94] Petroleum (Drilling and Production) Regulations, Regulation 15(2).

[95] Ibid., Regulation 25.

[96] Ibid., Regulation 36.

[97] Ibid., Regulations 17, 19, and 22.

[98] Environmental Impact Assessment Decree, section 2(2). Prior to the EIA Decree of 1992, certain similar requirements applied under the Petroleum Act and other legislation, such as the requirement under the Petroleum (Drilling and Production) Regulations to draw up an "oil field development programme," approved by the Director of Petroleum Resources, which should point out potential dangers to the environment and the appropriate solutions.

to give "prior consideration" to the environmental effects of any activity before it is embarked upon. An EIA is compulsory in certain cases, including oil and gas fields development and construction of oil refineries, some pipelines, and processing and storage facilities. The carrying out of EIAs is policed by the Federal Environmental Protection Agency, and by state environmental protection agencies.

As with the rest of the regulatory framework governing protection of the environment in Nigeria, there is in practice little enforcement of the requirements to carry out EIAs, either by FEPA or by the DPR's regulatory arm, the Petroleum Inspectorate, and virtually no quality control over the assessments carried out. As one study concluded: "Most state and local government institutions involved in environmental resource management lack funding, trained staff, technical expertise, adequate information, analytical capability and other pre-requisites for implementing comprehensive policies and programmes. In the case of the oil industry, overlapping mandates and jurisdiction between FEPA and the DPR frequently contribute to counterproductive competition."[99]

The Impact of Oil Operations on the Environment

The oil companies operating in Nigeria maintain that their activities are conducted to the highest environmental standards, and that the impact of oil on the environment of the delta is minimal. Shell, for example, has stated that "Shell Nigeria believes that most of the environmental problems are not the result of oil operations."[100] At the other extreme, Ken Saro-Wiwa, spokesperson for the Movement of the Survival of the Ogoni People (MOSOP) until he was hanged in November 1995, maintained that the environment in Ogoni has been "completely devastated by three decades of reckless oil exploitation or ecological warfare by Shell.... An ecological war is highly lethal, the more so as it is unconventional. It is omnicidal in effect. Human life, flora, fauna, the air, fall at its feet, and finally, the land itself dies."[101]

Environmental groups accuse the oil companies of operating double standards; of allowing practices in Nigeria that would never be permitted in North

---

[99] Environmental Resources Managers Ltd, *Niger Delta Environmental Survey Final Report Phase I, Volume I*, p.263.

[100] Shell International Petroleum Company letter to Prof. John Heath, December 22, 1994.

[101] Ken Saro-Wiwa, "My Story," text of statement to the Civil Disturbances Tribunal, reprinted in *Ogoni: Trials and Travails* (Lagos: Civil Liberties Organisation, 1996), p.42-3.

America or Europe. The companies deny this, although Shell, for example, has defended the idea of national rather than international environmental standards. At the annual general meeting for the Shell group in London in May 1996, group chairman John Jennings stated that "the charge of 'double standards' is mistaken, because it is based on the notion that there is a single, 'absolute environmental standard.' ... As long as we continue to improve, varying standards are inevitable." In the same vein, Group Managing Director CAJ Herkströter implied at the parallel annual meeting held in the Netherlands, that higher environmental standards could harm local economies: "Should we apply the higher-cost western standards, thus making the operation uncompetitive and depriving the local work force of jobs and the chance of development? Or should we adopt the prevailing legal standards at the site, while having clear plans to improve towards 'best practice' within a reasonable timeframe?"[102]

Shell admits, however, that its facilities in the delta are in need of upgrading: "Most of the facilities were constructed between the 1960s and early 1980s to the then prevailing standards. SPDC would not build them that way today."[103] Under pressure from international and national environmental groups, Shell has stated that it will finally bring its Nigerian operations (with the exception of gas flaring, for which see below) into line with Nigerian law—which in most respects refers to international standards—by the end of 1999.[104]

---

[102] Quoted in *PIRC Intelligence*, vol.11, issue 3, March 1997 (published in London by Pensions Investment Research Consultants). Principle 11 of the 1992 U.N. Rio Declaration on Environment and Development states that "Environmental standards, management objectives and priorities should reflect the environmental context to which they apply. Standards applied by some countries may be inappropriate and of unwarranted economic social cost to other countries, in particular developing countries." As noted above, however, Nigerian law at many points explicitly refers to international standards and requires companies operating in Nigeria to respect those standards.

[103] Shell International Petroleum Company, *Developments in Nigeria* (London: March 1995).

[104] Royal Dutch/Shell Group of Companies *Health, Safety and the Environment Report 1997* (London and the Hague, May 1997). Shell states that areas of noncompliance for which exemptions and waivers have been applied include effluent discharges in environments with levels which already exceed regulatory limits and areas where SPDC has not completed the installation of monitoring systems. SPDC is said to be working on bringing five main areas, currently covered by waivers, into compliance: produced water effluent limits (by the end of 1998); approved disposal facilities for produced sand, sludge and solid wastes (2000); oily waste water limits for flowstations (2000); gas flaring condition monitoring (1999); and environmental sensitivity index

Unfortunately, the oil industry's own evaluations of environmental damage, required for the production of EIAs, which might otherwise provide a useful basis for assessing environmental damage, are inadequate. According to a Dutch biologist formerly employed by SPDC for two years as head of environmental studies, for example: "There was/is a major problem with most of the environmental studies carried out in the Niger Delta, as they are carried out by Nigerian Universities or private consultancies, which have a generally low scientific level and little technical/industrial expertise."[105] A review of two of SPDC's EIAs for pipeline projects conducted for the Body Shop International in 1994 concluded that, while "SPDC's consultants have tried to be thorough," the assessments were "lengthy, generally poorly constructed, and therefore it is difficult to envisage how they could either assist the Nigerian planning authorities in determining authorisation of the development, or enable SPDC employees in Nigeria to better manage their (potential) environmental impacts." Furthermore, "there is little evidence that SPDC have been involved in the EIA process, that they acknowledge the potential impacts of their pipeline operations and that they have taken ownership of the mitigation measures necessary to minimise potential impacts."[106] The environmental impact assessment for the proposed liquefied natural gas project, carried out in 1995 on behalf of Nigeria LNG Ltd by SGS Environment Ltd, was also reviewed on behalf of Body Shop International. The review of the substantial document concluded that, although some sections of the report were of high quality, there were serious defects. Overall, "the Environmental Statements fall well short of what would be required in any developed country and do not allow the reader to make an informed judgement about the relative environmental benefits and costs of the scheme. It is normal practice to consider alternatives in an environmental assessment, but this has not been done. Significant issues have been overlooked or deferred to a later date."[107]

As a result of deficiencies in such studies and the paucity of independent academic research, there is little publicly available hard information on the state of

---

(ESI) mapping (2000). Tony Imevbore, Paul Driver, and Chris Geerling, "Environmental Objectives Discussion Document" prepared by SPDC for its April 1998 "Stakeholders EnvironmentalWorkshop" held in Port Harcourt, section 1.3.d.

[105] J.P. van Dessel, *The Environmental Situation in the Niger Delta, Nigeria* (Internal Position Paper prepared for Greenpeace Netherlands, February 1995), section 5.1.

[106] Environmental Resources Management, *Review of Environmental Statements* (London: Body Shop International, March 1994)

[107] Dr. Phil Smith, *Review of the Environmental Statements Prepared for Nigeria LNG Ltd by SGS Environment Ltd* (London: Aquatic Environmental Consultants, 1995).

the environment in the delta or the impact that oil production has had. Problems identified include flooding and coastal erosion, sedimentation and siltation, degradation and depletion of water and coastal resources, land degradation, oil pollution, air pollution, land subsidence, biodiversity depletion, noise and light pollution, health problems, and low agricultural production, as well as socio-economic problems, lack of community participation, and weak or non-existent laws and regulations.[108] Astonishingly, despite decades of oil exploration and production, neither the oil companies nor the Nigerian government have funded the scientific research that would allow an objective assessment of the damage caused by oil exploration and production.

Oil Spills and Hydrocarbon Pollution

According to the official estimates of the Nigerian National Petroleum Corporation (NNPC), based on the quantities reported by the operating companies, approximately 2,300 cubic meters of oil are spilled in 300 separate incidents annually. It can be safely assumed that, due to under-reporting, the real figure is substantially higher: conservative estimates place it at up to ten times higher.[109] Statistics from the Department of Petroleum Resources indicate that between 1976 and 1996 a total of 4,835 incidents resulted in the spillage of at least 2,446,322 barrels (102.7 million U.S. gallons), of which an estimated 1,896,930 barrels (79.7 million U.S. gallons; 77 percent) were lost to the environment.[110] Another calculation, based on oil industry sources, estimates that more than 1.07 million barrels (45 million U.S. gallons) of oil were spilled in Nigeria from 1960 to 1997.[111] Nigeria's largest spill was an offshore well blowout in January 1980,

---

[108] Environmental Resources Managers Ltd, *Niger Delta Environmental Survey Final Report Phase I, Volume I*, p.234; see also World Bank, *Defining an Environmental Strategy for the Niger Delta*. Recently, geologists meeting at a conference organized by the U.N. Environmental, Scientific and Cultural Organisation (UNESCO) in Ghana identified "a growing consensus ... that oil extraction has played a strong role in speeding up subsidence and that its effects will be felt for years to come." Shell is said to have conducted research on these effects, but has not published the results. Barry Morgan, "That sinking feeling puts heat on oil," *Upstream News* (Oslo) August 7, 1998.

[109] Moffat and Lindén, "Perception and Reality," p.532.

[110] Environmental Resources Managers Ltd, *Niger Delta Environmental Survey Final Report Phase I, Volume I*, p.249. There are 42 U.S. gallons to one barrel of oil.

[111] The data on which the calculation was based were complete through October 13, 1997, and include spills of over twenty-four barrels (1,000 U.S. gallons). Tanker spills are more likely to be reported accurately than pipeline spills. Unsurprisingly, perhaps, the total is much lower than that calculated by the DPR. *Oil Spill Intelligence Report*

when at least 200,000 barrels of oil (8.4 million U.S. gallons), according to oil industry sources, spewed into the Atlantic Ocean from a Texaco facility and destroyed 340 hectares of mangroves.[112] DPR estimates were that more than 400,000 barrels (16.8 million U.S. gallons) were spilled in this incident.[113] Mangrove forest is particularly vulnerable to oil spills, because the soil soaks up the oil like a sponge and re-releases it every rainy season.

Two serious spills took place in early 1998. On January 12, 1998, a major spill of more than 40,000 barrels of crude oil (1.7 million U.S. gallons) leaked from the pipeline linking Mobil's Idoho platform with its Qua Iboe onshore terminal in Akwa Ibom State. Mobil estimated that more than 90 percent of the oil had dispersed or evaporated naturally, though the spill traveled "hundreds of kilometers farther than expected," and some 500 barrels (21,000 U.S. gallons) washed ashore.[114] By the end of February 1998, about 14,000 claims for compensation had been submitted from individuals or groups, totaling an estimated U.S.$100 million. About twenty communities, with a total population of about one million, were considered to be the worst hit, especially at the mouth of the Pennington River.[115] Clean Nigeria Associates, an oil industry-funded spill-response cooperative, was mobilized to assist in containing the spill and dealing with its effects. However, shoreline cleanup had still not begun by January 28, because "staff had to train crew leaders and deliver appropriate gear to the sites," and as late as March some sites were still visibly contaminated.[116] Mobil had not responded to requests from Human Rights Watch for further information about this spill at the time of going

---

(Arlington, Massachusetts), White Paper Series, vol.1, no.7, November 1997.

[112] "Effect of Nigerian Spill Termed 'Minimal' as Last Known Patch Disperses," *Oil Spill Intelligence Report*, vol.21, no.4, January 22, 1998. Other major spills occurring at around the same time (including Gulf Oil and SPDC spills in 1978) made the period 1978 to 1980 the worst for spills in Nigerian oil producing history. Environmental Resources Managers Ltd, *Niger Delta Environmental Survey Final Report Phase I, Volume I*, p.250.

[113] Environmental Resources Managers Ltd, *Niger Delta Environmental Survey Final Report Phase I, Volume I*, p.250; J. Finine Fekumo, "Civil Liability for Damage Caused by Oil Pollution," in J.A. Omotola (ed.) *Environmental Laws in Nigeria including Compensation* (Lagos: University of Lagos, 1990), p.268.

[114] Edwin Unsworth, "Mobil Covered for Nigeria Spill,"*Business Insurance*, January 26, 1998; Reuters, January 20, 1998; "Effect of Nigerian Spill Termed 'Minimal.'"

[115] *Oil Daily*, February 27, 1998; "Effect of Nigerian Spill Termed 'Minimal.'"

[116] *Oil Spill Intelligence Report*, vol.21, no.4, January 22, 1998, and vol.21, no.5, January 29, 1998; Human Rights Watch correspondence with Environmental Rights Action; *Oil Daily*, February 27, 1998.

to press. On March 27, 1998, a further spill of 20,000 barrels (840,000 U.S. gallons) took place from Shell's Jones Creek flow station, Delta State, in the brackish water of the mangrove forest, killing large numbers of fish. Shell identified the cause of the spill as "pipeline failure" and closed in 110,000 bpd of oil from eight flowstations. According to Shell, relief materials, including food and water, were provided to the communities affected at the time, and clean-up of the spill has been completed. As of September 1998, production at Jones Creek remained closed, pending the outcome of a technical investigation into the cause of the spill.[117]

As a result of the small size of the oilfields in the Niger Delta, there is an extensive network of pipelines between the fields, as well as numerous small networks of flowlines—the narrow diameter pipes that carry oil from wellheads to flowstations—allowing many opportunities for leaks. In onshore areas, most pipelines and flowlines are laid above ground. Many pipelines and flowlines are old and subject to corrosion: fifteen years is the estimated safe lifespan of a pipeline, but in numerous places in the delta pipelines aged twenty or twenty-five years can be found. SPDC stated that it completed a program for the replacement of older pipelines in swamp areas during 1996, and claimed that as a result the volume of spills due to corrosion was reduced by 36 percent compared to 1995. The company also stated that it planned to renew and bury 2,188 kilometers of lines by the end of 1998, and that all would by then be buried.[118] Burial still requires clearing of the vegetation above the line, and though it reduces the chances of pollution through sabotage, it also makes leak detection more difficult.

DPR regulations require the body responsible for a spill to clean the site and restore it to its original state so far as possible. Soil at a spill site on land must contain no more than thirty parts per million (ppm) of oil after six months. SPDC official policy is that "All hydrocarbon and chemical spills in the vicinity of the company's operations shall be cleaned up in a timely and efficient manner."[119] According to Shell, "All spills are investigated." The company starts with "an immediate visit [to the] site to locate the source of the leakage and to stop it. This is followed with the initiation of clean-up actions."[120] However, in some cases it

---

[117] Attachment to Shell International Ltd letter to Human Rights Watch, September 7, 1998.

[118] SPDC states it replaced 295 kilometers of swamp lines in 1996, and that it has replaced more than 1,000 kilometers of flowlines altogether since 1993. SPDC, *People and the Environment: Annual Report 1996.*

[119] SPDC, *People and the Environment: Annual Report 1996.*

[120] Shell International Ltd letter to Human Rights Watch, February 13, 1998.

is clear that land affected by spills is not properly or promptly rehabilitated. At Kolo Creek flow station, a spill that Shell alleged was caused by sabotage occurred in July 1997, and was cleaned by putting contaminated soil into pits; one year later, during flood season, the community believed that a new spill had taken place when this oil was released back into the water.[121] In Aleibiri, Bayelsa State, community members alleged in August 1997 that a spill dating from March 1997 had not yet been cleaned up. SPDC, which stated that the spill was caused by sabotage (a claim contested by local residents), said that the delay had been "because the community prevented access to the site to determine the cause of the spill and to clamp the hole," demanding "payments to appease their deities, relief materials and immediate cash compensation," while "ethnic clashes between Ijaws and Itsekiris in April, May and June caused further delay," because, during the Warri crisis, "SPDC restricted operations in the Western Division to essential activities to minimize movements on the water and the risk of hijack and further hostage-taking."[122] Local activists contest this explanation, saying that the violence associated with the Warri crisis (see below) could not have prevented Shell gaining access to Aleibiri, many tens of kilometers away from the area of conflict. Shell states that the pipeline was finally clamped in July 1997, and that clean-up operations were to begin in August but were delayed until November because two barges and a crew boat were seized. In March 1998, local environmental activists reported that in the process of clearing the spill several hectares of forest had been set alight by a contractor who had collected contaminated material into heaps for burning. This method of clearing spills is not regarded as satisfactory by international standards, and in this case additionally appears to have been carried out in a negligent fashion, allowing a serious fire to occur. SPDC confirmed to an oil industry publication that a Shell contractor had set the blaze on March 25, damaging ten hectares, and that the procedures used were not in compliance with

[121] Environmental Rights Action, "Shell's Double Barrel Attack," ERA Field Report No. 12, August 17, 1998.

[122] Reuters, August 18, 1997; attachment to Shell International Ltd letter to Human Rights Watch, September 7, 1998.

their requirements.[123] Substantial losses were suffered as a result by several members of the community.[124]

The effect on the environment of the contaminated "formation water" (also known as "produced water") separated from the hydrocarbon fluids with which it is mixed underground and deliberately discharged from flow stations and terminals is largely unevaluated. Formation water is in some cases treated to remove residual oil, but in other cases released directly into the environment. While the water discharged generally contains low concentrations of oil, its large volume, together with occasional oil spillages, could well have long term effects, depending partly on the ecological setting in which the discharge is made. In offshore locations or in areas with rapid drainage increased dilution reduces the polluting effects of the water; on land and in the swamp, however, the cumulative effect "can be devastating at some locations."[125] A 1993 Shell environmental impact study near the Bonny terminal found high hydrocarbon content in the nearby creek indicating "poor or no treatment of effluent."[126] At Abiteye, on the Escravos River in Delta State, Chevron has for several years reportedly pumped hot untreated formation water directly into mangrove creeks, not even piping it into the main tidal channel where it would be diluted and cause less damage.[127] Another problem of unknown impact is the disposal of waste from oil facilities: according to a former employee,

---

[123] *Oil Spill Intelligence Report* fax to Human Rights Watch, April 21, 1998. Shell stated to Human Rights Watch "Normal practice today in respect of oil-impacted debris is to remove it from site for controlled incineration. Where logistics make this difficult, a mobile incinerator is usually taken to the site. The Aleibiri site was three kilometres from the nearest transport access point, ruling out both options. Instead it was agreed that the debris be burned on location, a practice that had been successfully implemented in similar locations. At Aleibiri, a site was chosen and a firebreak established according to standard practice. However, despite these precautions the fire did get out of control. SPDC has since that time conducted further investigations to find out what happened. The investigations traced the incident to poor supervision. SPDC has accordingly revised its procedure to include additional precautions whenever such operation is to be carried out." Attachment to Shell International Ltd letter to Human Rights Watch, September 7, 1998.

[124] Environmental Rights Action, "Shell's One Year Old Spill Sets Forest Ablaze," ERA Field Report No. 3, March 26, 1998.

[125] Environmental Resources Managers Ltd, *Niger Delta Environmental Survey Final Report Phase I, Volume I,* p.242.

[126] Moffat and Lindén, "Perception and Reality," p.532.

[127] Human Rights Watch interview with Bruce Powell, zoologist and expert on Niger Delta ecology, London, June 20, 1998.

SPDC, for example, had no adequate facilities for treatment of oily or chemical waste (including polluted soil and debris) in its eastern division in 1994.[128] Effluents from the refineries at Port Harcourt and Warri are usually discharged, after treatment, into adjoining creeks and rivers. Nearby communities have complained at the effects of these effluents on fish stocks.[129]

The DPR sets a limit of 20 ppm hydrocarbon contamination for effluent discharged to nearshore waters and 10 ppm for inland waters; FEPA's limit is 10 ppm for coastal (nearshore) waters. In its 1996 annual report on "People and the Environment," SPDC indicated that the water discharged at its terminals (at Forcados, Bonny, and Ughelli) did not meet the FEPA limits, although Bonny and Forcados were within the DPR limits.[130] In an internal document from 1993, SPDC claimed to meet the DPR limit of 20 ppm oil and grease in its effluent at the Bonny terminal, stating that the concentration routinely discharged was 7 ppm. However, during the same period, a Shell employee noted the presence of an oily sheen on the water immediately after discharge, suggesting a concentration of at least 50 ppm.[131]

Nigerian crude oil is very light (low density), with a rapid evaporation loss which could be up to 50 percent within forty-eight hours.[132] The oil companies therefore maintain that the effects of oil spills are largely temporary and localized. Shell states that "Complete rehabilitation after clean-up takes 12-18 months."[133] A study of a major 1970 spill at Ebubu, in Ogoni, on the other hand, carried out nineteen years after it had been set ablaze, leaving a five-meter thick crust, found that vegetation was recovering, but that vegetation in areas downstream of the spill was still being degraded due to a slow seepage of crude oil from the spill site.[134]

---

[128] Van Dessel, *The Environmental Situation in the Niger Delta, Nigeria*, section 5.5.1.

[129] Environmental Resources Managers Ltd, *Niger Delta Environmental Survey Final Report Phase I, Volume I*, p.247. Data on monitoring of discharged effluents from the refineries are known to exist but could not be accessed by the authors of the report.

[130] SPDC, *People and the Environment: Annual Report 1996*. The figures given were: Forcados, 16 mg/l; Bonny, 14.3 mg/l; Ughelli, 17 mg/l.

[131] SPDC, *PAGE [Public Affairs, Government and the Environment] Fact Book 1993*, section 3.3.1; Van Dessel, *The Environmental Situation in the Niger Delta, Nigeria*, section 5.4.

[132] Moffat and Lindén, "Perception and Reality," p.532.

[133] SPDC, *People and the Environment Annual Report 1996*, p.14.

[134] Emmanuel Asuquo Obot, A. Chinda, and S. Braid, "Vegetation recovery and herbaceous production in a freshwater wetland 19 years after a major oil spill," *African Journal of Ecology* 1992, vol.30, pp.149-156. The responsibility for the Ebubu-Ochani

This is an exceptional case, but studies have shown that the chronic occurrence of minor spills can have "greater detrimental effects on the environment than the more visible, large-scale spillages associated with tanker accidents and blowouts."[135] Even when oil-in-water values have dropped below detectable limits, oil-in-sediment values can remain high.[136] In the absence of serious independent scientific studies of the long term effects of hydrocarbon pollution in the Niger

spill has proved a controversial issue. Shell maintains that the spill was "discovered" in the early 1980s in thick forest, near Ejamah village in the Ebubu field on the edge of Ogoni, and that discussions with villagers subsequently established that the spill had occurred during the 1967-70 civil war, while all Shell staff were withdrawn from the area, and was accompanied by a fire that raged for several days. (Shell's account is not altogether consistent: in other versions it has stated more precisely that the spill occurred in 1970 and was caused by sabotage by the retreating Biafran army, which deliberately set the oil alight to provide a barrier to the advancing federal troops.) In 1983, the paramount ruler of Ejamah-Ebubu made a claim for ₦10 million (U.S.$111,100) against Shell for compensation for the spill; although the company acknowledged no responsibility, Shell states that, "as a gesture of goodwill," it agreed to try to clean up the spill, provide a water supply and pay ₦300,000 (U.S.$3,300) to the community. Shell later acquired the land for ₦77,000 (U.S.$850) and states that it awarded a clean-up contract which removed layers of oil and was completed in 1990. However, because of the depth of the crust, oil continued to leach into the environment during the wet season. A 1990 study carried out by the Institute of Petroleum Studies at the Rivers State University of Science and Technology recommended further clean-up measures. According to Shell, these measures were planned but shelved in 1993 when all staff were pulled out of the Ogoni area. Local residents, however, contradict this account, stating that the spill took place in 1970, after the end of the civil war and long after the federal army had retaken the area, and was the result of an explosion in the pipeline; the fire is alleged to have been a clean-up measure undertaken by Shell itself. See, "Flash Points in the Ogoni Story: What Happened and Lessons Learned," briefing available on the Shell web site (http://www.shellnigeria.com) as of October 1, 1997; and Shell International Petroleum Co Ltd, Complaint to the British Broadcasting Complaints Commission, November 1995, and response from Channel 4.

[135] R.J. Snowden and I.K.E. Ekweozor, "The Impact of a Minor Oil Spillage in the Estuarine Niger Delta," *Marine Pollution Bulletin* vol.18, no.11, November 1987, pp.595-599.

[136] C.B. Powell, S.A. White, B. Baranowska-Dutkiewicz, D.D. Ibiebele, M. Isoun, and F.U. Ofoegbu, "Oshika Oil Spill Environmental Impact: Effect on Aquatic Biology," in *The Petroleum Industry and the Nigerian Environment: Proceedings of an International Seminar, November 11 to 14, 1985, Kaduna* (published by the Petroleum Inspectorate, NNPC, and the Environmental Planning and Protection Division of the Federal Ministry of Works and Housing).

Delta, the damage caused by individual spills on the overall environment cannot be evaluated, though spills in other parts of the world have been noted to cause long term effects. Moreover, the lighter compounds that evaporate quickly (such as toluene and benzene) also have a relatively high solubility and can be toxic at very low concentrations.[137]

Whatever the long term impact on the environment, spills can be devastating for those directly affected, especially in the dry land or freshwater swamp areas, where the effects are concentrated in particular locations. Oil leaks are usually from high pressure pipelines, and therefore spurt out over a wide area, destroying crops, artificial fishponds used for fish farming, "economic trees" (that is, economically valuable trees, including those growing "wild" but owned by particular families) and other income-generating assets. Even a small leak can thus wipe out a year's food supply for a family, with it wiping out income from products sold for cash. The consequences of such loss of livelihood can range from children missing school because their parents are unable to afford the fees, to virtual destitution. Even if the land recovers for the following year, the spill has consequences over a much longer period for the families directly affected. Several farmers interviewed by Human Rights Watch affected by spills appeared dazed and practically unable to take in the consequences of a recent spill, or to estimate the costs, beyond a simple statement that they had no idea how they would now manage. In tidal salt water areas, where fishing grounds tend to be open, individual families are less likely to be totally wiped out, while spills will in any event disperse more quickly. Nevertheless, big spills can still have a significant economic effect: following the Mobil spill of January 1998, savings by fishermen into microcredit schemes set up at a B.P./Statoil development project at Akassa, on the Atlantic coast, dropped appreciably.[138]

Similarly, since in most areas of the delta drinking water is drawn straight from streams and creeks, with no other option available to the local people, a spill can cause severe problems for the population dependent on the water source affected, even if it disperses rapidly and the water soon returns to its previous condition. Crude oil contains thousands of different chemicals, many of them toxic and some known to be carcinogenic with no determined safe threshold for human

---

[137] Greenpeace U.K., "Greenpeace Oil Briefing No. 5: The Environmental Impacts of Oil," and "Greenpeace Oil Briefing No. 6: Possible Long Term Impacts of the Braer Disaster: Review of Previous Spills" (London, January 1993).

[138] Human Rights Watch interview with Bill Knight, project manager, B.P./Statoil development project in Akassa, London, June 29, 1998.

exposure.[139] Following the major Texaco spill of 1980, it was reported that 180 people died in one community as a result of the pollution.[140] On several occasions, people interviewed by Human Rights Watch said that spills in their area had made people sick who drank the water, especially children.[141] In January 1998, Nigerian opposition radio reported that about one hundred villagers from communities affected by a major Mobil spill of January 12 had been hospitalized as a result of drinking contaminated water.[142] Litigation against oil companies for compensation in the event of spills has also claimed for deaths of children caused by drinking polluted water.[143] Often, local residents complain that fish taste of paraffin (kerosene), indicating hydrocarbon contamination.

In many villages near oil installations, even when there has been no recent spill, an oily sheen can be seen on the water, which in fresh water areas is usually the same water that the people living there use for drinking and washing. In April 1997, samples taken from water used for drinking and washing by local villagers were analyzed in the U.S. A sample from Luawii, in Ogoni, where there had been no oil production for four years, had 18 ppm of hydrocarbons in the water, 360 times the level allowed in drinking water in the European Union (E.U.). A sample from Ukpeleide, Ikwerre, contained 34 ppm, 680 times the E.U. standard.[144] Similarly, a geographer based at Uyo University in Akwa Ibom State, who had studied the effect of oil operations since 1985, described to Human Rights Watch how soils in communities near to the Qua Iboe area where Mobil has its tank farm had very high hydrocarbon content, while local fauna and flora, including

[139] Greenpeace U.K., "Greenpeace Oil Briefing No. 7: Human Health Impacts of Oil" (London, January 1993).

[140] Fekumo, "Civil Liability for Damage Caused by Oil Pollution," p.268.

[141] For example, interviews at Edagberi, Rivers State, July 5, 1997, referring to a spill that took place in July 1996. The Director of Research at the California Air Resources Board stated to Greenpeace in 1993 that, faced with a situation similar to the Braer oil spill in the Shetlands, he would evacuate children living in the affected locality. Greenpeace U.K., "Greenpeace Oil Briefing No. 7: Human Health Impacts of Oil."

[142] Radio Kudirat Nigeria, January 30, 1998, as reported by BBC SWB, February 4, 1998.

[143] For example, *SPDC v. Chief Caiphas Enoch and two others* [1992] 8 NWLR (Nigerian Weekly Law Reports) (Part 259), p.335, in which five children are alleged to have died as a result of drinking oil-contaminated water.

[144] Stephen Kretzmann and Shannon Wright, *Human Rights and Environmental Information on the Royal Dutch/Shell Group of Companies, 1996-1997: An Independent Annual Report* (San Francisco and Berkeley, CA: Rainforest Action Network and Project Underground, May 1997), p.6. The E.U. standard is 0.05 ppm.

periwinkles—a major food source for the local people—had died out. Follow up research had, however, proved impossible for lack of resources.[145] Other studies have found hydrocarbon contamination of oysters and adverse effects on fisheries, but again further investigation is needed to ascertain the prevalence of such effects.[146]

The overall effect of oil spills on the delta is effectively unknown: "Although the effects of oil on mangrove environments are well known and a large number of studies appear to have been carried out in the Niger Delta, available information is not sufficient to assess the present condition of the region with respect to oil spills."[147] One zoologist, before his death perhaps the foremost expert on the ecology of the Niger Delta, commented to Human Rights Watch that "the bottom line is that the oil companies have never tried to find out what the effect of oil spills is; and those assessments that are done are useless and too late."[148] Therefore, although one study concluded that, "When assessing the impact of the oil industry on the environment of the delta, it appears that oil pollution, in itself, is only of moderate priority when compared with the full spectrum of environmental problems in the Niger Delta,"[149] this opinion, admittedly based on incomplete data, is challenged by environmentalists. The overall impact of oil spills is, in any event, irrelevant in assessing the impact of individual spills or the effect on a community of discharges from a particular flowstation. Moreover, as described below, it is also the case that many of the other environmental problems of the delta are due in whole or in part to the oil industry, and the distinction between hydrocarbon pollution and the other effects of oil operations and oil-led development is largely meaningless for the local communities.

Infrastructure Development

In addition to the direct pollution caused by oil production, the oil industry has had a profound effect on the environment of the Niger Delta through the infrastructure constructed to support oil exploration and production, and the immigration from other parts of Nigeria that has followed the economic opportunities provided by oil. Oil companies have constructed roads or dredged canals to their well heads and flow stations, and in some cases have built roads

[145] Human Rights Watch interview, July 8, 1997.

[146] Environmental Resources Managers Ltd, *Niger Delta Environmental Survey Final Report Phase I, Volume I*, p.179.

[147] Ibid., p.250.

[148] Human Rights Watch interview with Bruce Powell, London, June 20, 1998.

[149] Moffat and Lindén, "Perception and Reality," p.532.

specifically for communities (though often communities are bypassed by roads to oil facilities). These thoroughfares and others built by the Nigerian government with oil money and partly for the benefit of the oil industry have improved transportation dramatically in dry land areas of the delta region, and so increased economic activity in the affected communities, but at the same time roads have allowed cultivation and hunting in previously pristine forest and increased commercial logging activities. With the influx of comparatively rich, and almost all male, workers from the well-paid oil industry elite, has also come increased prostitution in previously isolated and stable communities.[150]

The lines cleared of vegetation for oil pipelines or seismic surveys[151] also become informal roads, which, though not paved, allow foot access for hunters into previously inaccessible forest regions. Although seismic lines are only needed temporarily and growth regenerates quickly in dry land and freshwater areas, mangrove forests have a very slow regeneration rate. Seismic lines a few meters wide cut through mangrove decades ago are still visible from the air: SPDC estimated in 1993 that since it had started operations onshore, 60,000 kilometers of seismic line had been cut, of which 39,000 kilometers were through mangrove; forthcoming three-dimensional surveys planned would cut a further 31,380 kilometers, of which 17,400 were to be through mangrove.[152] According to Shell, "In densely populated or environmentally sensitive areas, where explosions are not practical, vibrator trucks are used" rather than dynamite, which is used in "remote areas."[153] However, Human Rights Watch visited several villages in Nigeria where

---

[150] For one account, see, Ibim Semenitari, "Siege of the Sluts," *Tell*, February 23, 1998. For the effect of oil on local political economies generally, see below.

[151] Seismic surveys are one of the most important methods of surveying sites for oil deposits without actually drilling. Sound waves, usually generated by detonating dynamite a few meters below ground, are sent into the earth, and the time taken for them to be reflected by the different rock layers present is measured and gives an indication of where oil may be found. The most sophisticated seismic surveys are three-dimensional, in which seismic lines are laid out in a dense grid and the recorded data processed by computers. In order to carry out a seismic survey vegetation is cut back to ensure that the holes for the dynamite are sited in a straight line; these lines are referred to as "seismic lines." Shell publicity booklet, *Oil* (London: Shell International Ltd, 1990).

[152] SPDC, *PAGE Fact Book 1993* section 3.1.1. In recent years, Shell has introduced a program for replanting seismic lines in mangrove areas, though local environmental groups have claimed that it is poorly managed and ineffective.

[153] Shell publicity booklet, *Oil*.

dynamiting had taken place very close to human habitations, in some cases reportedly causing cracks in the walls of houses nearby.[154]

Roads and canals built by the oil companies can also be destructive in a more direct way than simply by promoting the mixed blessing of human access. In a number of cases, roads have been built on causeways across seasonally flooded plains, whose ecology depends on the changing hydrological conditions. Unless proper culverts are built under the causeways, as is all too often not the case, the drainage of the area is affected, causing permanent flooding on one side of the road and the drying out of the other. As a result, trees die, fishponds are destroyed, and seasonal fishing completely disrupted, often destroying a significant percentage of the income derived by local communities from the land or even the entire livelihood of some families. A typical case is that of Gbaran oil field in Rivers State. In 1991, a causeway to carry a road to the well heads was built on behalf of SPDC by Willbros West Africa Inc, a contractor to the oil industry with headquarters in the U.S. that has been involved in a number of incidents where protesters at the work they have been carrying out have been assaulted or killed by Nigerian security forces. According to local people, the causeway initially had no passages for water to pass underneath, blocking the drainage channel. Although, following protests from community members and environmental groups, culverts were eventually constructed, they were poorly designed, and the drainage of the area is still disturbed. Trees and other vegetation over a wide area have died from waterlogging, and seasonal fishing grounds have been destroyed, causing substantial economic damage to those whose land was affected.[155] At the time the

---

[154] For example, at Ozoro, Isoko North Local Government Authority, Delta State, where a survey by Seismographic Services Limited for SPDC was said to have caused cracks in the walls of a house visited by Human Rights Watch on July 21, 1997.

[155] Human Rights Watch interviews, Yenezue-Gene, July 5, 1997. In response to inquiries from Human Rights Watch, dodging the issue of the blockage of water passage and the level of damage done, Shell stated that: "Gbaran field development was planned in two phases. Phase I involved the accelerated construction of drilling locations and their access roads. The objective was to facilitate an early commencement of drilling operations. In this phase, three bailey bridges were constructed and the work was completed in 1990. The drainage structure provided at this stage was adequate but could not provide long term solutions to the drainage problem in the field. Phase II was planned to commence at the end of drilling operations and this involved detailed engineering design and construction of all required long-term facilities including drainage improvement works. After the completion of Phase I, work could not immediately commence on Phase II because of budget constraints that has become an industry problem, and low oil yield resulting from the drilling of Gbaran-5 (ex-Gbaran

culverts were cut, a young girl drowned when her canoe was capsized by the turbulence caused by the draining of the lake that had developed.[156] Farmers in Obite, Rivers State, in the Obagi oil field operated by Elf, also complained of flooding to Human Rights Watch.[157]

Canals can also disrupt delicate hydrological systems, especially when they are constructed in the border zone between fresh water and brackish water in the riverine areas. Such disruption can destroy long-established fishing grounds. A canal dug by Chevron near the remote village of Awoye, Ilaje/Ese-Odo local government area, Ondo State, has reportedly caused or accelerated erosion by the sea and has also destroyed the local hydrological system by allowing salt water into previous fresh water areas, creating a saltwater marsh in place of much higher biodiversity freshwater swamp. As a consequence, traditional fishing grounds and sources of drinking water have been wiped out: the damage is described by one expert on the Niger Delta environment as "one of the most extreme cases of habitat destruction" in the delta.[158]

Dredging destroys the ecology of the dredged area and the area where the spoils are dumped. Although dredged material is in principle dumped on land, some of it will inevitably slip back into the water, increasing turbidity, reducing sunlight penetration and thus plant life, and possibly driving away fish. Dredged materials in mangrove areas will turn acidic once exposed to oxygen, and silt dredged as a result of canalization and dumped on cultivated levees can decrease

---

VQTL-1) location." Phase II eventually began in 1995, and a number of bridges and culverts have been added, although several are outstanding. "Twelve claimants have been paid compensation; others are at various stages of processing, while incoming claims are being considered." Shell International Ltd letter to Human Rights Watch, February 13, 1998.

[156] Human Rights Watch interviews, Yenezue-Gene, July 5, 1997.

[157] Human Rights Watch interviews, July 4, 1997.

[158] Ebun-Olu Adegboruwa, "Report on Visit to Awoye Community," Gani Fawehinmi Chambers, Lagos 1997; Human Rights Watch interview, Bruce Powell, June 20, 1998. Chevron states that it has allowed access to a borehole at its nearby Opuekeba facilities since 1994: Chevron Nigeria Ltd letter to Human Rights Watch, June 29, 1998. Human Rights Watch has not itself visited the site. A major protest at Chevron's Parabe platform, offshore from the Ilaje area, took place in May 1998, by youths protesting habitat destruction, among other complaints (described below in the section on "Protest and Repression in the Niger Delta"). In September 1998, at least fifty died and thousands were displaced in the Ilaje-Ese-Edo local government area of Ondo State in armed clashes between Ijaw and Ilaje communities laying competing claims to Apata, an oil rig area located between them.

farm yields. Similarly, drilling for oil produces waste, largely mud, which in itself is relatively harmless, but in the large quantities produced can cause problems by changing acidity or saline levels of the soil or water, and by increasing turbidity of the water.[159] Site preparation for drilling often involves clearance of vegetation and dredging in the riverine areas.

Oil facilities can also prove hazardous in other ways. Flow stations and other facilities are often inadequately fenced. In Esit Eket, Akwa Ibom State, local residents told Human Rights Watch in July 1997 that five children had drowned since the beginning of the year in an unfenced flooded pit, roughly two meters by one meter, where SPDC used to have a "christmas tree" well head. They said no compensation from Shell had been paid for these deaths.[160]

Gas Flaring

Nigeria flares more gas than any other country in the world: approximately 75 percent of total gas production in Nigeria is flared, and about 95 percent of the "associated gas" which is produced as a by-product of crude oil extraction from reservoirs in which oil and gas are mixed.[161] About half this gas is flared by SPDC, in line with its share of oil production. Flaring in Nigeria contributes a measurable percentage of the world's total emissions of greenhouse gases; due to the low efficiency of many of the flares much of the gas is released as methane (which has a high warming potential), rather than carbon dioxide.[162] At the same time, the low-lying Niger Delta is particularly vulnerable to the potential effects of sea levels rising.

---

[159] Van Dessel, *The Environmental Situation in the Niger Delta, Nigeria*, section 5.3. SPDC claims that "Our long term target is to achieve a dry drilling location," and that, in 1996, "almost no mud discharges to the environment were made," while a "drilling waste management strategy" was prepared to meet DPR Environmental Guidelines and Standards. SPDC, *People and the Environment: Annual Report 1996*.

[160] Human Rights Watch interviews and site visit, July 8, 1997. The names of the children given were: Okon Mkpapa, Udong Ete, Ekpe Ekene Nsuwegh, Adia Haudeno, and Philip Sunday. All were one or two years old.

[161] Khan, *Nigeria*, p.162; SPDC, *Nigeria Brief: Harnessing Gas* (Lagos: SPDC, August 1996).

[162] The World Bank estimates that Nigerian gas flaring releases some 35 million tonnes of carbon dioxide annually. This represents 0.2 percent of total global man-made carbon dioxide emissions; of which the rest of Africa contributes 2.8 percent; Europe 14.8 percent; the USA 21.8 percent; and the rest of the world 60.4 percent. SPDC, *Nigeria Brief: Harnessing Gas*. See also World Bank, *Defining an Environmental Strategy for the Niger Delta*, and Moffat and Lindén, "Perception and Reality."

In 1969, Nigerian legislation required oil companies to set up facilities to use the "associated gas" from their operations within five years of commencement of production. In 1979, further legislation set a time limit of October April 1980 for companies to develop gas utilization projects or face fines.[163] However, without any gas utilization projects of its own, the government could not credibly enforce this legislation. After oil company lobbying, limited exemptions to this rule were granted in 1985, by an amendment and regulations which allowed flaring in certain cases; but in any event, the costs to the operating companies of ceasing flaring far outweighed the fines imposed.[164] Fines for gas flaring were raised in January 1998 from ₦0.5 to ₦10 (U.S.11¢) for every 1,000 standard cubic feet of gas.[165]

During 1996, SPDC committed itself to the elimination of gas flaring at its facilities by 2008.[166] In October 1996, Shell announced that it had awarded a U.S.$500 million contract for a new gas processing plant at Soku, Rivers State, which would supply the LNG plant at Bonny with a mixture of associated and non-associated gas. Together with two other gas facilities, at Odidi and Alscon, SPDC intends to collect 380 million standard cubic feet per day (scf/d) of associated gas, more than one third of the volume of gas currently flared by the company, before the end of the century.[167] Chevron's Escravos gas project, the first phase of which began exporting in September 1997, is intended to reduce flaring by 40 percent from its facilities.[168] Mobil's Bonny facility, which came on stream in July 1998 producing 50,000 bpd of LNG, collects associated gas and will reduce flaring from its Oso field.

Many communities in the Niger Delta believe that local gas flares cause acid rain which corrodes the metal sheets used for roofing. According to Shell internal documentation, due to the low content of sulphur dioxide and nitrous oxide in the

[163] Petroleum (Drilling and Production) Regulations, Regulation 42 (which came into force in November 1969), and the Associated Gas Reinjection Act, Cap.26, *Laws of the Federation of Nigeria*, 1990 (which came into force in 1979).

[164] Associated Gas Reinjection (Continued Flaring of Gas) Regulations, 1985; see also Khan, *Nigeria*, p.162. Because of the geology of Nigeria's oilfields, reinjection of gas is, according to the oil companies, not usually an economic option.

[165] Reuters, November 19, 1996; Environmental Rights Action, Niger Delta Alert No. 1, January 1998. NNPC is exempt from these fines, so the oil majors in theory pay in accordance with their share in the joint ventures.

[166] SPDC, *People and the Environment: Annual Report 1996.*

[167] SPDC Press Release, October 18, 1996; see also SPDC *Nigeria Brief: Harnessing Gas.*

[168] U.S. EIA, "Nigeria Country Analysis Brief."

gas, it is unlikely that flaring in fact contributes to acid rain, and various studies by different consultants have failed to prove a link.[169] One study of flares in the Niger Delta found that air, leaf and soil temperatures were increased up to eighty or one hundred meters from the stack, and species composition of vegetation was affected in the same area.[170] However, in one case, at Utapete flow station, on the Atlantic coast near Iko village, Akwa Ibom State, a flare was sited too low, so that sea water flooded the flare pipe at high tide, vaporizing the salt and shooting it over the village. Corrosion of the roofs in Iko was shown to be faster than in other areas. In 1995, SPDC closed the flare at Utapete, shortly after local environmentalists issued a report on its effects.[171] In other cases, inefficient technology in the flares means that many of them burn without sufficient oxygen or with small amounts of oil mixed in with the gas, creating soot that is deposited on nearby land and buildings, visibly damaging the vegetation near to the flare. Respiratory problems among children as a result are reported, but apparently unresearched.[172] The most noticeable yet generally unremarked effect of the flares is light pollution: across the oil producing regions, the night sky is lit up by flares, that, in the rainy season, reflect luridly from the clouds. Villagers close to flares complain that nocturnal animals are disturbed by this light, and leave the area, making hunting more difficult.

In some cases, gas flares are very close to communities. Shell claims that this is usually because settlements have grown up around the oil facilities; local communities dispute this claim. In any event, the flares are rarely if ever relocated, or even made safe by providing secure fencing. In July 1997, Human Rights Watch observed women climbing right into the bunded (walled) pit where a flare was burning, to spread out cassava for drying on the earth close to the flame. A malfunction in the flare or missed footing could have fatal consequences; it is also likely that the soot from the flare would contaminate the cassava.

---

[169] SPDC, *PAGE Fact Book 1993*, section 3.3.2; Environmental Resources Managers Ltd, *Niger Delta Environmental Survey Final Report Phase I, Volume I*, p.244.

[170] Augustine O. Isichei and William W. Sanford, "The effects of waste gas flares on the surrounding vegetation in South-Eastern Nigeria," *Journal of Applied Ecology* 1976, vol.13, pp.177-187.

[171] Environmental Rights Action, *sHell in Iko* (Benin City: Environmental Rights Action, July 10, 1995); Human Rights Watch interview with Bruce Powell, June 20, 1998.

[172] Human Rights Watch interviews, Uzere, Delta State, July 21, 1997.

Compensation for Land Expropriation

For oil production to take place, land is expropriated for the construction of oil facilities (a process referred to by the oil companies as "land take"). This land is taken under Nigerian laws which are both difficult to interpret definitively and provide for an extraordinary level of government control over land use and transfer. Although the Nigerian constitution provides that no right or interest in property may be acquired compulsorily except under a law providing for the payment of prompt compensation and for the amount of compensation to be determined by a court of law or other tribunal, this right has been substantially eroded in practice by laws passed by successive military governments.[173]

The principal statute governing real property in Nigeria is the 1978 Land Use Act (originally Decree No. 6 of 1978), which provides that:

> all land comprised in the territory of each State in the Federation are [*sic*] hereby vested in the Governor of that State and such land shall be held in trust and administered for the use and common benefit of all Nigerians.[174]

Under this law, land in urban areas is under the control and management of the state governor; all other land falls under the control of the local government authority. The governor has the absolute right to grant "statutory rights of occupancy" to any land, to issue "certificates of occupancy," and to demand payment of rental for that land. Local governments have the right to grant "customary rights of occupancy" to land not in urban areas. While the law is largely ignored in rural areas, where residents treat the land as their own, any transfer of occupancy rights theoretically requires the consent of the governor or

---

[173] Article 40 of the 1979 constitution (Article 42(3) of the 1989 constitution; Article 47(1) of the draft 1995 constitution) provides that:

> (1) No movable property or any interest in an immovable property shall be taken possession of compulsorily and no right over or interest in any such property shall be acquired compulsorily in any part of Nigeria except in the manner and for the purposes prescribed by a law that, among other things—
> (a) requires the prompt payment of compensation therefor; and
> (b) gives to the person claiming such compensation a right of access for the determination of his interest in the property and the amount of compensation to a court of law or tribunal or body having jurisdiction in that part of Nigeria.

[174] Section 1, Decree No. 6 of 1978, Cap. 202, *Laws of the Federation of Nigeria.*

local government authority. Equally, the governor may revoke a right of occupancy for reasons of "overriding public interest." Overriding public interest is defined in section 28 of the act to include "the requirement of the land for mining purposes or oil pipelines or for any purpose connected therewith." In addition, and in common with other military decrees suspending the provisions of the constitution or ousting the jurisdiction of the courts to inquire into executive acts, the Land Use Act is stated to have effect "notwithstanding anything to the contrary in any law or rule of law, including the Constitution ... and ... no court shall have jurisdiction to inquire into any question concerning or pertaining to the amount or adequacy of any compensation paid or to be paid under this Act."[175] The 1979 constitution itself specifically provides that nothing in the constitution shall invalidate the Land Use Decree.[176]

If land is acquired for mining purposes, the Land Use Act provides that the occupier is entitled to compensation as provided under the Minerals Act or the Mineral Oils Act (now superseded by the Petroleum Act). If compensation is due to a community, it may be paid "to the community," "to the chief or leader of the community to be disposed of by him for the benefit of the community," or "into some fund specified by the Military Governor for the purpose of being utilised or applied for the benefit of the community."[177] The Petroleum Act (originally Decree No. 51 of 1969), however, makes no provision for compensation to be paid for land acquisition. Section 1 of the act vests the entire ownership and control of all petroleum in, under or upon any land within the country or beneath its waters in the state. Although the act requires the holders of oil exploration licenses, oil prospecting licenses or oil mining leases to pay "fair and adequate compensation for the disturbance of surface or other rights" to the owner or occupier of any land or property,[178] nothing is due for expropriation of the land itself; thus for properties

---

[175] Section 27, Land Use Act.

[176] Article 274(5) of the 1979 constitution. This provision is repeated in Article 346(5) of the draft 1995 constitution.

[177] The act also provides for Land Use and Allocation Committees to be appointed by and advise the military governors on the management of the land, and to settle disputes as to compensation to be paid.

[178] Petroleum Act, Section 36. The Petroleum (Drilling and Production) Regulations, made under the Act, also provide that before entering or occupying any private land, oil companies are required to obtain written permission from the government and pay "fair and adequate compensation" to the lawful occupiers, presumably in respect of the rights mentioned in the primary legislation. Petroleum (Drilling and Production) Regulations, Regulation 17(c)(ii).

acquired since the Land Use Act came into effect rent is paid to the federal government only.[179] Since oil is federal property, land occupiers are entitled to no royalties for oil extracted from their land.

The Oil Pipelines Act, dating from 1956 but since amended, provides for compensation both in respect of surface rights and in respect of the loss of value of the land affected by a pipeline.[180] Disputes as to the compensation due may be referred to court, which "shall award such compensation as it considers just," taking into account not only damage to buildings, crops, and "economic trees," but also damage caused by negligence or disturbance, and the loss in value of the land or interests in the land.[181]

Land is acquired by the oil companies for oil operations from the Nigerian government under these laws, which in practice allow the government to expropriate land for the oil industry with no effective due process protections for those whose livelihoods may be destroyed by the confiscation of their land. While Human Rights Watch recognizes that every government has the right to acquire

---

[179] Before the Land Use Act came into effect, the Public Land Acquisitions (Miscellaneous Provisions) Act 1976 and other laws provided for compensation to be paid in respect of the land acquired itself. See J.A. Omotola, *Essays on the Land Use Act, 1978* (Lagos: Lagos University Press, 1984), chapter 5, "Compensation provisions under the Act."

[180] The Act provides: "The holder of a licence shall pay compensation:

(a) to any person whose land or interest in land (whether or not it is land in respect of which the licence has been granted) is injuriously affected by the exercise of the rights conferred by the licence, for any such injurious affection not otherwise made good; and

(b) to any person suffering damage by reason of any neglect on the part of the holder or his agents, servants or workmen to protect, maintain or repair any work structure or thing executed under the licence, for any such damage not otherwise made good; and

(c) to any person suffering damage (other than on account of his own default or on account of the malicious act of a third person) as a consequence of any breakage or leakage from the pipeline or an ancillary installation, for any such damage not otherwise made good."

Oil Pipelines Act, Cap.338, *Laws of the Federation of Nigeria*, 1990, section 11(5).

[181] Ibid., Section 20. "In determining the loss in value of the land or interest in land of a claimant the court shall assess the value of the land or the interests injuriously affected at the date immediately before the grant of the licence and shall assess the residual value to the claimant of the same land or interests consequent upon and at the date of the grant of the licence and shall determine the loss suffered by the claimant as the difference between the values so found, if such residual value is a lesser sum." Section 20(3).

land for public purposes, those affected should have the right to voice opposition to the acquisition, to challenge it before an impartial court, and to obtain adequate compensation. In practice, the decision as to the land that will be expropriated and the determination of such compensation as will be paid appears to be made by the oil industry itself.

According to Shell internal documentation, the oil company must first notify the government of the intention and purpose of a proposed acquisition, based on its own surveys of the area. The oil company also identifies the owners/occupiers of the land, notifies them of its intentions, and agrees a date for assessment of the property. Compensation for surface rights is valued in accordance with government rates which vary according to whether land is cultivated and what structures, fishponds, "economic trees," or other assets are present. Valuations are approved by the Divisional Land Board. Once compensation payments have been made to the occupiers for the surface rights, a one-off payment, a permit to take possession of the land is granted to the oil company.[182] SPDC states that its operations have taken approximately 280 square kilometers of land, or 0.3 percent of the total area of the Niger Delta and that measures are being undertaken to reduce the land taken, such as the introduction of "horizontal drilling," and to rehabilitate land no longer needed, for example by replanting land cleared for seismic surveys.[183]

While the total land take may seem small by these figures, the effect of land confiscation under the legal regime in place can be very serious for those affected. Since the Land Use Act and the other relevant law provides local communities with very limited rights over land they have traditionally used, both government agencies and private companies are largely able to ignore customary land use rights, in the oil areas as elsewhere. Because the government has complete control over land, it is easy for oil companies to ignore local concerns and to fail to ensure that local communities are fully consulted. Decisions relating to use of land are completely taken out of the hands of those who have lived on and used it for centuries. Moreover, whatever the total effect of land expropriations, the effect on individual landholders can be devastating, in some cases even destroying livelihoods, especially since there is heavy pressure on cultivable land across the oil producing regions. Community members also have a strong conviction, based on traditional land use arrangements, that the community in general should be compensated for land take and disturbance caused by oil activities.

---

[182] SPDC, *PAGE Fact Book 1993.*

[183] SPDC, *People and the Environment: Annual Report 1996.*

Compensation for Oil Spills

Compensation for pollution damage is equally plagued by problems of due process and difficulties in interpreting a series of overlapping statutes, combined with rules developed through the common law. The Petroleum Act does not explicitly refer to spills, but its requirement for oil companies to pay "fair and adequate compensation for the disturbance of surface or other rights" to the owner or occupier of any land or property affected by exploration or production has been held to apply to oil spills.[184] There is no statutory definition of fair and adequate compensation, but in the lead case interpreting this provision, *Shell Petroleum Development Company v. Farah*, the Court of Appeal, basing its judgment on English and Nigerian case law, stated that compensation should "restore the person suffering the damnum [loss] as far as money can do that to the position he was before the damnum or would have been but for the damnum."[185] The Petroleum (Drilling and Production) Regulations, made under the Act, provide only for compensation for interference with fishing rights.[186]

The Oil Pipelines Act explicitly provides that compensation is due "to any person suffering damage (other than on account of his own default or on account of the malicious act of a third person) as a consequence of any breakage or leakage from the pipeline or an ancillary installation, for any such damage not otherwise made good," and also provides, as stated above, for valuation to take into account damage to crops, buildings, "economic trees" and loss in value of the land.[187] The Federal Environmental Protection Agency Act, in addition to providing for criminal liability for contravention of its provisions, and for spillers to be responsible for the cost of rehabilitating land, states that companies violating its provisions or regulations made under it "shall be directed to pay compensation for any damage resulting from such breach thereof or to repair and restore the polluted environmental area to an acceptable level as approved by the Agency unless he proves to the satisfaction of the court that—(a) he used due diligence to secure

[184] Petroleum Act, Section 36.

[185] [1995] 3 NWLR (Part 382) p.148, at p.192. The *Farah* case arose from a blow out at Shell's Bomu II oil well in Tai/Gokana local government areas in Ogoni in 1970, though the case was not commenced until 1989. Shell has appealed from the Court of Appeal to the Supreme Court.

[186] Regulation 23 states that "if the licensee or lessee exercises the rights conferred by his licence or lease in such a manner as unreasonably to interfere with the exercise of any fishing rights, he shall pay adequate compensation therefor to any person injured by the exercise of those first-mentioned rights."

[187] Oil Pipelines Act, sections 11(5) and 20(2).

compliance with this Act; and (b) such offence was committed without his knowledge consent or connivance."[188]

Nigerian case law also incorporates liability for negligence, nuisance, trespass, and the rule in *Rylands v. Fletcher*, an English law case of 1866, which held that anyone bringing onto land, in the course of a "non-natural" use of the land, something "likely to do mischief if it escapes ... is *prima facie* answerable for all the damage which is the natural consequence of its escape."[189] The Nigerian courts have held that crude oil can (though does not always) fall into this category. The rule provides for strict liability; that is to say, it is not necessary to prove negligence on the part of the person allowing the damaging material to escape, once it has been shown that the use is "non-natural" and that the material is dangerous or "mischievous." However, "the owner of a dangerous thing is not liable if the thing has escaped through the independent act of a third party and there has been no negligence on his part ... in the absence of a finding that he instigated [the act] or that he ought to have provided against it."[190]

Compensation at uniform rates is paid by the oil companies for spillages, where they are not attributed to sabotage, as for land expropriated. The government sets compensation rates, but the oil companies pay higher rates which are agreed across the industry and are claimed by Shell to be "calculated at on-going market prices. Loss of revenue for the period and inconveniences are also incorporated into the compensation paid."[191] In September 1997, oil companies in Nigeria announced that they were increasing the rates of compensation paid in case of oil spillage or land acquisition by over 100 percent, to ₦500,000 per hectare (U.S.$5,600).[192] Elf states that "Compensations are paid either to the individual or family property, or to representatives with power of attorney in case of community property."[193] In theory, these rates can be challenged in the courts, which will

---

[188] Federal Environmental Protection Agency Act, section 36.

[189] (1866) LR1 Exch. 265. Oil naturally occurs in the ground, and therefore in its natural state would not come under the rule in *Rylands v. Fletcher*. However, once it has been channeled through pipes or gathered into tanks, its presence is no longer "natural" and the rule applies. However, the case law on the issue is not entirely consistent. See J. Finine Fekumo, "Civil Liability for Damage Caused by Oil Pollution," in Omotola (ed.) *Environmental Laws in Nigeria*.

[190] *SPDC v. Chief Graham Otoko and five others* [1990] 6 NWLR (Part 159), p.693, at p.724.

[191] Shell International Ltd letter to Human Rights Watch, February 13, 1998.

[192] Reuters, September 2, 1997.

[193] Elf Petroleum Nigeria Ltd letter to Human Rights Watch, May 8, 1998.

apply general rules for assessing damages in tort (civil wrong) cases, but in practice, the standardized rates are applied.[194]

When spills occur, the usual procedure is that the company will be informed by the community which sees itself as the "host community" to the company, or by the community which will suffer most from the spill. The company will send its representatives to assess the extent of the spill, and the community will be instructed to approach one of the company's registered and approved claims agents. Alternatively, the community may approach its own lawyers and hire its own claims agents for the purpose of a legal case, but few communities are able to pay legal fees up front, and so their only possibility may be to make deals with lawyers which mean that, in the event of success in court, much of the award may be taken by the legal team. Law cases are so protracted that they offer, in reality, no alternative to the company-controlled procedure.

Even when compensation is agreed in principle at oil company rates, compensation payments rarely reflect the true value of the loss to the local community.[195] There are constant disputes as to what is included and to the rates paid. The oil companies allege that local communities greatly inflate their claims, including old equipment among items that are damaged by a spill: for this reason, for example, Shell states that there is no payment for damaged fishing nets "collected after any spillage has been contained."[196] Communities claim on the other hand that the compensation they receive when a claim is finally agreed is nothing compared to the loss they suffer overall and that the oil companies refuse to take into account the particular circumstances of each case, applying uniform rates whatever the loss suffered in practice: while villagers are often unaware of the full environmental consequences of oil pollution, they are well aware of the economic effect of spills on their income derived from farming or fishing.

It is also probable that the amounts theoretically paid out by the oil companies are plundered along the way by claims agents and others and do not reach the people who have actually suffered from oil company activity. Landholders in Osubi, Delta State, affected by land taken to construct an airport for Shell in 1997-

[194] See J.A. Omotola, "The Quantum of Compensation for Oil Pollution: An Overview," in Omotola (ed.), *Environmental Laws in Nigeria.*

[195] In 1995 the World Bank estimated that the value of forest products was at least fifty times the government rate for compensation. World Bank, *Defining an Environmental Development Strategy*, p.93.

[196] Reuters, October 5, 1997, quoting a SPDC spokesperson in connection with demands by members of the Peremabiri community for compensation for fishing nets allegedly damaged in a June 1997 spillage.

98 were reportedly paid sums from ₦20 (U.S.22¢) to ₦200 (U.S.$2.20) for nut and rubber trees worth several thousand naira annually to their owners.[197] In any event, cash payments can rarely compensate for the continuing income supplied by assets such as economically valuable trees which have been destroyed.

Sabotage

SPDC claimed in 1996 that sabotage accounted for more than 60 percent of all oil spilled at its facilities in Nigeria, stating that the percentage has increased over the years both because the number of sabotage incidents has increased and because spills due to corrosion have decreased with programs to replace oil pipelines.[198] Of oil spills during 1997, Shell stated that 63,889 barrels, or almost 80 percent of a total 80,412 barrels, were spilled due to sabotage.[199] Other oil companies similarly report sabotage to their pipelines and installations.[200] Shell states that "sabotage is usually easy to determine, since there is evidence of cleanly drilled holes, hacksaw cuts, cutting of protective cages to open valves, etc. In the few cases where the evidence is unclear, ultrasonic soundings are taken for further clarification."[201] Similarly, Shell claimed that 60 percent of spillages in Ogoni from 1985 to the time it ceased production in the area were caused by sabotage.

The claims of sabotage are hotly disputed by the communities concerned. Community leaders point out that, given the fact that compensation payments are

---

[197] Environmental Rights Action, "Shell's Airport at Osubi—The Killing of Sleep," ERA Monitor Report No. 5, April 1998. Shell stated that a total of ₦194.7 million (U.S.$2.16 million) was approved in compensation for the loss of use of land and crops, although a small percentage of this remained in a holding account pending negotiations with a claimant who had begun a court action. "Osubi Airport Project: Shell Nigeria's Response to Allegations by ERA," SPDC Press Release, March 23, 1998.

[198] SPDC, *People and the Environment: Annual Report 1996.*

[199] SPDC letter to Environmental Rights Action, August 19, 1998. The data given were as follows:

1997 oil spills (barrels)	**Land**	**Swamp**	**Total**
Corrosion	4,205	7,327	11,532
Operations	4,415	413	4,828
Sabotage	52,676	11,213	63,889
Other	44	119	163
Total	61,340	19,072	80,412

[200] With the exception of Mobil, which has most of its operations offshore and which stated to Human Rights Watch that no act of sabotage had occurred at any of its facilities. Mobil Producing Nigeria Unlimited letter to Human Rights Watch, February 10, 1998.

[201] Shell International Ltd letter to Human Rights Watch, February 13, 1998.

paid late and are inadequate even if it is proved the company is at fault, there is little for them to gain from polluting their own drinking water and destroying their own crops—though they agree that this argument may not apply to those who are contractors involved in cleaning up spills. In 1996, the British Advertising Standards Authority reviewed the claim that 60 percent of spills in Ogoni were caused by sabotage, following complaints from members of the public and from Friends of the Earth, and concluded that "the advertisers had not given enough information to support the claim and asked for it not to be repeated."[202] Statistics from the Department of Petroleum Resources indicate that only 4 percent of all spills in Nigeria were caused by sabotage during the period 1976 to 1990; these statistics include offshore spills, which have been by far the largest, and are unlikely to be caused by sabotage.[203]

In cases of sabotage, in accordance with Nigerian law, the oil companies do not pay compensation for spills, on the grounds that to pay compensation creates an incentive to damage oil installations and harm the environment. However, even if a spill is caused by sabotage, the person carrying out the sabotage is not necessarily the person who suffers the damage. In many cases, it appears that sabotage is carried out by contractors likely to be paid to clean up the damage; sometimes with the connivance of oil company staff. A former adviser to a state petroleum minister commented as follows, repeating the gist of many similar reports to Human Rights Watch: "It is true that there is a lot of sabotage, but often it is the chiefs who do it. The oil company then settles the chiefs [i.e. pays them off] by giving them the contract to clean up, but they tell the youths they have received nothing. Then the youths protest and cause damage and the chief gets more money. If the government and the oil companies did development projects properly it would not happen."[204]

Part of the problem is that there is no independent confirmation that spillages have been caused by sabotage: although the Department of Petroleum Resources is supposed to confirm sabotage and community members may also be invited to

---

[202] The Advertising Standards Authority, *ASA Monthly Report*, no.62 (London, July 1996), pp.40-41.

[203] Environmental Resources Managers Ltd, *Niger Delta Environmental Survey Final Report Phase I, Volume I*, figure 14.5, p.253. The other causes recorded were corrosion (33 percent), equipment failure (38 percent), blow-out (20 percent), accident from third party (1 percent), operator or maintenance error (2 percent), and "natural" (stated as 0 percent, presumably 3 percent intended). Sixty-nine percent of total spills during the same period were offshore, 25 percent in swamp, and 6 percent on land.

[204] Human Rights Watch, interview, July 7, 1997.

inspect the damaged installation, often no genuinely independent experts are present. Typical is the case of a landholder in Obobura, Rivers State, in the Obagi oil field operated by Elf.[205] On December 31, 1996, a spillage occurred at a well head on his land, spraying crude oil over a wide area and destroying crops and fishponds. The spill was cleared up within one month, apparently by shoveling off the surface layer of oil and burning it on site, a method of cleanup which is not in compliance with international best practice. Local contractors were hired for this work, though not the family who owned the land; when they protested that they should be employed and attempted to stop clear-up work, a small detachment of Mobile Police came to warn them off and guard the site. The landowner hired a lawyer who wrote to Elf on January 9, 1997, demanding compensation. The reply, dated February 4, 1997, states (in full, as to its substantive content):

> Investigation into the alleged spillage shows that some unknown person(s) cut and removed the nipple valve in the Surface Safety Valve (SSV) sensing line at the well head. Consequently, crude oil, under high pressure, jet out, affecting an area of about 100m by 150m. Thus it is a case of established sabotage, the Department of Petroleum Resources (DPR) supports our stand. We are therefore not liable to your clients in respect of their claim for compensation and wish that the issue be allowed to rest.[206]

Five members of the landholder's family, who deny responsibility for the sabotage—logically, considering the damage to their crops and the lack of any benefit received—were arrested on January 4, 1997, apparently on suspicion that they were responsible for the sabotage, and held overnight at Akabuka police station. They were released the next day, without charge, but only after payment of ₦1,000 (U.S.$11) for each person.[207]

Human Rights Watch is not in a position to comment on the cause of the spillage that led to this incident. However, given that the Department of Petroleum Resources is close to the oil companies, there was no independent confirmation of the allegation that the spill was caused by sabotage. No opportunity for an independent assessment was offered to the family affected, and the information

---

[205] Human Rights Watch interviews, July 4, 1997.

[206] Letter dated February 4, 1997, from Elf Petroleum Nigeria Ltd (signed E. Chiejina), reference RC/LC 97/18, to C.V. Goodwill and Co, Port Harcourt.

[207] Those arrested were Pastor P.N. Orji, Christopher Nwubio, Isaiah Samuel, Abel Orji and Chief S.U. Amirize. Human Rights Watch interviews, July 4, 1997.

given to their lawyer which is said to "establish" sabotage is too cursory to be convincing. Moreover, the letter states that "unknown person(s)" cut the valve, suggesting that there was no evidence against those arrested. In correspondence with Human Rights Watch, Elf essentially repeated the information in the letter written to the lawyers for the family, but gave no new details.[208]

The Petroleum Production and Distribution (Anti-Sabotage) Act of 1975, a military decree of the regime led by Gen. Murtala Mohammed, defined an offense of "sabotage" for the first time:

> Any person who does any of the following things, that is to say—
> (a) wilfully does anything with intent to obstruct or prevent the production or distribution of petroleum products in any part of Nigeria; or
> (b) wilfully does anything with intent to obstruct or prevent the procurement of petroleum products for distribution in any part of Nigeria; or
> (c) wilfully does anything in respect of any vehicle or any public highway with intent to obstruct or prevent the use of that vehicle or that public highway for the distribution of petroleum products,
> shall, if by doing that thing he, to any significant extent, causes or contributes to any interruption in the production or distribution of petroleum products in any part of Nigeria, be guilty of the offence of sabotage under this Act.

Any person who aids, incites, counsels or procures any other person to do any of these things is equally guilty of sabotage. The decree also allows the head of state to constitute a military tribunal to try persons charged with offenses under the act, and states that those convicted may be sentenced either to death or imprisonment for a term not exceeding twenty-one years.[209] The Criminal Justice (Miscellaneous Provisions) Act of 1975, passed by the same regime, makes any person who "destroys, damages or removes any oil pipeline or installation connected therewith"; or who "otherwise prevents or obstructs the flow of oil along any such pipeline or interferes with any installation connected therewith" guilty of an offense. The offense is punishable by a fine or ten years imprisonment in the first

[208] Elf Petroleum Nigeria Ltd letter to Human Rights Watch, May 8, 1998.

[209] Section 1, Petroleum Production and Distribution (Anti-Sabotage) Decree no.35 of 1975 (Cap. 353, *Laws of the Federation of Nigeria*).

case, or a fine or three years imprisonment in the second.[210] These laws were followed by the Special Tribunal (Miscellaneous Offences) Decree No. 20 of 1984, which created a range of offenses triable by "miscellaneous offenses tribunals" and provides that:

> Any person who wilfully or maliciously—
> (a) breaks, damages, disconnects or otherwise tampers with any pipe or pipeline for the transportation of crude oil or refined oil or gas; or
> (b) obstructs, damages, destroys, or otherwise tampers or interferes with the free flow of any crude oil or refined petroleum product through any oil pipeline,
> shall be guilty of an offence and liable on conviction to be sentenced to imprisonment for life.[211]

Unauthorized importation or sale of petroleum products or their adulturation were also made offenses.[212] The decree provides that the constitutional bill of rights shall not apply to anything done under its authority, and that the courts may not inquire into any such actions.[213] While the decree did not explicitly repeal the earlier legislation relating to sabotage, it did provide that any person who "was arrested, detained or charged with an offence under any other enactment amounting to an offence under this Act" should rather be tried under the Special Tribunal (Miscellaneous Offences) Decree.[214] Insofar as the offenses overlap, therefore, they

---

[210] The Criminal Justice (Miscellaneous Provisions) Decree no.30 of 1975 (Cap. 78, *Laws of the Federation of Nigeria*), Section 3(1) and (2).

[211] Section 3(7), Cap. 410, *Laws of the Federation of Nigeria.* The maximum sentence was originally the death penalty but was reduced to life imprisonment by the Special Tribunal (Miscellaneous Offences) (Amendment) Decree no.22 of 1986, which also provided for an appeal to a Special Appeal Tribunal. The original decree was promulgated by the regime of Mohammadu Buhari, the amendment by Ibrahim Babangida. Miscellaneous offenses tribunals, composed of one judge, three members of the armed forces and one police officer, may be created by the president and commander in chief of the armed forces for any state.

[212] Ibid., sections 3(17) and (18).

[213] Ibid., section 11.

[214] Section 12(2) provides that "Any person who on or at any time after 31st December 1983 was arrested, detained or charged with an offence under any other enactment amounting to an offence under this Act shall be liable to be tried and convicted in accordance with the relevant provisions of this Act and any charge or information pending against him in or before any court or tribunal shall as from the

are triable before a miscellaneous offenses tribunal, and subject to the penalties applicable under the decree, though the status of the previous laws appears to be uncertain.

According to Shell, "prosecutions for sabotage are extremely rare since, in order to obtain a conviction, the perpetrators must either be caught in the act or there must be other evidence to place them at the scene of the crime. Also, since the law provides severe penalties, it has not been in the interest of sustained community relations to press for charges, even when there is circumstantial evidence."[215] Chevron confirmed that the company "has not been able to prosecute in cases of sabotage," and that it was not aware of any prosecutions by the Nigerian authorities: "While it is usually not too difficult to determine sabotage, there are often very few evidences to identify who is responsible."[216] Elf stated that "Sabotage cases are normally reported to the police, but we do not enforce prosecution for the interest of peace."[217]

The Niger Delta Environmental Survey

As a result of the focus on Shell's activities in Nigeria brought by the activities of Ken Saro-Wiwa and the Movement for the Survival of the Ogoni People (MOSOP), Shell led a move to establish a Niger Delta Environmental Survey (NDES).[218] Shell announced the initiative, designed to head off international criticism of its Nigerian operations, on behalf of its joint venture with NNPC, Agip and Elf, on February 3, 1995, and the NDES steering committee held its first meeting on May 24, 1995. Originally financed only by the SPDC joint venture, the steering committee—urged by local and international environmentalists—insisted on the need for greater independence. Eventually, the NDES was established as an independent corporate entity, a company limited by guarantee, and all members of the Oil Producers Trade Section of the Lagos Chamber of Commerce agreed to make financial contributions, as did the Rivers State and Delta State governments.

---

making of this Act, abate."

[215] Shell International Ltd letter to Human Rights Watch, February 13, 1998.

[216] Chevron Nigeria Ltd letter to Human Rights Watch, February 11, 1998.

[217] Elf Petroleum Nigeria Ltd letter to Human Rights Watch, May 8, 1998.

[218] SPDC's February 3, 1995, press release announcing the establishment of the NDES made clear the pressure Shell felt it was under by referring to "recent politicized and emotive campaigning [which] has clouded some very important issues concerning the development of this region."

Although the survey had been originally conceived of by Shell as a purely technical collection of scientific data on the environment in the delta, the steering committee decided that the more pressing need was for an evaluation of the socio-economic and human dimensions of the environmental degradation visible in the delta.[219] The mission statement eventually adopted by the NDES states that the aims of the survey were: "In concert with communities and other stakeholders to undertake a comprehensive environmental survey of the Niger Delta, establish the causes of ecological and socio-economic change over time and induce corrective action by encouraging relevant stakeholders to address specific environmental and related socio-economic problems identified in the course of the Survey, to improve the quality of life of the people and achieve sustainable development in the region."[220] The survey was intended to be "both people and community centred" and to "involve all stakeholders, particularly communities in the Niger Delta, in the process of conceptualising and implementing the Survey and secure their full participation in gathering the data, and in interpreting and using them."[221] With this strong community focus, based on participatory rural appraisal techniques, the NDES was expected to provide:

a. a comprehensive description of the area, ecological zones, boundaries, and different uses of renewable and non-renewable natural resources;

---

[219] SPDC's February 3, 1995, press release stated that the survey would "catalogue the physical and biological diversity of the 70,000 square kilometre Niger Delta" including information on "population growth, migration, farming, deforestation, soil degradation, oil activities, road building and other factors, over time." The change of focus from this approach to one which centered on the human consequences of environmental degradation and oil activities was largely the work of two members of the steering committee: Professor Claude Ake of the Centre for Advanced Social Science in Port Harcourt, and Struan Simpson of the Conservation Foundation in London. Professor Ake resigned from the committee in November 1995, in the wake of the execution of Ken Saro-Wiwa and eight other Ogoni activists, and in protest at Shell's response to the executions (he later died in a November 1996 plane crash). The Conservation Foundation withdrew its support for the project, and Dr. Simpson resigned, in December 1997, as a result of the survey's failure to make progress in achieving its terms of reference.

[220] NDES, "The Niger Delta Environmental Survey: Background and Mission," NDES Briefing Note 1, October 1995.

[221] Ibid.

b. an integrated view on the state of the environment and its relationship to local people;
c. an analysis of the causal relationships between land use, settlement patterns, industry and the environment, to provide a base line for future development planning;
d. an indicative plan for the development and management of the Niger Delta.[222]

Thus, the NDES aimed to "recommend reform of policies and practices which encourage social dislocation and environmental degradation; address poverty-induced causes of environmental degradation and social tension; improve public sensitivity and understanding of environmental issues and the application of this understanding; and strengthen the capacity of the people to identify and deal with environmental problems, in their local space and their own cultural idiom."[223]

With such an ambitious brief, it was perhaps inevitable that the NDES failed to fulfil its promise. SPDC had originally intended that the survey would be completed within two years, and the timetable eventually scheduled was for a preparatory phase from February to October 1995 (establishing a steering committee, defining terms of reference, and selecting managing consultants to conduct the survey); phase one, from November 1995 to April 1996; and phase two, from twelve to eighteen months after phase one. However, this schedule soon began to slip, as problems in the management of the survey became increasingly apparent. Phase one of the survey was eventually carried out between February and July 1996, by Euroconsult, a Dutch environmental consultancy, which produced a two volume report on "the definition, description of the Niger Delta and the assessment of data."[224] The report was seriously criticized by Nigerian environmentalists involved in the process, and by some personnel within SPDC, for failing to provide a clear idea of what had been achieved so far and what the next stages should be. Although a follow up report was prepared, disagreements between Euroconsult and the steering committee continued, and the contract with Euroconsult was not extended.

---

[222] NDES, The Niger Delta Environmental Survey: Terms of Reference," April 3, 1996.

[223] NDES, "The Niger Delta Environmental Survey: Background and Mission."

[224] G.O. Onosode, Chairman, Niger Delta Environmental Survey, "Text of Press Briefing on the Niger Delta Environmental Survey (NDES)," Sheraton Hotel, Lagos, September 10, 1996.

In September 1997, a fresh four-volume report was completed by Environmental Resources Managers Ltd, a Lagos-based consultancy, which was stated finally to represent the completion of phase one of the survey. Phase two of the survey is supposedly underway, though in effect the project appears to have ground virtually to a halt. Nigerian environmentalists express great skepticism as to the independence of the NDES from the oil industry—which funds it—in practice, and its ability to carry out its mandate effectively. What was initially a promising project which community members themselves, consulted for virtually the first time about their own environment, reportedly felt could make a positive contribution to improvement of their circumstances and the management of the delta, has degenerated into an opportunity for patronage for its members. A comprehensive and independent assessment of the impact of the oil industry on the ecology and communities of the Niger Delta that involves communities themselves in the process is badly needed; the NDES was the first attempt to carry out such an assessment, but its structure was always problematic for this task and it has apparently failed.

VI. OIL COMPANIES AND THE OIL PRODUCING COMMUNITIES

The coming of the oil industry has transformed the local economy of the oil producing communities. Although the changes are not as profound as those among previously uncontacted peoples of the Amazon rainforest living in areas where oil has been discovered[225]—the Niger Delta was one of the first parts of Nigeria to have extensive contact with Europeans, and was profoundly affected by the slave trade (from which some local leaders profited, while other communities in the hinterland were victims), and subsequently exported oil palm derivatives and other local products—the sheer quantities of cash involved in the oil industry cannot but dramatically affect local economic opportunities and power relations between those who lose or gain from those opportunities. In some respects, the oil economy has had beneficial effects, creating job opportunities and educational and infrastructure development in areas which would otherwise likely have been far more marginalized within the Nigerian state. Overall, however, the effects of oil are at best ambivalent, and most local activists argue that they have proved negative for the communities where oil is produced.

Minorities in the Oil Producing Regions

The peoples living in the oil producing communities largely belong to ethnic groups other than the three major groups (Yoruba, Igbo, and Hausa-Fulani) that dominate Nigeria. They speak a diverse range of languages and dialects: at least five major language groups are represented in the delta states.[226] The largest of these groups are the Ijaw, who collectively form Nigeria's fourth largest ethnic group but are themselves divided, as a consequence of the difficult territory which they inhabit, into subgroups speaking mutually unintelligible dialects of the Ijaw language (by some definitions thus themselves different languages).[227] There are

---

[225] See Judith Kimmerling, *Amazon Crude* (New York: Natural Resources Defense Council, 1991).

[226] In addition to members of the Igboid and Yoruboid language groups, Ijoid, Edoid and Delta Cross dialects are represented.

[227] Ijaw (sometimes spelled Ijo), has four main groups of dialects, each of which may itself be considered a language (that is, speakers within the dialect group cannot understand speakers of another dialect group, though they can, generally, understand other dialects within the group): Eastern Ijaw (including Kalabari, Bile, Okrika, Ibani and Nkoro); Nembe-Akassa; Izon (including Bumo, Oporoma, Olodiama, Eastern Tarakiri, Basan, Apoi, Ikibiri, Ogboin, Ekpetiama, Kolokuma, and Gbanrain, all spoken in Yenagoa local government area); and Kabou, Western Tarakiri, Tungbo, Oiyakiri,

estimated to be approximately eight million people (there are no reliable census data) who would describe themselves as Ijaw, largely living in the riverine areas of what are now Bayelsa, Delta and Rivers States, as well as in Port Harcourt, Warri, and other towns on dry land. The division between the riverine and upland areas is of major cultural and geopolitical importance in the debates over the rights of the oil areas.

Other ethnic groups on dry land in what is now Rivers State include the Ogoni, numbering some 500,000 (themselves divided between four separate dialect groups); several groups speaking languages related to Igbo, including the Etche, Ndoni, and Ikwerre; a number of communities speaking dialects falling into a Central Delta language group; the Andoni, who speak a Lower Cross dialect, and others.[228] In Delta State are found the Itsekiri (whose language is related to Yoruba), the Urhobo, Edo, Isoko (in the Edo language group centered on Benin), and others. In the Cross River valley toward the Cameroon border, now Akwa Ibom and Cross River States, live the Efik, on the coast; the Ibibio; and, further north, a large number of ethnic groups, some of whose languages are spoken by no more than a few tens of thousands of people: the Willink Commission estimated that there were seventeen major languages and some 300 of lesser importance in the region.[229] In addition, there are large numbers of Igbo immigrants into the minority areas, especially to the British-created town of Port Harcourt, while oil is also produced in some areas of the majority Igbo Imo State.

At the time of the Willink Commission representatives of the Ijaw already complained that the particular problems of those living in the creeks and swamps of the delta were not understood, indeed deliberately neglected, by both the regional and federal governments.[230] A number of indigenous rulers of the Ijaw coastal communities, many of whom had concluded "treaties of protection" with the British in the eighteenth and nineteenth centuries, argued that the British should revoke the treaties, allowing them to revert to their previous position of independence, rather than become part of one Nigerian state. The commission rejected this contention, nor did it recommend the creation of a separate state for

---

Kumbo Mein, and Iduwini, all spoken in Sagbama local government area); and Inland Ijaw (including Biseni, Okodia, and Oruma). This categorization is already a simplification of the situation on the ground. E.E. Efere and Kay Williamson, "Languages," in E.J. Alagoa and Tekena N. Tamuno (eds.), *Land and People of Nigeria: Rivers State* (Port Harcourt: Riverside Communications, 1989).

[228] Ibid.

[229] Willink Commission Report, chapter 5, paragraph 4.

[230] Ibid., chapter 6, paragraph 18; chapter 7, paragraphs 14-19.

the riverine Ijaw areas;[231] however, it did recommend the creation of a federal board to consider the problems of the Niger Delta and "to direct the development of the areas into channels which would meet their peculiar problems," and the assumption of joint federal and regional responsibility for "the development of special areas."[232] Between 1956 and 1959, twelve provinces with provincial assemblies were also created out of the Eastern Region, in a further move to allay the fears of minorities.

Following independence, the federal government passed the Niger Delta Development Act in 1961, establishing a Niger Delta Development Board. The board had powers only to undertake surveys and make recommendations to the federal and regional governments.[233] It was based in Port Harcourt, not itself in the Niger Delta "special area." Despite this gesture, dissatisfaction among the delta peoples remained. In February 1966, shortly after the first coup, and before the outbreak of the Biafra war, Isaac Boro, Sam Owonaro, and Nottingham Dick, leading a group of about 150 youths known as the Delta Volunteer Service, proclaimed a "Niger Delta Republic" intended to comprise mainly the Ijaw.[234] The "twelve day revolution" was soon crushed by the Nigerian army and the leaders convicted of treason and sentenced to death; but, with the outbreak of the war, Boro, Owonaro, and Dick were released by Gen. Yakubu Gowon and joined many others in the riverine area in opposing what they perceived as the threat of the Igbo domination in the intended Biafra state. In September 1966, a delegation of "Rivers Leaders of Thought" presented a "Rivers State Memorandum" to General Gowon. In 1967, Rivers State was created, though it could only begin to function

[231] In the delta area the idea of a Rivers State took concrete form from 1953, with the formation of the Council of Rivers Chiefs, later renamed the Rivers State Congress and then Rivers Chiefs and Peoples' Congress. In 1957, the Niger Delta Congress (NDC) was formed as a political party, under the leadership of Chief Harold Dappa-Biriye, prominent in the Rivers State movement. The NDC formed an alliance with the Northern Peoples' Congress (NPC), as support against the majority southern parties. A parallel movement existed for the creation of a Calabar-Ogoja-Rivers (COR) State, as a more viable alternative. V. Reggie-Fulaba and A.I. Pepple, "Regional Government," and Ben Naanen and A.I. Pepple, "State Movements," both in Alagoa and Tamuno (eds.), *Rivers State*.

[232] Willink Commission Report, chapter 14, paragraph 28.

[233] Alagoa and Tamuno (eds.), *Rivers State*, introduction.

[234] In October 1998, the name of the Niger Delta Volunteer Force was resurrected by a coalition of youth groups involved in the closure of flow stations and demanding increased investment in the oil producing regions.

with the defeat of the secessionists by federal troops in the greater part of the state by September 1968.[235]

During the civil war, the minority groups of the delta were generally sympathetic to the federal cause, fearing domination in an Igbo state; the government of the secessionist Biafra state accordingly treated minority leaders with suspicion, and many were detained, tortured, even executed. With the defeat of Biafra, and reconstruction of the southeastern region, the minorities were once again integrated into a wider federal system, though demands for greater autonomy and recognition of the role played by the economic resources of the Niger Delta in the national economy continued. With each round of state creation, the Ijaws of the riverine areas made their case, though not until October 1996 were these demands answered by the federal government, with the creation of Bayelsa State out of the riverine areas of Rivers State. The Ijaws in Delta State, however, were excluded from the new government unit, which in any event almost totally lacks the infrastructure and personnel necessary to develop and administer policies for the area. The Bayelsa State capital, Yenagoa, was when the state was created little more than a crossroads, bus terminal and landing stage at the junction of the dry land and riverine areas.

The creation of Bayelsa State has not silenced the debate over revenue allocation to the oil producing communities, and petitions to government continue to demand better terms. Manifestoes by groups such as the Southern Minorities Movement and the Ijaw National Congress were submitted to the constitutional conference of 1994 to 1995. A seminar attended by representatives of the oil companies, NNPC, and leaders from oil producing communities in April 1997 issued a statement recommending that the federal government allocate a percentage of royalties on oil to them, suggesting that "the royalties percentage could be withheld as sanctions for acts of vandalism against properties of oil companies."[236] In March 1998, a meeting called by oil minister Dan Etete among representatives of Royal Dutch/Shell and military administrators of the oil producing states

[235] For the first fifteen months of its existence, the Rivers State government functioned in internal "exile." With the mid-1967 restoration of federal control over Bonny, on the Atlantic coast, the governor of the new state, Navy Lt. A.P. Diete-Spiff, established a civilian administration in Bonny under a sole administrator, Ken Saro-Wiwa, later to lead the Movement for the Survival of the Ogoni People.

[236] Reuters, April 27, 1997. While Human Rights Watch does not take a position on the percentage of oil money that should be paid to the oil producing areas, we note that this suggestion would imply that whole communities would be held hostage for individual acts of sabotage, perpetuating many of the injustices that exist today.

announced the creation of a new body, comprising representatives of government, oil companies and host communities, to coordinate provision of social investment in the oil producing areas. The Department of Petroleum Resources was given three months "to work out strategies for achieving observable results."[237] Minority resentment of the federal government and of Yoruba and Igbo domination of the oil industry remains a potent force: with the death of General Abacha and the inauguration of a new transition program, demands for greater attention to be paid to the oil producing communities by the federal government and the oil companies have surged once again.

Social and Economic Conditions in the Oil Producing Communities Today

Despite the vast oil wealth of the oil producing areas, the Niger Delta region remains poor—though detailed, accurate data on the economic situation do not exist. GNP per capita is below the estimated national average of U.S.$260, and is lower still in the riverine and coastal areas. Unemployment in Port Harcourt, the capital of the region, is at least 30 percent. Education levels are below the national average, already low: approximately three quarters of Nigerian children are believed to attend primary school, and national adult illiteracy is estimated at 43 percent, but in parts of the delta attendance at primary school drops to less than a third and illiteracy is presumably correspondingly higher (this is by contrast to the position at independence, when the delta still benefitted in terms of western education from its earlier contact with European missionaries).[238] The poverty level is exacerbated by the high cost of living: the influx of people employed in the well-paid energy sector has made Port Harcourt and the other urban areas of the region among the most expensive in Nigeria. The oil sector employs only a small percentage of the workforce: a labor aristocracy of high wages surrounded by a great mass of un- or under-employed.

The state governments report that only 20 to 25 percent of rural communities and 45 to 50 percent of urban areas have access to safe drinking water; in all likelihood this is an overestimate. Proper sanitation is available to less than 25

---

[237] Reuters, March 13, 1998; text of Nigerian TV broadcast, March 13, 1998, as reported by BBC SWB, March 24, 1998.

[238] World Bank, *Defining an Environmental Development Strategy*, p.2-3; World Bank, *World Development Report 1997*, Table 1; see also, Uche Onyeagucha, Oronto Douglas, and Nick Ashton-Jones, *The Human Habitat of Port Harcourt* (Benin City: Environmental Rights Action, 1995). The northern state of Sokoto, however, has fewer schools per capita than Delta or the old Rivers State. Environmental Resources Managers Ltd *Niger Delta Environmental Survey Final Report Phase I, Volume I*, p.164.

percent of the population; in Port Harcourt, the region's biggest city, there is no city-wide sewage system. This situation is common to much of Nigeria but worse in the delta regions, where it is additionally exacerbated in the areas of regular flooding. Water related diseases are widespread and probably the "central health problem in the Niger Delta."[239] State programs for immunization of children have declined drastically in recent years: in Rivers State 85 percent of children were immunized in 1989, dropping to 15 percent in 1991; in Delta State 80 percent of children were immunized in 1990, dropping to 40 percent in 1993.[240] As in the rest of Nigeria, electricity supply from the national grid is erratic; in any event, most of the riverine and coastal areas are not connected to the grid, and depend on kerosene stoves and lamps or private generators for power.

In Rivers, Bayelsa, and Delta States, estimated on the basis of the 1991 census to have a total population of up to seven million, about 70 percent of the population lives in rural delta communities.[241] While overall population densities are not high, because of the high percentage of land not suitable for settlement, densities per habitable area are very high. Higher flood levels, projected as a result of upstream dam siltation, threaten to increase densities still further in those areas. Higher population densities have in turn increased the human and economic impact of seasonal inundations during which periods water levels can rise eight to ten meters above their lowest dry season levels.

Local population growth coupled with the influx of people from other parts of Nigeria, pushed by pressure on land elsewhere or pulled by the economic opportunities offered by the energy sector, has put serious pressure on agricultural land. New roads built by the oil companies to access their facilities are swiftly followed by agricultural development and settlement. As a result of pressure on land, farmers are forced to shorten the periods during which fields are allowed to lie fallow; fertilizers are not available to the great majority of farmers. Reduced sedimentation, caused by the construction of dams, is also believed to have contributed to decreased fertility. Yields have declined as a result: in the oil producing communities decreases in yield have often coincided with the beginning of oil production, and are usually attributed to the activities of the oil companies, though it is difficult to disentangle the different causes.[242]

---

[239] World Bank, *Defining an Environmental Development Strategy*, p.71.

[240] Ibid., p.70.

[241] Ibid., p.2.

[242] Ibid., p.16.

Several hundred thousand people make a living through fishing. Fish catches in the delta region are believed to be well above sustainable levels, though statistics are unreliable.[243] Most fishing is carried out on a small-scale basis by self-employed fishermen and women using wooden canoes, rather than by commercial enterprises; however, commercial trawlers do operate offshore. The dams on the Niger and Benue Rivers and their tributaries have contributed to declining fish stocks, by reducing floods and nutrient inputs. Local fishermen complain at reduced catches in recent years, and attribute the decline to pollution from oil operations—both oil spillages and other effects such as increased turbidity of the water caused by dredging or traffic of large motor-powered craft. Again, lack of proper research makes it difficult to evaluate the overall contribution of hydrocarbon pollution to declining fish catch. In individual cases, however, oil spills can kill large numbers of fish in a small area. While spills in the open sea or in large creeks in tidal areas disperse fairly quickly, oil spilled in freshwater swamps or affecting fishponds in forest areas is confined to a small area. Moreover, although the effect of fish kill as a result of a spill can be mitigated by fishing elsewhere in the sea or large creeks, where access is usually open for those fishing from a particular community, the effect of a spill can destroy much of the livelihood for those affected in the freshwater swamp, where fishing areas and fishponds belong to particular families.

The forests of the Niger Delta of all types provide important sources of food and income to local communities. Mangrove has over seventy major uses: non-timber forest products collected from the mangrove forests include medicines, dyes, thatching, and food species as diverse as monkeys or periwinkles. In the freshwater swamp forests, raffia palm, mango, ogbono (bush mango; a common food ingredient in the local diet and sold across Nigeria), land snails, and other products are all significant.[244] Destruction of "undeveloped" forest is thus as important to local communities as destruction of cultivated land.

Oil Company Relations with the Oil Producing Communities

Shell's statement of general business principles recognizes "society" as one of the five groups to which Shell companies owe a responsibility (the others are shareholders, customers, employees, and those with whom they do business). Shell companies "take a constructive interest in societal matters which may not be

[243] Moffat and Lindén, "Perception and Reality," p.529.

[244] Environmental Resources Managers Ltd, *Niger Delta Environmental Survey Final Report Phase I, Volume I*, p.131.

directly related to the business," and "provide full relevant information about their activities to legitimately interested parties, subject to any overriding considerations of business confidentiality and cost."[245] Chevron's statement on "mission and vision," which it calls "The Chevron Way," commits Chevron to be "Better than the Best," a philosophy which means, amongst other things, that "communities welcome us." Chevron companies stated aim is to "Communicate openly with the public regarding possible impact of our business on them or the environment,"[246] to "establish an enduring and mutually beneficial relationship with the people," and to be the "petroleum company of choice in Nigeria."[247] Chevron supplied Human Rights Watch with a range of publications produced in Nigeria, apparently aimed at informing local communities about their operations. Mobil, Agip, and Elf did not supply us with any similar company policy document, either on international or national policies; previously acquired copies of Mobil's policies on business ethics and related matters do not refer to policies on community relations.

The oil companies have formal structures through which their relations with local communities are supposed to be channeled. SPDC's official policy is that contacts with the oil producing communities are conducted through Community Relations Committees, consisting of the chief, elders and "representatives of relevant groups."[248] Shell also claims that "Many SPDC employees are themselves members of communities in the oil producing regions, where they live and work. SPDC is therefore well aware of the problems affecting the communities of the Niger Delta."[249] SPDC first began to appoint community liaison officers in 1992, and attributes a drop in the time taken to resolve disputes to their appointment.[250] There are about twenty community liaison officers in the eastern division, and

---

[245] Royal Dutch/Shell Group of Companies, *Statement of General Business Principles* (London and The Hague: Shell, March 1997).

[246] Chevron, *The Chevron Way*, (San Francisco: Chevron, 1995).

[247] NNPC/Chevron Joint Venture, *Community Development Philosophy* (Lagos: Chevron Nigeria Ltd, November 1997).

[248] SPDC, *PAGE Fact Book, 1993* section 3.1.1.

[249] Shell International Petroleum Company, *Operations in Nigeria* (London: May 1994).

[250] According to Shell, stepped up efforts to improve relations with communities resulted in a drop in the volume of oil of which the delivery was deferred due to community disturbances, from 6.6 million barrels in 1995 to 1.1 million barrels in 1996; the length of time taken to resolve community disturbances fell from seventeen days in 1995 to five days in 1996. However, the widespread disturbances of 1997 and 1998 may well have reversed this decline. SPDC, *People and the Environment: Annual Report 1996*; Human Rights Watch meeting with SPDC, Port Harcourt, July 28, 1997.

presumably a similar number in the western division. Though their appointment represents a recognition of the need for better communication with the communities, the liaison officers have, however, been appointed from among Shell's technical staff, and do not have specialized training in development issues. They receive only a few weeks of training maximum, sometimes as little as one week. From all accounts, they show little interest in changing their approach from the past.[251]

Mobil, stating that "Mobil cares for all its publics, particularly the communities," claims to have had "an enviable and unrivaled policy on community relations for many years."[252] Mobil says it has public relations committees in all of the four communities closest to its operations (Eket, Esit Eket, Onna, and Ibeno, in Akwa Ibom State). Mobil has also recently established a public relations committee in Bonny, where a terminal for its Oso natural gas project is being constructed. According to Mobil, "The committee members are elected by their respective communities. The committees are responsible for sampling opinions from their communities to determine what projects they want Mobil to carry out. The projects are prioritized and discussed with Mobil External Affairs staff. Projects are executed based on our community relations budget."[253] Residents of the areas where Mobil operates, however, criticize the public relations committees for being "packed" with Mobil contractors, turning themselves into "employment agencies, contract conduits and distortion and bribe-stricken organizations."[254]

Similarly, Chevron states that, "As a matter of course, we hold quarterly meetings with community representatives. ... Chevron has no hand in the selection of community representatives. Communities elect their representatives at Town Hall meetings and forward their names to us. Most communities hold elections

---

[251] Ibid., and interviews with individuals and nongovernmental organizations involved in negotiations with Shell. For a general overview of Shell's community relations and other issues, see Doris Danler and Markus Brunner, *Shell in Nigeria* (Lagos and Cologne: Bread for the World, August 1996).

[252] Mobil Producing Nigeria Unlimited letter to Human Rights Watch, February 10, 1998. Since Mobil's operations are mostly offshore, it is much less exposed to the community protests that have affected Shell or to sabotage.

[253] According to Mobil, development projects include provision of health care facilities and potable water, construction of roads, electrification, building and rehabilitation of schools, support for teachers and doctors in schools, clinics and hospitals, and scholarships for tertiary institutions. Mobil Producing Nigeria Unlimited letter to Human Rights Watch February 10, 1998.

[254] Human Rights Watch interviews, July 8, 1997; Martin Usenekong, "Dilemma of Public Relations Committees," *Pioneer* (Uyo), February 13, 1998.

every two or three years. ... We also hold town hall meetings and public enlightenment forums on a regular basis." Chevron's "Community Relations Officers are recruited based on their academic qualifications and experience in relationship building. More than 75% of our Community Relations staff come from host communities."[255] Despite these efforts, Chevron admitted to Human Rights Watch, in the context of a particular incident of hostage taking, that "We have restricted our operational activities in the Ilaje area [Ondo State] because of the great difficulties in reaching meaningful and lasting agreements with the communities."[256]

Elf "has created the positions of Community Relations Officers, who are EPNL permanent staff and are dedicated to the host communities and project sites. These officers have proven experiences, having interacted with these communities for nothing less than 10 years. They also possess a good knowledge of the company and its operations. In addition they have opportunities for external training courses. EPNL deals primarily with host families, Community Development Committees and ... Consultative Committees. We also dialogue with elders, youth organizations and environmental agencies. EPNL discusses development projects / community affairs with the consultative committees. Each representation to this committee is selected by the various host communities. It has a two year tenure."[257] Elf further maintains that its community relations policy "meets the fundamental basis for enabling work environment by: (i) being proactive; (ii) identifying with the needs and aspirations of host communities i.e. the provision of socio-economic infrastructure; (iii) being conscious of the need to protect the environment; (iv) close collaboration with government agencies, community leaders, youth organizations, etc; (v) principles of dialogue."[258]

It is Human Rights Watch's understanding that Agip has similar structures. However, Agip's response to our correspondence did not supply information requested on community relations structures.

Despite the stated policies of some of the oil companies, the oil companies and their contractors are typically perceived as arrogant and dismissive by local communities. Those who negotiate with the communities are frequently described as unsympathetic or hostile, and in allegiance with local chiefs and contractors. A chief in Obite village near the Elf's gas project, asked by the community to

---

[255] Chevron Nigeria Ltd letter to Human Rights Watch, March 11, 1998.

[256] Chevron Nigeria Ltd letter to Human Rights Watch, June 29, 1998.

[257] Elf Petroleum Nigeria Ltd letter to Human Rights Watch, May 8, 1998.

[258] Ibid.

negotiate with C&C Construction, a contractor to Elf, for development spending in the village, complained that it was impossible to fix a meeting with the company's representatives.[259] Another man, from Egbema village in Rivers State, part of whose land had been taken to form the nearby Agip compound, complained that "At times they invite us to discuss our problems with them, but when we go there they take us for a joke."[260] The headquarters of the oil companies in Port Harcourt are difficult to gain access to without an appointment; perhaps understandably from the point of view of the oil companies, yet increasing the impression of inaccessibility from the point of view of the communities. Oil company workers at remote flow stations typically live on barges in virtual isolation from local communities, obtaining their food, water, and other supplies from company suppliers rather than local retailers. Roads to oil facilities often, if not usually, bypass nearby villages; leading to great resentment when, as is often the case, the road to the flow station is tarred while the road into the village remains a dirt track. If oil workers fall sick, they are airlifted to company hospitals in Port Harcourt or Lagos; the local people, meanwhile, have little or no health care available to them other than traditional remedies.

As a government inquiry concluded in January 1991, there is "a lack of meaningful contact and consultation between the Oil Company/Companies and the Communities in which the Oil Companies operate and therefore lack of understanding between both parties. Where there is such lack of understanding there is always confusion, disorder and all that makes for disturbances."[261]

Employment

It is a constant complaint of communities that they have no permanent staff working for the oil companies and that not enough casual labor is used. The oil companies respond that it is not possible to employ community members without appropriate qualifications within the company, while there are only a limited number of jobs available, including casual labor. Their perspective is that "Many youths who do not have the required skills erroneously believe that it is their birth right, coming from an oil producing area, to be employed by an oil company or its contractor."[262]

---

[259] Human Rights Watch interview, July 4, 1997.

[260] Human Rights Watch interview, July 4, 1997.

[261] *Report of the Judicial Commission of Inquiry into the Umuechem Disturbances* (Port Harcourt: Rivers State Government, January 1991).

[262] Chevron Nigeria Ltd letter to Human Rights Watch, March 11, 1998.

It is the stated practice of oil companies and their contractors to hire unskilled workers on a temporary basis from the communities where construction work or other projects are being carried out. Skilled workers are in principle hired "on merit." The companies also point to scholarships they fund to enable local community members to get the necessary training. Community members point out, however, that scholarships are usually allocated to those in favor with the individuals in charge of awarding them, often members of the local elites who benefit from oil company activity, and that they are mostly restricted to primary school level. Furthermore, due to the system of patronage that operates, even those with qualifications often do not have opportunities to seek permanent employment with the oil companies, since they have few contacts among senior staff.

Development Projects

Over the last two decades successive Nigerian governments have allowed the country's infrastructure to decline. Roads are poorly maintained and potholed; the national electricity grid provides intermittent power, at best; water and sewerage systems are in such poor condition as to threaten the population's health; and education and health facilities are understaffed and in disrepair. The Niger Delta is no exception to this state of affairs. Although there are some initiatives by OMPADEC, or by the state administrations, these are woefully inadequate to provide even for basic needs of the inhabitants of the region; as they are elsewhere in Nigeria. While blaming the military government and its civilian allies for this state of affairs, the people of the delta also feel that the oil companies have a responsibility to develop the communities in which they work, a responsibility separate from and not alternative to that owed by the government.

The oil companies claim that they are caught between the oil producing communities and the federal government, with the communities demanding that the oil companies provide development assistance for them since the federal government, which is properly responsible, has not done so. The federal government has also made statements that the oil companies should share responsibility for development in the areas where they operate: in April 1997, for example, oil minister Etete stated that oil companies should be "socially responsible citizens," and "oil companies' profits should be reinvested in these communities to alleviate the negative impact of their operations."[263] A government-backed judicial inquiry concluded that Shell "does not owe any legal

[263] James Jukwey, "Nigerian Troops Head to Oil Town to Restore Order," Reuters, April 23, 1997.

obligation to the ... Community to provide any socio-economic or social amenities," but emphasized that the company was obliged to pay "adequate compensation for lands acquired for oil operations and for crops and trees on such lands; to pay adequate compensation for damage done to farms by oil spillage/blow-out; to pay adequate compensation for pollution of water, rivers and streams by oil spillage and such other liabilities as may be stipulated by law." Instead, "the compensations paid for these deprivations are just pittance, meagre pittance, on which the people cannot subsist for even six months, and they become frustrated with life."[264]

Although the oil companies maintain that they should not be responsible for development projects in the oil producing areas, they nonetheless claim to spend substantial amounts of money for the benefit of the local communities, in addition to what they see as already adequate compensation paid for damage caused by oil operations.

SPDC claims to have had an "active community assistance programme" for more than twenty years, although this program involved fairly small amounts of money until recently.[265] Increasing community unrest led to strategy reviews of SPDC's community relations in 1992 and the adoption of its first formal five year "Public Affairs Plan."[266] The plan, clearly developed as a crisis response to the pressures being put on Shell domestically and internationally by the campaigns of the Movement for the Survival of the Ogoni People (MOSOP), resulted in the expansion of SPDC's community assistance program and the appointment of a new Health, Safety, Environment and Community Affairs manager. From a level of U.S.$330,000 in 1989, according to Shell, the community assistance budget rose to U.S.$7.5 million in 1993 and to more than U.S.$36 million in 1996.[267] Shell states that its "choice of development projects is essentially based on the needs of the people and in agreement with their communities,"[268] and that, during 1997:

> the company provided 71 classroom blocks—thereby putting a roof over the heads of more than 12,500 children. It sponsored 252 science teachers in 51 schools in rural areas, which these teachers would

---

[264] Rivers State Government, *Report of the Judicial Commission of Inquiry into the Umuechem Disturbances*.

[265] Shell International Petroleum Company letter to P.V. Horsman, Oil Campaigner, Greenpeace, October 20, 1993.

[266] SPDC, *PAGE Fact Book 1993*, section 6.1.

[267] Ibid., section 6.6; SPDC, *People and the Environment: Annual Report 1996.*

[268] Shell International Ltd letter to Human Rights Watch, February 13, 1998.

> otherwise have avoided. It played a major role in providing training, organising logistics, supplying syringes, needles and vaccines for the immunisation of more than 300,000 children against childhood diseases. It donated drugs to treat outbreaks of cholera in Ogoniland, and in Bayelsa State. The 14 hospitals supported by the company in the Eastern Division treated some 40,000 outpatients, admitted some 3,000 patients, delivered around 600 babies, undertook almost 300 surgeries, and treated over 15,000 children in Infant Welfare Clinics.[269]

Local activists and community members counter that these projects are achieved more on paper than in reality, and that much of the money supposedly spent in fact goes missing, leaving substandard facilities of little use to the communities, such as hospitals without water or electricity.[270]

Mobil claims to have spent an average of U.S.$8 million annually on community development projects between 1994 and 1997.[271] Between 1990 and 1997, Chevron Nigeria Ltd reports that it spent approximately U.S.$28 million on community development and other assistance to its host communities, as "agreed to by the communities and requested of us by the people."[272] All the oil companies undertake development projects in the communities in which they operate, rather than in the oil producing region in general; Mobil, which operates mostly offshore, spends its development budget in the four closest local government areas. Elf's annual budget on development projects is stated to be U.S.$4.5 to 5 million per year.[273] Agip claims to have invested "more than U.S.$2.5 million a year" over the

---

[269] SPDC, "Response to Environmental Rights Action (ERA) Monitor Report No. 3, Shell and Community Support in the Niger Delta," 1998.

[270] Environmental Rights Action, "Report to the Ecumenical Council for Corporate Responsibility," April 1998.

[271] Mobil Producing Nigeria Unlimited letter to Human Rights Watch February 10, 1998.

[272] The individual projects planned for 1998, according to Chevron, included ten blocks of six classrooms each, five three-bedroom bungalows for teachers, three science blocks and laboratories, three secondary school dormitories, five steel boat-landing jetties, three town halls and civic centers and water projects in nine communities. Chevron states that there are other health and agricultural projects that will begin in 1999 and future years. Chevron also has a "youth skills acquisition training project" for youths from its host communities. Letter from Chevron Nigeria Ltd to Human Rights Watch, March 11, 1998.

[273] Elf Petroleum Nigeria Ltd letter to Human Rights Watch, May 8, 1998.

past ten years in its "Green River Project," and to have provided infrastructure and development projects, as well as educational scholarships.[274]

However, the money spent on "development" in the delta has been largely misspent. In practice, according to community members, contractors, and oil industry employees spoken to by Human Rights Watch, much development spending gets diverted into the pockets of oil company employees or local contractors or chiefs, or is spent to pay off those who might otherwise be troublemakers. While school buildings have been erected, and water pumps and pipes installed, much of the money has gone to waste. There is little evidence of the development of a proper plan for development in consultation with local communities as to what their real needs are. In each community the effect has been to create an elite group which has benefitted substantially from the presence of the oil companies, and a great mass of people who have seen only damage to their livelihood. Wholly inappropriate development projects abound, such as an SPDC fish processing plant in Iko, Akwa Ibom State, far from any potential markets, without electricity to provide cold storage, and without any suitably qualified local people to run the plant. It stands empty, like many other projects. Nearby is a small hospital, also built by SPDC, which has no running water and no toilet; and no patients on the day Human Rights Watch visited it (though there was a nurse present, and the building did appear to be in good repair generally). Virtually every community in the delta has a non-functioning water or electricity scheme or other project sponsored by one or other of the oil companies or by OMPADEC and since abandoned. Alternatively, a large and expensive project such as a jetty is provided, not because it is a community priority, but because a large contract provides opportunities for equally large rake-offs.[275]

---

[274] Nigerian Agip Oil Co Ltd letter to Human Rights Watch, July 7, 1998. Details of the Green River Project were not supplied.

[275] According to a report for the Niger Delta Environmental Survey: "In the eyes of the community, causes of dissatisfaction include the following complaints:

- contracts are sometimes awarded to opinion leaders/chiefs in the oil producing communities who collect contract fees and abandon the project sites,
- some opinion leaders/chiefs collude with contractors to falsely certify job completion in order to share a percentage of the contract sum to the detriment of the community,
- oil companies sometimes initiate and execute ill-defined projects which may quickly be abandoned or vandalised by people in the community including influential individuals who then blame the oil companies in order to mobilise their communities in fresh demands for projects,
- projects are overvalued to obtain kickbacks,

Not surprisingly therefore, communities remain dissatisfied despite the large amounts disbursed: research carried out for SPDC in its areas of operation in the Niger Delta found that 84 percent of the respondents felt that oil company activities *adversely* affected the economies of the host communities and 69 percent felt that there was a high level of deprivation and neglect.[276]

In recent years, Shell has changed the language it uses from "community assistance" to "community development" and has engaged in a review of the company's development program. Shell reported to Human Rights Watch that:

> An overall audit of all projects carried out in the past five years has been recently completed. This audit was independently verified by the international audit firm of KPMG: 47% of the projects were fully successful in meeting the needs of the communities, and a further 35% were partially successful in doing so.[277]

The success of the projects, as evaluated in this audit, varied by the type of project undertaken: 58 percent of water projects, for example, were judged unsuccessful, and only 18 percent fully successful; by contrast 73 percent of agricultural projects were deemed fully successful, and only 2 percent unsuccessful.[278] Human Rights

---

- not all the community assistance projects may get to the target communities,
- the projects may not have been initiated by the people,
- the dubious or corrupt role of opinion leaders/chiefs who collude with others to cheat or defraud companies,
- the projects are not economically viable, self-sustaining or easily maintained, so that they break down soon after installation and commissioning, and
- projects are initiated and executed without consultation with the benefiting community (e.g. the case where items of hospital equipment were provided whereas the community has no health institution)."

Environmental Resources Managers Ltd, *Niger Delta Environmental Survey Final Report Phase I, Volume I*, p.228.

[276] Environmental Resources Managers Ltd, *Niger Delta Environmental Survey Final Report Phase I, Volume I*, p.226, citing a 1994 report for SPDC (emphasis added).

[277] Shell International Ltd letter to Human Rights Watch, February 13, 1998.

[278] The audit reportedly involved some 60 personnel, who visited 425 projects (45 percent of the total listed) across Shell's operational area and completed questionnaires designed to assess their success. KPMG's verification of this exercise was based on field visits carried out between October 13 and 27, 1997, to 181 projects split between Shell's east and west divisions. SPDC, *SPDC Community Assistance Projects Review 1992-1997* (Lagos: SPDC, November 1997).

Watch has not itself collected data to enable it to evaluate the audit. No other oil company operating in Nigeria has reported any similar reevaluation of its development spending.

The Effect of the Oil Economy on Community Politics

The corruption pervading the Nigerian political system applies not only to the sums of millions of dollars that can be involved at federal level, but feeds down into each community in the delta, where oil money flows into the hands of local elites in the same way as it does to national elites. Contractors working in the oil industry report that oil company employees in middle management routinely take a percentage of the value of a contract, effectively selling the contract to the highest bidder—rather than the lowest, according to the usual practice of tendering. This system applies equally to development projects as to contracts directly connected to the construction or management of oil facilities: in 1995, a European Shell executive was quoted anonymously in the London *Sunday Times* as stating "I would go so far as to say that we spent more money on bribes and corruption than on community development projects."[279] Local contractors, often traditional leaders, in turn take their own percentages before passing a share of the benefit of the oil money to their own supporters; and so on down the chain. A small elite in each oil producing community thus becomes rich, and is prepared to tolerate the inconveniences of oil company presence—such as environmental pollution—for the sake of continued financial gain.[280]

---

[279] "Shell axes 'corrupt' Nigeria staff," *Sunday Times* (London), December 17, 1995.

[280] Local government in Nigeria is carried out by local government authorities (LGA) which are responsible for local facilities and infrastructure. Each LGA is headed by a chairman, who is advised by councilors. Local government elections were held in March 1997, as part of the discredited "transition program" of Gen. Sani Abacha, and those elected had little legitimacy. (See Human Rights Watch/Africa, "Transition or Travesty?") Following the death of General Abacha, local government councils were dissolved and civil servants appointed to manage their business, pending fresh elections under the program announced by his successor, Gen. Abdulsalami Abubakar: elections for new local government councils were held on December 5, 1998. In addition, different ethnic groups and communities in Nigeria have traditional leaders or chiefs chosen according to their particular traditions, as they have evolved over the years in symbiosis with colonial and independent central governments. These traditional leaders are also recognized by the federal or state governments, according to a scheme developed by the British under the system of "indirect rule" through local leaders, and may be paid a small stipend, which varies by the seniority of the particular title. In the Niger Delta chiefs are generally chosen within communities by partly consultative processes, though

Because of this relationship, oil companies are always able to show that some members of the community support their presence. In response to questions raised by Human Rights Watch relating to the Gbaran oil field, for example, SPDC carried out its own investigations, which resulted in letters from local traditional leaders copied to Human Rights Watch acknowledging payments made by Mife Construction (Nig) Ltd (the contractor for SPDC) toward the cost of annual festivals. Shell stated that "since the inception of the project, the overall relationship between the community and MIFE has been cordial."[281] Shell also states that the company has been invited by some local leaders to resume its production in Ogoni, closed since major protests took place in 1993.[282] Similarly, Chevron stated, in correspondence with Human Rights Watch about a May 1998 incident when its Parabe platform, offshore from Ondo State, was invaded by about 200 youths, that it has always dealt with representatives appointed by the local onshore communities who "completely dissociated themselves" from the group known as "Concerned Ilaje Citizens" responsible for occupying the platform and warned Chevron against dealing with them. Local activists stated to Human Rights Watch that the representatives cited by Chevron are contractors and others who have always cooperated with the oil company.[283]

Those traditional leaders and contractors who benefit from the presence of the oil companies have every interest in their operations, even if the majority of the people do not. Where respect for such traditional leaders has not completely broken down, as happened in Ogoni, they often act as intermediaries between the oil companies and the general population in the event of protest, assisting in the resolution of disputes. Nevertheless, it is also clear that the great majority of the inhabitants of the oil producing communities regard the oil industry with hostility,

---

descent is also a factor. Their status is thus somewhat ambivalent: while they receive recognition from government, they also have some genuine respect within communities, though this can be jeopardized by a too-close relationship with, for example, the oil companies. In general, however, there is palpable distrust of traditional leaders and other "elders" within communities from the "youths" who are excluded from this system but may have more education and are anxious for power relations to be democratized at local level.

[281] Letter from Shell International Ltd to Human Rights Watch, February 13, 1998.

[282] MOSOP alleges that many Ogonis have been forced to sign statements indicating that they want Shell to resume production in Ogoni; even so, it is clear that some Ogonis, those who stand to benefit, do want Shell to return.

[283] Letter from Chevron Nigeria Ltd to Human Rights Watch, June 29, 1998; interviews with members of Environmental Rights Action.

regarding it as destructive and exploitative, and deeply resenting the wealth of those in the industry or with contacts to it, compared to the poverty of those who live close by. Those who are excluded from the system of mutual financial benefit between local elites and oil company staff become increasingly resentful of their exclusion, and protests involving closure of flow stations, hostage taking, or occupation of company property result.[284] There is a clear correlation between such protests and subsequent provision of development projects, and many community members feel that protests are therefore the only way to get heard.[285] Alternatively, individuals hope that if they are able to attract enough attention they may finally be offered a contract or other sweetener: they are thus themselves coopted into the system.

The presence of oil has also exacerbated political disputes in the delta region over territory or other rights. While territorial disputes in the delta predate the discovery of oil, and while they continue in other parts of the Nigerian federation, it is undoubtedly the case that many of the conflicts between neighboring communities in the delta are fueled by the presence of oil. Even though the oil industry is blamed for a range of ills and for not doing enough for the areas where it operates, communities are also aware of the potential benefits of having a pipeline travel through their land or a flow station, and the opportunities for compensation payments and contracts that will result even if the cash input only reaches a few. Hence, disputes between communities which have been latent can be stirred up by the suggestion that an oil installation is planned, as well as by damage caused by oil pollution.[286]

---

[284] "Internal divisions within the community also seem to have increased, most frequently between the youths and the chiefs, between youths and the community urban and local elites, between youths and professional claims agents and the community, as well as between different youth groups.... Thus in most cases, the conflict is directed against the chiefs who are seen as the focal point of authority and patronage." Environmental Resources Managers Ltd, *Niger Delta Environmental Survey Final Report Phase I, Volume I*, p.230. While the term "youths" usually refers to young men, it is also used to refer in general to those who are not part of the patronage system, and can include individuals well into middle age.

[285] Environmental Resources Managers Ltd, *Niger Delta Environmental Survey Final Report Phase I, Volume I*, p.230.

[286] "Inter-community conflicts had occurred frequently even before the exploitation of petroleum. However, they have become much more rampant since oil exploitation started. The conflict is usually over land where petroleum is found, or where there are other forms of oil-related installations. Virtually all neighbouring villages in the Niger Delta where oil has been found have experienced such conflicts. Such conflicts are

In a document written in response to allegations over its role in the Ogoni crisis, Shell directly addressed this issue, stating that:

> [The problems of the Niger Delta] include the provision of basic infrastructure such as water, electricity, health and education; and land and mineral rights. They are further complicated by the resurgence of ethnic conflict between different communities and ethnic groups—conflicts which, in Nigeria, unfortunately have a long history. These ethnic conflicts have been well documented by the Nigerian media. They report that the reasons behind the conflicts are, to a large extent, disputes between neighboring communities over territory. SPDC is in no way involved in such conflicts. It is totally unjustified to suggest that Shell, by virtue of endeavoring to carry out its legitimate business of oil exploration and production, is in some way responsible for such conflicts or the level of the Nigerian government's response to them because of its need to maintain oil production.[287]

Human Rights Watch documented the involvement of Nigerian soldiers in attacks on the Ogoni by a neighboring ethnic group, the Andoni, during the height of the Ogoni crisis. The attacks were apparently designed to punish the Ogoni for their resistance to oil production and to justify a security crackdown to maintain "law and order" and, hence, oil revenues.[288]

Oil production generates conflict on a lesser scale on a regular basis. For example, at Elele-Alimini, in Rivers State, a spill occurred from the SPDC Mininta-Rumuekpe pipeline on May 8, 1997. The oil spilled onto land belonging to two local families, on which a third family from a neighboring village had by tradition rights to keep fishponds. The oil destroyed a large area of forest and the fishponds within it. In discussions over the incident, it was reportedly alleged by Shell to one of the landholder families that the spill had been caused by sabotage carried out by the tenant family, though no evidence was put forward, and tensions between the

---

usually settled in the courts of law or through violence. There is considerable evidence that most of the court cases between villages in the area are related to this dispute over oil rights." Ibid., p.258.

[287] Shell Briefing Note, *Operations in Nigeria.*

[288] Human Rights Watch/Africa, "The Ogoni Crisis: A Case Study of Military Repression in Southeastern Nigeria," *A Human Rights Watch Short Report*, vol.7, no.5, July 1995.

two villages had risen as a result.[289] Similarly, in July 1997, two rival factions in Igwuruta, Ikwerre local government authority, Rivers State, were reported to have clashed over the award of contracts by SPDC, causing other residents to flee their homes.[290] On February 23, 1998, communities in Onna local government authority, one of the communities affected by the Mobil oil spill of January 12, were reported to be split between factions disputing the right to be acknowledged as the legitimate negotiators for the people of the area.[291] In September 1998, in the Ilaje-Ese-Edo local government area of Ondo State, at least fifty died and thousands were displaced in armed clashes between Ijaw and Ilaje communities laying competing claims to Apata, an oil rig area located between them. Soldiers and police were deployed to the area by the military administrator of Ondo State, Col. Moses Fasanya.[292]

Local community members regularly assert that the oil companies use the award of contracts or development projects in a deliberate effort to divide the communities among and within themselves and thus rule them without serious challenge to their operations. Whatever the intentions of the companies, division and conflict within and between communities can often result from or be exacerbated by their presence.

The Warri Crisis

One example of the oil industry being caught up in and contributing to a conflict, and ultimately to violent military or police action, was the "Warri Crisis" of 1997. Since before independence there have been tensions surrounding the arrangements for the government of the region surrounding Warri, the second most important "oil town" after Port Harcourt: in part, these conflicts arose from British mismanagement or deliberate attempts to play one ethnic community off against another.[293] Like Port Harcourt, Warri is on the border between the dry land and riverine areas of the delta. Warri itself is claimed by the Itsekiri, a small ethnic

---

[289] Human Rights Watch interviews, Elele-Alimini, July 11, 1997.

[290] Joseph Ollor Obari, "Rival Groups Clash Over Shell Contracts," *Guardian* (Lagos), July 16, 1997.

[291] "Oil Spill Largesse Tears LGA Apart," *Pioneer* (Uyo), February 23 to March 1, 1998.

[292] Onyema Omenuwa, "Riverine War in Ondo," *The Week* (Lagos), October 5, 1998; AFP, September 29, 1998; Alex Duval Smith, "Nigerian warriors seek spiritual aid as oil discovery stokes land dispute," *Guardian* (London), October 8, 1998.

[293] Environmental Resources Managers Ltd, *Niger Delta Environmental Survey Final Report Phase I, Volume I*, p.148.

group claimed by some to be of Yoruba origin. To the north, on land, are the Urhobo, related to the Edo-speaking peoples of Benin City. To the south, in the swampy riverine areas, are members of the "Western Ijaw."[294]

Violence flared up in Warri in March 1997, over the issue of the relocation of a local government headquarters from Ogbe-Ijaw, an Ijaw town, to Ogidigben, an Itsekiri area. Similar local government relocations, carried out as part of the rearrangement of state and local government in General Abacha's "transition program" supposedly designed to restore civilian rule, caused violent clashes in other parts of Nigeria. From March to May, widespread clashes continued, in which hundreds of people died on either side.

During the violence, six Shell flow stations were seized by a number of youths on March 22, and 127 SPDC staff held hostage. A seventh flow station was later also closed down. Shell's output in Nigeria was cut by some 210,000 bpd.[295] Three people were reported injured during an incident on Monday March 24, although the SPDC staff were eventually released unharmed in stages, the final batch on Thursday March 27. In late April, it was reported that a number of SPDC flow stations in Ogidigben were seized by youths, this time demanding compensation from SPDC for their grievances, again forcing Shell to stop production for several days. As a result of these disturbances, Shell declared the suspension of its exports from its Bonny terminal for several days from April 1, 1997, on grounds of *force majeure*,[296] and again from April 29 till May 28, 1997,

[294] In 1952, the traditional leader of the Itsekiri, previously known as the Olu of Itsekiri, was given instead the title of Olu of Warri, thus implying—positively in the eyes of the Itsekiri and negatively in the view of the Urhobo and Ijaw—rights of control not only over the Itsekiri, but also over the other ethnic groups living in the Warri area. The change of title provoked riots in Warri. The 1957 Chiefs' Law (Cap. 19), however, excluded Ijaw areas from the Olu of Warri's authority. During the investigations of the Willink Commission, the Itsekiri argued that the Warri administrative district, which they regard as their ancestral territory, should be excluded from the proposed Mid-West State and included in what was then the Ondo Province of the Yoruba Western Division.

[295] Reuters, March 27, 1997. During the same period, villagers protesting a merger of two communities into one local government area in Bayelsa State closed five flow stations in Nembe Creek. In May 1997, youths occupied the same five flow stations in Nembe again forcing Shell to stop production. Reuters, March 28 and May 13, 1997. In July 1997, SPDC reported that the Warri River flow station, abandoned during the Warri crisis, had been vandalized, and 80 percent of the facility destroyed. Reuters, July 11, 1997.

[296] Roland Gribben, "Shell Delays Oil Exports after Nigerian Protests," *Daily Telegraph* (London), April 2, 1997.

of some cargoes from its Forcados terminal, announcing that there would be delays of several days in loading.[297]

A task force was appointed to handle the crisis, headed by Brigadier General Karmasche.[298] A dusk to dawn curfew was imposed in March for several weeks, and a fast navy attack ship sent to the area in April. Soldiers were also deployed in Warri town in late April to restore order.[299] The Warri refinery was closed for several days during May, when the violence prevented vessels from reaching the port, although it reopened when the navy provided escorts for ships loading refined products: the chief of defense staff, Maj. Gen. Abdulsalami Abubakar (now head of state), assured oil companies that ships moving in and out of Warri would have "adequate protection."[300]

The Delta State government under Col. J. Dungs appointed a commission of inquiry into the conflict, chaired by Justice Alhassan Idoko, which met during June and July. Mr. Chukwudozie Okonkwo, a representative of SPDC, was reported on June 25 to have confirmed to the commission in his oral testimony that SPDC had given the youths ₦100,000 (U.S.$1,111) "to look after the flow stations" during their occupation.[301] Shell confirmed to Human Rights Watch that a sum of ₦100,000 had been paid, to "people from the community" who were asked to guard the facilities while Shell staff were not present, and were accordingly paid "the equivalent of the money the company would have paid its security personnel at the stations."[302] Shell stated repeatedly that the Warri crisis was nothing to do with oil production, but rather that "Shell was just there. Invading oil installations was seen as a good way of bringing attention to protesters' demands."[303] "The hostages were released when SPDC agreed to pass on the demands of those holding the staff hostage (for the local government headquarters not to be relocated) to the authorities."[304]

---

[297] Reuters, May 5, 1997.

[298] *Energy Compass*, vol.8, no.32, August 8, 1997.

[299] James Jukwey, "Nigerian Troops Head to Oil Town to Restore Order," Reuters, April 23, 1997.

[300] Radio Nigeria, May 2, 1997, as reported by BBC SWB, May 6, 1997.

[301] *Nigeria Today*, June 25, 1997. Human Rights Watch has attempted to obtain a copy of the report of the commission, which was presented to Col. Dungs, but has been unable to do so.

[302] Shell International Ltd letter to Human Rights Watch, February 13, 1998.

[303] *Oil and Gas Journal*, March 31, 1997.

[304] Shell International Ltd letter to Human Rights Watch, February 13, 1998.

However, the commission also heard a number of allegations from representatives of the Ijaw and Urhobo communities that both SPDC and Chevron unfairly favored the Itsekiri community in handing out contracts and employment opportunities; in particular, channeling benefits through the Olu of Warri, Atuwatse II, the Itsekiri leader.[305] Shell responded to this allegation by referring to its competitive tendering process, under which "award of contracts is based on value for money, reflecting cost, technical competence, and ability to deliver on time, among other criteria."[306] In meetings with Human Rights Watch, Shell has also stated that in case of complex technical tasks, it can be difficult to find local contractors able to carry out the project to the required standard. Whatever the truth of the allegations, which are certainly plausible given similar allegations raised in communities across the oil areas, it is clear that the possible financial reward connected to contracting to the oil industry, in an otherwise impoverished region, has great potential to exacerbate tensions between different communities, thus contributing to the level of violent clashes between neighboring villages or ethnic groups in the delta region.

Violence continues in the region to date, leading to clamp-downs by the authorities: the military task force remains deployed.[307] In October 1998, a curfew was declared in Warri town by the new military administrator, Navy Commander Walter Feghabor, after at least five people were shot dead in clashes between Ijaws and Itsekiris and a large number of houses set on fire; violence nevertheless continued, with attacks on leaders of each community.[308]

---

[305] Oma Djebah, "At the Commission, Endless Claims over Warri," *Guardian* (Lagos), July 2, 1997.

[306] Shell International Ltd letter to Human Rights Watch, February 13, 1998.

[307] In September 1997, at least three people died in a raid by soldiers on an the Ijaw community of Ekeremor Zion, and fifty-eight were reported arrested, while substantial damage was done to the village. The clashes apparently resulted from the kidnapping by youths of four soldiers from the Warri task force during the previous month; one of the soldiers was reported to have been later found dead, and his colleagues carried out an indiscriminate reprisal raid. Environmental Rights Action later ascertained that some of the soldiers involved in the raid had been dismissed and others jailed by the military authorities. Reuters, October 1, 2 and 3, 1997; Radio Kudirat Nigeria, October 2, 1997 (Nigerian opposition radio), as reported by BBC SWB, October 2, 1997; Environmental Rights Action "Shell's Airport at Osubi"; communications from Environmental Rights Action to Human Rights Watch. Franklin Atake, a retired judge and spokesman for the Itsekiri ethnic group, was detained for five days in October 1997 by the military administrator of Delta State.

[308] AFP, October 22 and 23, 1998.

VII. SECURITY

The oil companies operating in Nigeria have a legitimate interest in ensuring security for personnel, flow stations, pipelines, and other oil facilities. In recent years, the number of cases of hostage taking and intimidation of oil company staff has increased, as have incidents in which flow stations are temporarily closed by community members protesting an alleged injustice; in addition, sabotage certainly does occur, even if the figures are contested, and the oil companies must try to prevent damage of this kind in order to protect the environment as well as their own profit. Equally, the Nigerian government has a legitimate interest to exploit its oil resources, to protect the operations of its joint venture partners, and to ensure that the oil companies themselves protect those operations. For these reasons, security agreements between the oil companies and the Nigerian government are inevitable. If the multinationals are in Nigeria at all, then they must have arrangements or understandings with the Nigerian government for their security; they must also have internal guidelines in relation to the deployment and use of security guards, police or other protection. Human Rights Watch is concerned, however, at the level of secrecy which surrounds such arrangements. Although the oil companies with which we corresponded gave us some information about their security arrangements, all—including Shell, which divulged the most—failed, despite requests, to give us access to the relevant parts of their Memorandum of Understanding or Joint Operations Agreement with the government which govern security and the internal guidelines relating to protection of their facilities.

Security Arrangements for Oil Facilities

All the oil companies in Nigeria hire "supernumerary police," sometimes known as "spy police," to protect their installations. These police are recruited and trained by the Nigerian police force, but paid for by the oil companies, at rates well above those paid by the Nigerian government. They remain accountable to Nigerian police command structures.[309] According to Shell, the supernumerary

---

[309] The Police Act (originally promulgated in 1943, republished by Decree No. 41 of 1967) provides (according to a 1965 amendment) for the appointment of supernumerary police by the inspector-general of police on the application of "any person ... who desires to avail himself of the services of one or more police officers for the protection of property owned or controlled by him." A police officer appointed in this way "shall be employed exclusively on duties connected with the protection of that property," and "shall be a member of the Force for all purposes and shall accordingly be subject to the provisions of this Act and in particular the provisions thereof relating to discipline." The

police deployed at its premises are, in general, unarmed, and patrol inside the perimeter fence of oil installations, with instructions not to attempt to exercise jurisdiction outside the company property. Local activists challenge this statement, stating that the oil company police, including those at Shell installations, are frequently armed. As of mid-1997, SPDC stated that it employed 594 supernumerary police, of which the company said ten to twenty were armed, after application from Shell to the authorities for them to do so. In addition, Shell stated to Human Rights Watch that 186 armed members of the regular Nigerian police force, employed by the Nigerian government rather than Shell, were deployed to SPDC facilities, including several dog handlers. Both sets of police officially report to the commissioner of police and operate according to the procedures and practices of the Nigerian police, though SPDC decides where they are to be deployed. If not employed on "visible duties" some of these police may be in plainclothes, engaged in investigation such as uncovering theft.[310] Shell said it has no official policy on engaging informers, though it has "all kinds of links" with the communities where it works, including "surveillance guards," who are farmers paid to look after pipelines or well heads on their land. Shell stated that the only private security companies engaged by Shell work on barriers at entrances to Shell property and similar duties. A large proportion of Shell staff work on security (including internal duties unrelated to public order): of a total SPDC 11,372 workforce in mid-1997 (of which 41 percent were contractors), 20 percent were security staff.[311]

Chevron Nigeria stated in correspondence with Human Rights Watch that it has "a running contract with some private security companies for the protection of Company assets against theft and to control access to our premises. CNL does not have a running contract with any Government Security agency."[312] Mobil only divulged that "Under the Joint Operations Agreement and also in the interest of Mobil employees, contractors and in order to safeguard our facilities against theft and sabotage, we make efforts to provide adequate security facilities in our areas

---

person for whom they are appointed is responsible for the cost of uniforms and for payment to the officers designated. Police Act, section 14.

[310] In 1997, a visiting environmentalist from the U.S. was confronted by a man in plain clothes claiming to be "Shell police" at a Shell installation in Port Harcourt. He produced an identification card showing a picture of him in Nigerian police uniform and the Shell logo. Kretzmann and Wright, *Human Rights and Environmental Operations Information on the Royal Dutch/Shell Group of Companies 1996-1997*, p.10.

[311] Human Rights Watch meeting with SPDC, Port Harcourt, July 28, 1997.

[312] Chevron Nigeria Ltd letter to Human Rights Watch, March 11, 1998.

of operations. We do have a security department."[313] Elf did not give any details of its security measures, stating only that "We do not involve the military neither in providing security for our operations nor during demonstrations," and that "EPNL uses landlords and community guards to secure its well heads and installations."[314] In a later letter, Elf stated that these local guards "are supervised by the site managers. These guards are paid 500% above the national income wage or according to the industry standards."[315] Agip did not respond to questions about security.

The oil companies state that they are under a legal obligation to notify the government if there is a threat to oil production, though there is some confusion as to the basis for the obligation. When asked the specific legal provision in meetings with Human Rights Watch, SPDC cited the Nigerian criminal law of conspiracy, under which, if the company failed to notify the authorities of actions that could amount to criminal offenses (such as damage to property), the company itself could be charged with an offense. Chevron, on the other hand, referred to "laws relating to economic sabotage, kidnap, and high sea piracy based on which [the Nigerian government's] agencies are deployed to oil installations."[316] In addition, according to Shell, since the companies operate under joint venture agreements, "the authorities have the right to know when production is threatened."[317] In relation to a specific incident at Chevron's Parabe platform, the company stressed again that it is "required by regulation and agreement to report to our partner when an incident such as the Parabe hostage situation occurs.... CNL has no paid soldiers of its own."[318] The detailed terms relating to security in the MOUs or JOAs by which the joint ventures are governed are not public.

The companies also emphasize their commitment to avoid violent confrontations between protesters and security forces. In the case of Shell, "We only notify the authorities and we assume responsibility, as operator, to resolve problems through dialogue and negotiations. In most cases the authorities do not intervene and, when we become aware that they are considering doing so, we prevail on them not to—because the process of dialogue yields results acceptable

---

[313] Mobil Producing Nigeria Unlimited letter to Human Rights Watch, February 10, 1998.

[314] Elf Petroleum Nigeria Ltd letter to Human Rights Watch, May 8, 1998.

[315] Elf Petroleum Nigeria Ltd letter to Human Rights Watch, November 23, 1998.

[316] Chevron Nigeria Ltd letter to Human Rights Watch, March 11, 1998.

[317] Shell International Ltd letter to Human Rights Watch, February 13, 1998.

[318] Chevron Nigeria Ltd letter to Human Rights Watch, June 29, 1998.

to both sides."[319] Shell states that the company's staff "emphasize to the police the need for restraint and tact so as to avoid violence."[320] Accordingly,

> Staff members are not authorized to call the police to intervene during demonstrations and the use of MOPOL [Mobile Police] or the military is prohibited. It is the brief of the CLO [community liaison officer] in such cases to contact the most influential indigenes or organization of the area to kick off a dialogue. If that fails, the CLO and government relations officials of the company go to the Chairman of the Local Government Authority and to the State Government when necessary. If the case goes beyond the Local Government Authority, the Department of Petroleum Resources (DPR) and the Police are notified by SPDC as a statutory requirement (but not invited to quell the demonstration).[321]

In another document, Shell has stated that "a call for external police protection (i.e. use of police other than those assigned to guard Shell's premises and people) is to be made only as a last resort if this is necessary in order to protect lives."[322] Shell has also stated that the company has "never requested military force for assistance" and would not do so.[323] In meetings with Human Rights Watch Shell has stated that its contractors are bound by the same rules relating to security as its own staff. In March 1998, in response to allegations that it had made payments to soldiers protecting an airport construction project at Osubi, Shell admitted using external police protection in circumstances short of a threat to life, stating that "Fourteen armed policemen from the regular Nigerian Police Force are currently on site protecting contractor equipment from vandalisation. They were moved to the site on 8 February during an industrial dispute between the contractor and some of the workforce when a threat was made to vandalize a dredger. The dispute was

---

[319] Shell International Ltd letter to Human Rights Watch, February 13, 1998.

[320] SPDC, "Response to Human Rights Watch/Africa publication — The Ogoni Crisis: A Case Study of Military Repression in Southeastern Nigeria, July 1994 [*sic*]," attached to SPDC letter to Human Rights Watch, July 6, 1995.

[321] Shell International Ltd letter to Human Rights Watch, February 13, 1998.

[322] Complaint submitted to the British Broadcasting Complaints Commission, November 1995; reply of Shell International Limited to response of Channel 4, June 10, 1996.

[323] SPDC letter to Human Rights Watch, July 6, 1995. As noted below, soldiers have been reported at Shell sites on several occasions.

resolved on 26 February, but the policemen will remain there until it is considered that this threat is no longer there. This dispute did not involve the communities. In fact, the communities helped to resolve the problem. Before this industrial dispute, there had been no police at the site." [324]

Chevron similarly states that:

> In the event of a demonstration, employees and contractors alike are firstly counseled to remain calm and do nothing that would further aggravate a tense situation. All personnel are advised to assemble in designated safe areas where they would be adequately protected. If the situation warrants it, work could be shut down and employees evacuated. ... Employees and contractors are not normally authorised to have direct dealings with military or civilian authorities in the event of demonstrations. ... Any crisis of such proportion as cannot be managed by the Chevron Security is made known to the appropriate government agencies. ... Whenever the need to request for help arises, CNL Security insists on exercising reasonable control over those deployed to assist, ensuring that no more than the minimum force required to bring a situation under control is applied.[325]

According to Mobil's response, "When demonstrations do occur, we prefer dialogue and resist using any force to settle disputes. ... We definitely oppose the use of force by the military or any other authority."[326] In this regard, "Employees are instructed to be calm and never engage in physical force. ... We have always prevented any confrontation between our security personnel even when there are demonstrations. We have never supported the use of force to handle dispute. Mobil advises the appropriate authorities where violence is a real threat."[327] Elf states that "When there is a blockade, protest or demonstrations, Community Relations Officers approach the venue peacefully to create an atmosphere for dialogue.... We do everything possible to maintain peace through dialogue or negotiation, and this has yielded positive results all the time."[328]

---

[324] "Osubi Airport Project: Shell Nigeria's Response to Allegations by ERA," SPDC Press Release, March 23, 1998.

[325] Chevron Nigeria Ltd letter to Human Rights Watch, March 11, 1998.

[326] Mobil Producing Nigeria Unlimited letter to Human Rights Watch, February 10, 1998.

[327] Ibid.

[328] Elf Petroleum Nigeria Ltd letter to Human Rights Watch, May 8, 1998.

Shell also maintains that it has on occasion taken political risks in order to avoid confrontation, citing the 1994 strike by oil workers related to the previous year's annulment of elections aimed to install a civilian government, during which SPDC "shut in more than half its production ... in order to prevent confrontation between security forces and staff. This was done despite considerable pressure from the government to keep the oil flowing."[329] Similarly, during the Warri crisis, when seven flow stations were closed, it said "the company asked the authorities not to intervene by force, but rather leave it to dialogue with the host communities. As a result, 127 hostages were freed without any serious incident."[330]

Despite requests, none of the oil companies provided Human Rights Watch with copies of internal directions relating to the handling of protests or deployment of security, though Shell did confirm in meetings that such documents existed, and states that its guidelines have been reviewed against the U.N. Basic Principles on the Use of Force and Firearms by Law Enforcement Officers, the U.N. Code of Conduct for Law Enforcement Officials, and the U.N. Pocket Book on Human Rights for the Police.[331] Allegations regarding illicit payments to the military or the import of weapons are described below, in the section on the role and responsibilities of the international oil companies.

Special Task Forces

In addition to the regular security arrangements made between the oil companies and the Nigerian government, the Nigerian government has created a number of special security units and initiatives to protect oil installations: oil is the lifeblood of the Nigerian federal government, and any threat to oil revenues is viewed in the most serious light. The best known of these special units is the Rivers State Internal Security Task Force, a paramilitary force created in response to the protests led by the Movement for the Survival of the Ogoni People

---

[329] SPDC, *Shell in Nigeria*, December 1995.

[330] Shell International Ltd letter to Human Rights Watch, February 13, 1998.

[331] Shell, *Profits and Principles—does there have to be a choice?* (London: Shell International, May 1998), p.38. In correspondence with the Ecumenical Council for Corporate Responsibility, Shell quoted a paragraph from SPDC's guidelines on the use of external security, on which its comments to Human Rights Watch are clearly based: "Under no condition or circumstance must SPDC, or any contractor working, or about to work for SPDC, engage, or cause to be engaged, the services of any military or paramilitary force (e.g. MOPOL), for the protection of SPDC facilities and work locations or, for the protection of transportation to and from such facilities and locations." SPDC, "Response to Environmental Rights Action," p.2.

(MOSOP), with a well-earned reputation for brutality. The Task Force was now withdrawn to barracks in September 1998, and the situation in Ogoni greatly improved.

The government regularly emphasizes its commitment to the forceful protection of oil company activities. In August 1996, after arresting nine youths in connection with sabotage of a Shell pipeline, a press release from the police command in Rivers State warned "community and opinion leaders that the command will deal ruthlessly with anyone caught."[332] In April 1997, oil minister Etete warned local communities that "The present administration will not tolerate a situation where every political grievance is taken out on the oil installations and operations of oil companies." Community leaders should restrain their youths, since "Host communities should relate with operators in the oil industry as frequent unrests in the oil producing communities are not conducive to sustainable development[*sic*]."[333] In March 1998, Etete again stated that destruction of oil company property would meet "the full wrath of the law," emphasizing the identity of interests between the government and the oil companies by stating that "the oil joint venture companies are partners of government; any destruction of their equipment is like destroying government property."[334] In September 1998, the coordinator of the "Naval Information Unit," Lt.-Cdr. Kabiru Aliyu stated that the navy would deal with any youths involved in attacks on oil installations as "economic saboteurs" and that they would be "decisively dealt with."[335]

In August 1997, the government of Bayelsa State announced the formation of a new security outfit known as "Operation Salvage," with the aim of protecting oil installations.[336] Press reports stated that the announcement was in the presence of oil company representatives. However, Shell stated to Human Rights Watch that "SPDC was not present at the announcement of the formation of the Bayelsa Security Task Force. However, we and other companies operating in the area were subsequently invited to a meeting with the State Government to discuss the matter and to sign a proposed memorandum of understanding (MOU). At the meeting we were informed that the primary purpose of the task force was crime prevention,

---

[332] Reuters, August 30, 1996.

[333] James Jukwey, "Nigerian Troops Head to Oil Town to Restore Order," Reuters, April 23, 1997.

[334] *Platts Commodity News* (London), March 25, 1998

[335] Philip Nwosu, "Navy Reads Riot Act to Youths in Oil-Producing Areas," *Post Express Wired*, September 6, 1998.

[336] Environmental Rights Action, "Don't Militarize Bayelsa," Press Statement, August 12, 1997.

although a role in protecting oil facilities was also mentioned. For that reason, SPDC refused to sign the MOU."[337]

A similar unit, named "Operation Flush," has been established in Rivers State. Special anti-crime task forces, with names such as "Operation Sweep" or "Operation Storm," exist in other (non-oil producing) states, and have reputations as being among the most abusive Nigerian security force outfits. In December 1997, it was reported that the federal government was planning to establish a new naval base in Bayelsa State, "in view of the economic importance of the state"; in March 1998, the minister for internal affairs also stressed the need for "increased security operations" in Rivers State; in April 1998, the Delta State military administrator suggested the creation of a national coast guard, comprising the army, navy, airforce, police, customs and related agencies, to police the delta, "especially economic activities"; in November 1998, the government once again promised to "beef up" security in the oil areas, and it was reported that several hundred soldiers, including a number recently returned from peacekeeping duties in Sierra Leone, had been deployed to the delta, while the Nigerian navy would also be fortified to prevent disruptions to production.[338] On December 30, 1998, as Ijaw youths protested at several locations across the delta, both army and navy deployed large numbers of personnel, reported as up to 15,000, into the region.[339]

---

[337] Shell International Ltd letter to Human Rights Watch, February 13, 1998.

[338] "Nigerian Government to Build Naval Base in Bayelsa State," Kaduna Radio Nigeria, December 5, 1997, as reported by FBIS, December 7, 1997; "Minister Urges Increased Security in Rivers State," Lagos Radio Nigeria, March 22, 1998, as reported by FBIS, March 24, 1998; *Nigeria Today*, April 17, 1998; *Nigeria Today*, October 28, 1998; *Opecna Bulletin*, November 27, 1998.

[339] Environmental Rights Action, "Unprecedented State of Emergency Declared in Niger Delta," Press Statement, December 31, 1998; Reuters, December 31, 1998.

VIII. PROTEST AND REPRESSION IN THE NIGER DELTA

While all the oil companies that responded to Human Rights Watch's request for information stated that their policy was always to oppose the use of force against protesters at oil installations, the response from the military regime has been invariably repressive when community members attempt to demand better treatment from the government or the international oil companies. The following section describes well known protests, including the campaign by the Movement for the Survival of the Ogoni People (MOSOP), as well as lesser known attempts to obtain compensation by local communities, and the response from the security forces to these actions. While information relating to the oil companies' response is included, where available, the next chapter considers the role and responsibilities of the oil companies in more detail.

Umuechem

On October 30 and 31, 1990, a protest took place at Shell's facility at Umuechem, east of Port Harcourt, Rivers State, that led to the police killing some eighty unarmed demonstrators and destroying or badly damaging 495 houses. This incident was the first to bring the situation in the Niger Delta to international attention, and remains the most serious loss of life directly involving oil company activities. Youths from the Umuechem community demanded provision of electricity, water, roads, and other compensation for oil pollution of crops and water supplies. On October 29, 1990, the divisional manager of SPDC's eastern division had written to the Rivers State commissioner of police to request "security protection," with a preference for the paramilitary Mobile Police, in anticipation of an "impending attack" on SPDC's facilities in Umuechem allegedly planned for the following morning.[340] Following peaceful protests by village youths on SPDC's premises on October 30, SPDC again made a written report to the governor of Rivers State, a copy of which was sent to the commissioner of police. On October 31, Mobile Police attacked peaceful demonstrators with teargas and gunfire. They returned at 5 a.m. the next day, shooting indiscriminately, in a purported attempt to locate three of their members who had not returned the previous evening. A judicial commission of inquiry established by the government found no evidence of a threat by the villagers and concluded that the Mobile Police

---

[340] Letter from J.R. Udofia, SPDC Divisional Manager (East) to the Commissioner of Police, Rivers State, October 29, 1990. The Mobile Police are a paramilitary body with a reputation for brutality and abuse of power.

had displayed "a reckless disregard for lives and property."[341] No compensation has been awarded for the attack to those whose relatives were killed or homes destroyed; nor have the perpetrators been brought to justice.[342]

The Ogoni Crisis

The most significant effort to target oil production in an attempt to highlight minority grievances has been that led by the Movement for the Survival of the Ogoni People (MOSOP), founded in 1990 by leaders of the Ogoni ethnic group, including Ken Saro-Wiwa, a well-known author who became its spokesperson. In August 1990 MOSOP adopted an "Ogoni Bill of Rights," which listed the grievances of the Ogoni people and demanded "political autonomy to participate in the affairs of the Republic as a distinct and separate unit," including "the right to the control and use of a fair proportion of Ogoni economic resources for Ogoni development." MOSOP's political demands were targeted at the Nigerian federal government, but it also accused Shell of "full responsibility for the genocide of the Ogoni."[343] In October 1990, MOSOP sent the Ogoni Bill of Rights to then head of state Gen. Ibrahim Babangida, but received no response. In December 1992, MOSOP sent its demands to Shell, Chevron, and NNPC, the partners in the joint ventures operating in Ogoni, together with an ultimatum to pay back royalties and compensation within thirty days or quit Ogoni.

On January 4, 1993, at the start of the U.N.'s International Year of the World's Indigenous Peoples, MOSOP held a mass rally in Ogoni attended by hundreds of thousands of people—one half or more of the total Ogoni population. Mobilization continued throughout the year, and MOSOP decided, controversially, to boycott the June 12, 1993 elections. Shell withdrew its staff from Ogoni in January 1993 and ceased production at its facilities there (about 3 percent of its total production in Nigeria) in mid-1993, citing intimidation of its staff. Active Shell pipelines continue to cross Ogoni, however, carrying oil produced at other oil fields.[344]

---

[341] Rivers State Government, *Report of the Judicial Commission of Inquiry into the Umuechem Disturbances*.

[342] Anyakwee Nsirimovu, *The Massacre of an Oil Producing Community: The Umuechem Tragedy Revisited* (Institute of Human Rights and Humanitarian Law: Port Harcourt, November 1994).

[343] Ken Saro-Wiwa, *Genocide in Nigeria: The Ogoni Tragedy* (Port Harcourt: Saros, 1992), p.81.

[344] SPDC, *Nigeria Brief: The Ogoni Issue* (Lagos: SPDC, January 1995).

This demonstration of organized political opposition to both government and oil companies resulted in a military crackdown in Ogoni. Ken Saro-Wiwa and other MOSOP leaders were detained several times during 1993. A Rivers State Internal Security Task Force, a military unit, was created in January 1994 specifically to deal with the Ogoni crisis. In May 1994, following the brutal murder by a mob of youths of four prominent Ogoni leaders, who had been associated with a faction of MOSOP that had differed with Saro-Wiwa on the organization's tactics and strategy and had been regarded by some in MOSOP as government collaborators, the repression of MOSOP activities intensified. Ken Saro-Wiwa and several other Ogoni activists were immediately arrested in connection with the four murders, despite a lack of credible evidence to connect them to the deaths. In 1995, Human Rights Watch published a report on the Ogoni crisis which documented detentions, harassment, and extrajudicial executions of MOSOP activists by the Task Force and other security force units, as well as security force involvement in violent clashes between the Ogoni and neighboring ethnic groups.[345] Sixteen members of the MOSOP leadership were put on trial for the May 1994 murders, and nine, including Ken Saro-Wiwa, were eventually convicted and sentenced to death by a special tribunal established for the case, whose procedures blatantly violated international standards of due process.[346] One leading jurist concluded:

> The judgement of the Tribunal is not merely wrong, illogical or perverse. It is downright dishonest. The Tribunal consistently advanced arguments which no experienced lawyer could possibly believe to be logical or just. I believe that the Tribunal first decided on its verdicts and then sought for arguments to justify them. No barrel was too deep to be scraped.[347]

---

[345] Human Rights Watch/Africa, "The Ogoni Crisis"; see also *Ogoni: Trials and Travails* (Lagos: Civil Liberties Organisation, 1996).

[346] Ibid., see also Michael Birnbaum Q.C., *Fundamental Rights Denied: Report of the Trial of Ken Saro-Wiwa and Others* (London: Article 19, June 1995), and Michael Birnbaum Q.C., *A Travesty of Law and Justice: An Analysis of the Judgment in the Case of Ken Saro-Wiwa and Others* (London: Article 19, December 1995). A fact-finding team appointed by the U.N. Secretary-General, which traveled to Nigeria in April 1996, noted numerous defects in the trial process under international law, while concluding in addition that "the special tribunal ... had no jurisdiction to try Mr. Ken Saro-Wiwa and the others." Annex to U.N. Document A/50/960.

[347] Birnbaum, *Travesty of Law and Justice*, p.2.

Without the right to an appeal, the "Ogoni Nine" were executed on November 10, 1995.

Following the execution of Saro-Wiwa and his codefendants, and the flight of many other leadership figures into exile, MOSOP lost its driving force. Twenty former activists in MOSOP, who were detained at various times in 1994 and 1995, were held in Port Harcourt prison, in deteriorating health, until September 1998, charged with murder in connection with the killings of May 1994 for which Ken Saro-Wiwa and his codefendants were hanged.[348] They were held under a "holding charge" before a magistrates court, since the government did not reconstitute the special tribunal before which the earlier trial was held.[349] Hundreds of other Ogonis have been held in detention for periods ranging from a few hours or days to several months over the last few years. Nevertheless, protests continued at a lower pitch over the following years, and Ogoni activists continued to organize events to coincide with January 4, "Ogoni Day," and November 10, the anniversary of the executions.

Human Rights Watch visited Ogoni in July 1997, and spoke to eyewitnesses about several cases in which individuals marked as MOSOP activists had been extrajudicially executed, beaten, or detained by members of the security forces. In raids by the security forces on houses where such activists live, police or soldiers often assaulted all members of the household indiscriminately. Meetings of Ogoni organizations regarded as subversive, including MOSOP and its affiliates, had been broken up if held in public.

In one raid on October 14, 1996, soldiers came to the home of an activist, burst into his bedroom and beat him and his wife severely. They stripped them both naked, and then went to a nearby compound where the wife's mother lived, teargassed the premises and beat the mother also. The wife, who was pregnant, was admitted to the village clinic for two weeks, suffering from internal bleeding

---

[348] Their names are: Samson Ntignee, Nyieda Nasikpo, Nwinbari Abere Papah, Samuel Asiga, Paul Deekor, Godwin Gbodor, John Banatu, Adam Kaa, Porgbara Zorzor, Friday Gburuma, Kagbara Basseeh, Blessing Israel, Bariture Lebee, Babina Vizor, Benjamin Kabari, Taaghalobari K. Monsi, Bgbaa Baovi, Baribuma Kumanwee, Michael Dogala, and Kale Beete.

[349] The practice of filing "holding charges" before magistrates' courts, even when those courts do not have jurisdiction to try the case (as in the case of murder) is a common practice of the Nigerian police, despite criticisms from human rights organizations and rulings of the Court of Appeal that no such procedure exists in Nigerian law. The charge is used to obtain an order that the accused be kept in custody pending the preparation of the case before the tribunal in which it will be heard.

as a result of her injuries. Her mother was treated by traditional medicine, but was unable to stand up properly for two months, and was still unable to carry heavy objects when Human Rights Watch interviewed her nine months later. The husband was detained for several months.[350]

In many cases, the eyewitnesses spoken to by Human Rights Watch knew the names of those who had carried out the killings or beatings, who are notorious for similar assaults in Ogoni. Despite this, there was no prospect of bringing the perpetrator to justice; lawyers in the community were too frightened to assist victims in civil cases, while the chances of internal disciplinary proceedings within the security forces were virtually zero. While the situation in Ogoni has improved in recent months, the chances of redress for past violations remain slim. In a rare case in which disciplinary action was promised, Maj. Obi Umahi, commander of the Rivers State Internal Security Task Force, said that he would bring a soldier before a court martial in connection with the shooting and killing at a Task Force roadblock on July 12, 1997, of an Ogoni man, Barile Ikogbara, and the wounding of two others. However, MOSOP alleged that Umahi had attempted to cover up the killing by offering the family money in return for not speaking to the press.[351] Nothing further has been reported in relation to whether any disciplinary action was in fact instituted. Often, when people are killed by the security forces, the body is not released to the family. Several of those Human Rights Watch spoke to had petitioned the commissioner of police or Major Umahi in cases where members of their family had been killed, but they had been intimidated to such an extent that they had given up even seeking release of the body for burial.

There was another crackdown in Ogoni around January 4, 1998, when once again Ogonis attempted to celebrate what has been known since 1993 as "Ogoni Day," and once again the security forces did all they could to prevent them. According to reports from MOSOP's London office, confirmed by human rights activists in the region, the Internal Security Task Force began a fresh roundup of suspected activists in late December. On January 3 and 4, several tens of people were detained, and arrests continued during the following days. On January 3, Batom Mitee, the brother of Ledum Mitee, who was tried with Ken Saro-Wiwa but acquitted, was detained at his hotel in Bori, the main Ogoni town. Eyewitnesses reported that he had been severely beaten with rifle butts and electric cables, as had

---

[350] Human Rights Watch interviews, July 12, 1997.

[351] MOSOP Press Statement, July 14, 1997; Reuters, July 19, 1997; and Joseph Ollor, "MOSOP, Rights Group Fault Handling of Ogoni Man's Death," *Guardian* (Lagos), July 22, 1997.

Tombari Gioro, who was detained with him. MOSOP reported that two people were killed by security forces around Ogoni Day: Beatrice Nwakpasi, who was shot when soldiers opened fire into a group of dancing people on January 4; and Daniel Naador, who was arrested and beaten, and died on January 17 as a result of his injuries.[352]

MOSOP reported that on March 22, 1998, members of the Rivers State Internal Security Task Group and Operation Flush, an anti-crime unit in Rivers State, raided Ledum Mitee's residence in Port Harcourt and ransacked the entire property, also beating a twelve-year-old girl on the premises. Barileresi Mitee, another of Ledum's brothers, and Akpan George, a neighbor, were arrested and taken away. Batom and Barileresi Mitee, Akpan George, and Tombari Gioro, together with a number of other Ogonis, remained in detention until May 1998.[353]

Following the death of General Abacha in June 1998, the situation in Ogoni improved significantly. Nevertheless, MOSOP reported a series of new raids by the Internal Security Task Force in Sogho community on August 5, 6 and 7. A seventy-three year old man, Michael Nkpagayee, was said to have been severely beaten on August 6 and died on August 10 from his injuries. At least fourteen others were injured during the attack, including a fourteen-year-old boy whose leg was broken, and five were detained in Bori military camp.[354]

On September 7, 1998, the twenty Ogonis held on "holding charges" in connection with the 1994 murders were released unconditionally, and other detainees soon after.[355] On September 12, the Rivers State Internal Security Task Force was withdrawn to barracks (including military camps within Ogoni), and on September 15, a demonstration of several thousand Ogonis went ahead without incident. At the end of October 1998, Ledum Mitee, acting president of MOSOP, returned to Ogoni from exile in Britain. On November 10, tens of thousands of Ogonis publicly commemorated the third anniversary of the executions of Ken Saro-Wiwa and his eight co-defendants, for the first time able to do so in public:

---

[352] Amnesty International, "Urgent Action," UA 16/98, January 16, 1998; MOSOP press releases January 12, 1998 and list of detainees faxed by MOSOP to Human Rights Watch, February 20, 1998. Whenever Human Rights Watch has been able to check cases of detention, beating, or summary execution alleged by MOSOP, they have proved correct.

[353] MOSOP Press Statements, March 20 and 23, 1998.

[354] MOSOP Press Statement, August 11, 1998.

[355] "Ogoni 20 Free!" MOSOP Press Release, September 8, 1998.

Mitee called for Shell to "clean up the mess you have made by Ogoni Day January 4, 2000, or clear out once and for all."[356]

Attempts to Duplicate the MOSOP Protests

Across the Niger Delta, local people mention the name of Ken Saro-Wiwa with respect and admiration and ask how they can duplicate the success of MOSOP in closing down oil production in the Ogoni area. A variety of different ethnic associations have made representations to the government of Nigeria and the oil companies, presenting demands for recognition of their particular problems. Several of these associations have made explicit reference to the Ogoni situation.[357] While similar associations have demanded recognition since at least the time of the debates leading up to Nigerian independence in 1960, the more recent demands have been noticeably radicalized by MOSOP's own bill of rights. No other group has yet managed to match the cohesion and organization of MOSOP. However, the problems of communication and mobilization are much greater for the people living in the riverine areas than for the Ogonis, on dry land and only a half-hour by bus from Port Harcourt.

In October 1992, for example, the Movement for the Survival of the Izon (Ijaw) Ethnic Nationality in the Niger Delta (MOSIEND) presented an "Izon People's Charter" to "the government and people of Nigeria." The charter included an extensive discussion of state creation since independence and of the revenue allocation formulae applied to oil income, and demanded compensation for the oil revenue derived from their territory, as well as "political autonomy as a distinct and separate entity"outside the Nigerian state, with rights to control and use of oil, gas and other resources, based on agreements during the constitutional discussions leading up to independence and pre-colonial agreements with the British.

Similarly, on November 1, 1992, fifty-two traditional leaders from the Ogbia (an Ijaw subgroup, in whose territory the first Nigerian oil well at Oloibiri is situated) signed the Charter of Demands of the Ogbia People, drafted by the Movement for Reparation to Ogbia (Oloibiri) (MORETO). The demands listed include the repeal of the constitutional provisions giving ownership of minerals to the federal government and "a restoration of our rights to at least 50% of oil

[356] "Ogoni Rights Group Leader Returns from Exile," Lagos Radio Nigeria Network, as reported by FBIS, November 28, 1998; "Executions Remembered in Ogoniland," BBC News, November 10, 1998; AFP, November 10, 1998; MOSOP Press Statement, November 10, 1998.

[357] For example, "The Ogonis: A Case of Genocide in Rivers State," leaflet distributed by the Council for Ikwerre Nationality, 1994.

exploited in our land"; payment to the landlords of the area "all rents and royalties from the revenue from our crude oil since 1956," an amount "conservatively estimated at £226.5 billion"; the payment of "the sum of £35.5 billion for the restitution of our environment and devastated ecology and for our development and protection against future effects of oil exploitation."[358]

In August 1997, over a thousand people joined a rally at Aleibiri, Bayelsa State, for the launch of a new movement, Chikoko, named after the term for the soil the mangrove grows in. Unlike similar organizations, the Chikoko Movement aims to unite different ethnic groups, rather than representing one in particular. It describes itself as "a representative mass organisation for the defence of the rights of the ethnic minority nationalities in the rich Niger Delta Area," standing for the "struggling unity of these ethnic minority nationalities against our common oppressors," including the "Nigerian State," "the ruling Nigerian elites in and out of uniform," and "their Trans-national Oil corporation collaborators." The Chikoko Movement calls for "the right to self-determination of the constituent ethnic nationalities of Nigeria to be recognised and enshrined in a new democratic Nigerian constitution," and "an immediate end to all environmentally damaging economic activities by Trans-national oil corporations in the Niger Delta Area," as well as the "abrogation of all obnoxious laws like the Land Use Decree and the Petroleum Decree that rob our people of the right to control our land and mineral resources for sustainable development of our area."[359]

In December 1998, a gathering of Ijaw youths from different communities adopted a "Kaiama Declaration" which stated that "All land and natural resources (including mineral resources) within the Ijaw territory belong to Ijaw communities and are the basis of our survival" and demanded "the immediate withdrawal from Ijawland of all military forces of occupation and repression by the Nigerian state." Accordingly, "Any oil company that employs the services of the armed forces of the Nigerian state to 'protect' its operations will be viewed as an enemy of the Ijaw people." The meeting "agreed to remain within Nigeria but to demand and work for Self Government and resource control for the Ijaw people. ... the best way for Nigeria is a federation of ethnic nationalities. The federation should be run on the basis of equality and social justice."[360] On January 1, 1999, the Ijaw Youths Council formed at Kaiama launched "Operation Climate Change, a programme of

---

[358] *Charter of Demands of the Ogbia People*, 1992.

[359] The Chikoko Movement, "Reclaiming our Humanity," and "Enough is Enough," leaflets published August 1997.

[360] Text of Kaiama Declaration, December 11, 1998.

direct action [which] will involve activities aimed at extinguishing gas flares," by January 10, 1999.

Targeting of Community Leaders and Environmental Whistle-blowers

Potential or actual community leaders from human and environmental organizations, and especially from political movements attempting to organize resistance to the oil industry, have faced regular harassment from the authorities.[361] While the situation for well-known activists has improved since General Abubakar became head of state, less well-known individuals are still targeted: as one youth put it "As soon as you raise your head there is trouble."[362] The following are examples of the many incidents of detention of activists from the delta region over the last few years.

- Nnimmo Bassey, director of Environmental Rights Action (ERA), one of the most outspoken groups criticizing oil company activities, was detained from June 5 to July 19, 1996, in Lagos, after being picked up at the international airport while on his way to an environmental conference in Ghana. He was detained again on October 26, 1997, and held for two days, after being picked up at the airport while returning from an environmental conference in Ecuador. His passport was retained by the State Security Service (SSS) on his release.
- Godwin Uyi Ojo, project officer with ERA, was detained from January 25 to February 10, 1996 in Lagos, and questioned about materials on the situation in Ogoni in his possession.
- Patrick Naagbanton of the Rivers Coalition and the Rivers State chapter of the Civil Liberties Organization and Uche Ukwukwu of the Niger Delta Human and Environmental Rescue Organization (ND-HERO), both activists protesting abuses in the delta region, including by the oil companies, were

---

[361] Two prominent union activists also spent several years in prison under the Abacha government following a nationwide strike of oil workers in protest at the cancellation of the 1993 elections. Frank Kokori, secretary-general of the National Union of Petroleum and Natural Gas Workers (NUPENG) was arrested on August 20, 1994; Milton Dabibi, former secretary-general of the Petroleum and Natural Gas Senior Staff Association of Nigeria (PENGASSAN) was arrested in January 1996. Both were held without charge until June 1998. General Abacha also dissolved the national executives of NUPENG and PENGASSAN and appointed sole administrators for the unions; these decrees have been repealed by General Abubakar.

[362] Human Rights Watch interview, July 4, 1997.

detained from November 7 to 17, 1996, in Uyo, Akwa Ibom State, where they were distributing leaflets calling on students to commemorate the anniversary of the execution of the Ogoni Nine. Other members of ND-HERO were beaten or detained for shorter periods in Port Harcourt during the same period.

- Bariara Kpalap, director of programs for ND-HERO and an Ogoni, was arrested on October 13, 1996 and held for almost a year in Afam camp, near Port Harcourt.
- On July 7, 1997, Chief Matthew Saturday Eregbene, head of the Oil Producing Communities Development Organisation and spokesperson for four communities which had won an award of ₦30 million (U.S.$333,000) against Shell in court (described below) and given SPDC a deadline of July 8 to pay the sum awarded or cease production, was detained by members of the SSS in Asaba, capital of Delta State. He was held overnight and released.
- Anyakwee Nsirimovu, director of the Institute for Human Rights and Humanitarian Law in Port Harcourt, was detained for two days at the border with the Benin Republic in July 1996, as he was returning from a human rights course in Canada. He was detained again in Port Harcourt for several days in January 1998, after issuing a statement protesting the security crackdown on Ogoni Day.
- Batom Mitee, brother of Ledum Mitee, a co-defendant with Ken Saro-Wiwa and himself a leader in MOSOP, was detained from January 3, 1998, to May 1998.
- Isaac Osuoka, an activist with ERA seconded to coordinate the African section of Oil Watch, an international coalition of organizations protesting the effects of oil company operations on the communities in which they operate, was arrested on May 26, 1998, while he was attending a conference of the African Forest Action Network in Lagos, and was held until June 26. On May 28, Bamidele Aturu, a lawyer contracted by ERA on Osuoka's behalf, was also arrested as he attempted to secure bail for his client at Surulere police station, Lagos; he was released on June 8.[363]

The offices of human rights, environmental, and other nongovernmental organizations in Port Harcourt and other towns in the region were regularly raided under the Abacha government—as in Lagos and elsewhere in Nigeria. Members of the State Security Service (SSS) visited the offices of the Institute of Human

---

[363] Human Rights Watch press releases, June 1 and 2, 1998.

Rights and Humanitarian Law on dozens of occasions during 1997 and 1998, often confiscating materials from the office. The offices of Environmental Rights Action in Port Harcourt and Benin City have also been the subject of SSS raids, as have the offices of ND-HERO and the residence of Dr. M.T. Akobo, chairman of the Southern Minorities Movement. In February 1998, Felix Tuodolo, energy and climate change project officer with ERA, was evicted from his home on the grounds of security force harassment of others living in the same compound. On occasion, the security forces have also arrested, beaten or intimidated relatives of activists: in November 1997, the mother and sister of Ogoni student activist Sunny Kogbo were detained in the days before the anniversary of the 1995 executions. Even development organizations not involved in any sort of political activism have in the past been threatened by a visit from the security forces. The same process operates at all levels: a chief in Obite, who by his own admission took a "low profile" but had been educated in Europe and the U.S. and was therefore regarded as a potential spokesperson by his community, described how his house had been searched by police a few months before we interviewed him, on the allegation that he was handling firearms and stolen goods. Some of his possessions had been taken away but later returned.[364]

Foreigners visiting the oil producing communities, especially whites, who are conspicuous, are automatically suspicious. In May 1998, Shelley Braithwaite, a visiting doctoral student based in the U.K., was questioned in Ogbia town in the Niger Delta, after spending a day collecting water and soil samples from the surrounding creeks. Members of the State Security Service and uniformed police spent one hour attempting to find out her purpose in the delta, how she had met her guide there, and whether her "mission" was anything to do with the oil companies, since "the only white people who come to the area want to cause trouble for the oil industry."[365]

Journalists in Nigeria under the Abacha government were frequently the target of arbitrary detention for criticizing the government. Those reporting on developments in the oil communities have also been subject to harassment.

- In July 1997, at the launch of the Chikoko movement, five journalists from the Nigerian press were arrested at Ogbia town and questioned for several hours (Joseph Ollor-Obari of the *Guardian,* Doifie Ola of the *Post Express*, Wisdom Dike of *The Week*, Casmir Igbokwe of *Tempo/PM News*, and

[364] Human Rights Watch interview, July 4, 1997.

[365] Statement by Shelley Braithwaite for Human Rights Watch, August 17, 1998.

Tokunbo Awosakin of *This Day*). The rally was relocated to Aleibiri as a result of the security crackdown.

- In March 1998, Chidi Nkwopara, Imo State correspondent for the *National Concord*, and Donatus Njoku, a reporter with the *Statesman* were arrested while visiting Agip's Akri flow station in Oguta, Imo State, to investigate a blow out which took place on March 6, reportedly damaging a large area of land. They were detained overnight and allegedly accused of espionage.[366]
- On March 9, 1998, Sam Akpe, a journalist with the Akwa Ibom State government-owned newspaper, the *Weekend Pioneer*, was reported to have suspended without pay on the orders of the military administrator after writing an article in the March 6 edition entitled "The Spill Continues" about the effects of the January Mobil spill. Akpe was also accused of taking bribes from Mobil, in what he claimed to be a groundless campaign to discredit him.[367]

Day-to-day Protest and Repression in the Oil Producing Communities

Virtually every oil producing community—on the basis of Human Rights Watch's own investigations and on reports from human rights and environmental activists working in the region—has experienced an incident along the following lines. Community members stage a protest demanding compensation for oil company activities (often stated to have been promised in prior agreements) in the form of cash, development projects, or employment, or calling for environmental cleanup; in response to the protest, members of the Mobile Police or other security forces come to the scene; the security forces carry out indiscriminate beatings, arrests and detentions; the protest is then abandoned. In some cases, oil companies have apparently responded to the demands to some extent, in others they have been ignored. This cycle remains the same today.

As an indication of the frequency with which oil companies face serious protests at their activities, the following incidents resulting from community demands of oil companies were reported in the international press. Because such incidents are often only reported if the oil stops flowing, they represent only the most serious threats to oil production and are not a complete record: Human Rights Watch has not been able to investigate these disturbances itself.

---

[366] IFEX (International Freedom of Expression Exchange) Alert, April 1, 1998.

[367] *Media Monitor* (Lagos, Independent Journalism Centre), August 3, 1998.

- In March 1997, youths captured a barge delivering goods to a Chevron installation. The crew of seventy Nigerians and twenty expatriates were held hostage for three days by youths demanding jobs on the vessel. Following negotiations, in which money was paid to the protesters, the barge was allowed to go offshore, when the navy then boarded it and rescued the hostages.[368]
- In August 1997, the Iyokiri community in Rivers State blocked access to SPDC employees seeking to repair a leak, demanding compensation be paid first, causing three flow stations to be closed for several days.[369]
- In September 1997, the 10,000 bpd Diebu flow station in Bayelsa State was closed for several weeks as a result of a dispute with the Peremabiri community which was demanding compensation for fishing nets damaged by an oil spill in June.[370]
- In October 1997, the Odeama flow station in Bayelsa state was closed for several days by youths demanding that fifty of them be employed by SPDC.[371]
- In October 1997, youths in Gelegele village, near Warri, Delta State, halted production for several days at a well yielding up to 2,000 bpd operated by Dubri Oil Company, an indigenous Nigerian operator. The youths were protesting the effect of the gas flaring on their village.[372]
- In November 1997, Nigerian opposition radio reported that about 3,000 people from Ekakpamre village near Ughelli in Delta State had forced the closure of Ughelli West flow station for several days, demanding ₦20 million (U.S.$222,000) compensation for encroachment on their land, a new access road and other projects. Shell confirmed that about 6,500 bpd had been shut in by the protest.[373]
- From November 25 to December 23, 1997, Tunu and Opukoshi flowstations, together pumping 80,000 bpd, were closed by villagers, forcing Shell to

[368] James Jukwey, "Nigerian Navy Rescues Hostages on Oil Barge," Reuters, March 14, 1997; *Oil and Gas Journal*, March 31, 1997.

[369] Reuters, August 19 and 20, and September 1, 1997.

[370] Reuters, October 6, 1997.

[371] Reuters, October 9, 1997.

[372] Reuters, October 21, 1997.

[373] Reuters, November 12 and 14, 1997; Radio Kudirat Nigeria, November 13, 1997, as reported by BBC SWB, November 17, 1997.

declare on December 19 that it would be unable to meet all commitments on time at its Forcados terminal from December 21, to January 11.[374]

- From December 13 to December 17, 1997, thirteen employees of Western Geophysical were held hostage by youths in a barge off the coast of Ondo State.[375]
- Odeama Creek flowstation, pumping 18,000 bpd, was closed for several days in January 1998 by youths demanding environmental tests, a reduction of gas flaring, clean water supply and other projects from Shell.[376]
- From January 20, 1998, Texaco's offshore Funiwa platform was occupied for about one week by youths from the neighboring Koluama community, shutting in about 55,000 bpd.[377]
- In March 1998, SPDC reported that it had shut in 200,000 bpd at its Tora manifold in the Nembe area, after youths had protested calling for compensation, jobs and development projects.[378]
- From March 10 to 20, 1998, Texaco's Funiwa platform was again occupied for over a week by youths from Koluama, causing an eleven day slippage in the export loading schedule from the Pennington terminal.[379]
- From April 28 to May 11, 1998, Shell's flowstations at Odidi and Egwa in Delta State were closed by protesting youths.[380]
- From May 25 to June 2, 1998, youths occupied Chevron's Parabe Platform, offshore from Ondo State, and held workers hostage (see below for further details).

Since the death of Gen. Sani Abacha in June 1998, the relaxation of repression signaled by the withdrawal of the Internal Security Task Force from Ogoni, and the institution of a more credible program to hand over power to civilian government by new head of state Gen. Abdulsalami Abubakar, oil stoppages have escalated. At the end of August 1998, Nigeria was losing 800,000 bpd, and disruption continued at high levels for the rest of the year; though

[374] Reuters, December 19 and 24, 1997.
[375] *Independent* (London), December 16, 1997; PR Newswire, December 17, 1997.
[376] Reuters, January 21, 1998.
[377] Reuters, March 12, 1998.
[378] Reuters, March 12, 1998.
[379] Reuters, March 12 and 20, 1998.
[380] Reuters, May 11, 1998.

operators were able to compensate by boosting output elsewhere and overall production in fact increased from July to November.[381]

- In June, 1998, villagers protesting a spillage closed four wells and disrupted exports from Agip's Brass terminal, and the military administrator of Bayelsa State declared a curfew.[382] Exports were stopped again due to protests in August.[383]
- In July 1998, SPDC reported that 40,000 bpd had been shut in at its Nun river flowstation; the previous week, youths at Nembe hijacked a helicopter and forced the evacuation of staff.[384] 60,000 bpd production from Nembe was again closed for several days in August.[385]
- In late July and August, 1998, a number of workers were held hostage for several weeks on two oil support vessels working for Texaco to repair wells producing 3,000 bpd at the Okubie platform, near the community of Kolomo, in connection with disputes over compensation payments following a leak which had affected the coastline of six communities. Further hostage taking incidents occurred in August.[386]
- Disturbances at Nembe shut in at least 440,000 bpd of output and forced both Shell and Agip to declare *force majeure* on exports in early October 1998.[387] Ten Shell facilities, producing about 200,000 bpd, were still shut in as of mid-November.[388]
- On October 9, approximately 400 youths occupied Shell's Forcados terminal for several hours, protesting non-payment of compensation for Mobil's

---

[381] *Energy Compass*, vol.9, no.41, August 28, 1998, and vol.9, no.45, November 6, 1998. Production was estimated to have risen from 1,999,000 bpd in July to 2,074,000 bpd at the beginning of November. Only Shell's Forcados and Bonny Medium crude streams were down.

[382] Reuters, June 28 and 30, 1998.

[383] Reuters, August 26, 1998.

[384] Matthew Tostevin, "Nigeria's Southern Oil Region on the Boil," Reuters, July 23, 1998.

[385] Reuters, August 21, 1998; *Lloyd's List*, August 26, 1998.

[386] *Lloyd's List*, July 27 and 31, 1998; Reuters July 23 and 24, 1998; Reuters, August 17, 21 and 24, 1998.

[387] *Energy Compass*, vol.9, no.41, October 9, 1998.

[388] Reuters, November 11, 1998.

January oil spill. Fifteen Shell flow stations remained closed for much of the following month.[389]

- On October 14, youths seized control of two Chevron flow stations, at Abiteye and Olero Creek, near Escravos on the Atlantic coast, taking some thirty workers hostage for two days.[390]
- From November 12 to 18, eight oil workers employed by Texaco were held hostage by youths from the community of Foropah, near Warri, demanding social investment in their village and compensation for a recent oil spill.[391]
- On December 9, youths again occupied Shell's Forcados terminal protesting the Mobil spill, but were removed one day later.[392]

The incidents described below were investigated by Human Rights Watch in July 1997 and are described in chronological order, together with information Human Rights Watch has received relating to more recent incidents from 1998. In each case, the oil company involved was invited to comment on our findings, and any information supplied is incorporated in our account. Although the overall political climate in Nigeria has changed dramatically since these cases were investigated, the situation in the delta communities has changed little, and incidents of the type described here continue to occur on a regular basis.

The cases we investigated can be grouped under two broad thematic headings. On the one hand, there are those incidents where community members have made demands for compensation for oil company activities, whether in the form of cash payments following spillages or land expropriation, development projects in communities close to oil installations, or employment of local community members when work is being carried out in the vicinity. On the other, there is the general and apparently untargeted harassment of community members that is consequent on the security provided for oil operations.

In many incidents, oil companies describe protests by local youths as purely criminal in purpose, aimed at extorting benefits to which they are not entitled from the oil industry. These same incidents are described by the youths involved as a fight for their rights. According to Chevron, for example, "In some cases, the youths simply try to extort money from personnel working on barges and drilling

---

[389] AFP, October 11, 1998; Hilary Andersson, "Nigerians turn to magic in fight against oil firms,"*Independent* (London), November 7, 1998..

[390] AFP, October 14, 1998.

[391] AFP, November 12 to 18, 1998.

[392] Reuters, December 9, 1998; AP, December 10, 1998.

rigs without reason or based on some fabricated excuse."[393] Thus, "Because of the level of poverty in most of the remote areas, there are ... many cases of unscrupulous claims for compensation for damages that cannot be substantiated."[394] While Chevron identifies the disproportion between the wealth of the oil company and the poverty of the oil producing areas as an important contributor to conflict, it sees the protests that result as criminal only. The youths who make what Chevron describes as "unscrupulous" claims put it differently: "We have committed ourselves to the fight against environmental degradation, social and economic injustice in our land. Chevron pays soldiers to kill us and has bribed the police to keep us away."[395] Or, more generally, "When we demand our rights, they [the oil companies] just send the Mobile Police."[396]

Suppression of Demands for Compensation:
Damages, Development Projects, and Employment

During June and July 1995, there were major disturbances in Egbema, Imo State, after youths demonstrated against Shell, demanding, among other issues, the installation of a gas turbine to supply electricity for the community. The first protest happened on June 14 and 15, when youths occupied the residential area at the flow station for two days. Youths interviewed by Human Rights Watch admitted that a certain amount of property was stolen from the flow station at this point, mostly bedding and food. Two weeks later a further protest took place, when community members marched to the gate of the Shell premises, which by this time were guarded by a large number of Mobile Police.[397] The police responded violently to this protest, carrying out indiscriminate beatings and arrests and using teargas freely. Many were beaten who were not involved in the protest but were simply passersby. More than thirty people were arrested, of whom about eight were women, and some were teenagers. They were detained at Owerri for one to three weeks, and charged with sabotage, though the case was later adjourned indefinitely. A number of Mobile Police remained stationed in the community for

---

[393] Chevron Nigeria Ltd letter to Human Rights Watch, March 11, 1998.

[394] Chevron Nigeria Ltd letter to Human Rights Watch, March 11, 1998.

[395] Environmental Rights Action, "Chevron's Commando Raid," ERA's Environmental Testimonies No. 5, July 10, 1998.

[396] Human Rights Watch interview, Tuomo, July 15, 1997.

[397] Shell stated to Human Rights Watch that the divisional police officer, who witnessed the protest, reported it to his superiors at the state headquarters, who decided to send the Mobile Police, without consulting SPDC. Shell International Ltd letter to Human Rights Watch, February 13, 1998.

several months. In response to Human Rights Watch's inquiries, Shell stated that it was not aware of any arrests, and that: "The issue was amicably settled with the community after the meeting with the Governor."[398] While there are always differences of interpretation of events, this incident was clearly a major event in the life of the community, and Human Rights Watch finds it extraordinary that SPDC has no knowledge of the arrests. Since 1995, SPDC has undertaken a number of development projects in the area, including the initiation of a youth training scheme organized through the chief.[399]

On August 24, 1995, conflict between a Shell contractor and a local community over employment opportunities led to the killing of a teacher at Iko, Akwa Ibom State. There had been serious disturbances in Iko in 1987, when Mobile Police had burnt forty houses to the ground following a protest against Shell, and in 1995 the village of Iko was still badly affected by a malfunctioning flare which was flooded by salt water at high tide, allowing salt from sea water to be vaporized and shot out over the village, killing vegetation and corroding sheet metal roofing.[400] In August 1995, Western Geophysical, a seismic survey company, came to the nearby Utapete flow station, close to the Atlantic coast, to carry out a three-dimensional survey on behalf of SPDC.[401] According to community members, the company was approached to seek employment for local people in carrying out the survey: villagers reported to Human Rights Watch that representatives of Western Geophysical accordingly came to the village accompanied by a number of naval officers and negotiations took place with community leaders in the chief's house. Eyewitnesses described how, some time after the Western Geophysical representatives had left, a detachment of Mobile Police came to the community, fired teargas and beat people at random. During this incident, a school teacher from the village, Emmanuel Nelson, who had been interpreting during the meeting, was beaten to death. Up to twenty people were

---

[398] Shell International Ltd letter to Human Rights Watch, February 13, 1998. For more on the meeting with the governor, see below.

[399] Human Rights Watch interviews, including with some of those detained, July 19, 1997.

[400] Environmental Rights Action, *sHell in Iko*; Human Rights Watch interview with Bruce Powell, June 20, 1998.

[401] A major confrontation took place in 1987 between the community and the Mobile Police, in which a large number of houses were burnt down. Many of these houses are still not rebuilt, while some of those who lived in them have moved away to a nearby community and not returned. See, Environmental Rights Action, *sHell in Iko*.

detained, beaten, and put in police vehicles, although they were released at the next village, on the appeal of two senior members of the community.[402]

Shell, responding to Human Rights Watch on the basis of information it stated was supplied by Western Geophysical, described the incident differently. According to Shell, youths seized three vehicles belonging to Western Geophysical on August 23, and on August 24 blocked the main access road, and detained four of seven boats, in order "to highlight their displeasure over the number of job opportunities allocated to their community by the contractors." As a result of this situation, Western Geophysical asked the navy to try to recover their boats and to guard their houseboats; the navy was called rather than police as a result of the terrain, and Shell denies that navy representatives were present during negotiations with the community.[403] Furthermore, the company states that the Mobile Police were called in by the navy, not by SPDC or Western Geophysical, and arrived in Iko "some five and a half hours after the navy had been informed of the incident." Western Geophysical confirmed that they had been approached for assistance in the burial and transport of a body, but "this request was denied as we believe that this incident is unrelated to Western's seismic activities."[404]

Human Rights Watch spoke to several eyewitnesses who described the beating to death of Emmanuel Nelson on August 24, 1995, and believes their accounts to be accurate, and that the death was closely linked to Western Geophysical's activities near the village. Furthermore, regardless of any acts of force, such as boat seizures, carried out by local youths, it is clear that the response of the security forces to the dispute between the community and Shell's contractor was indiscriminate violence against the community as a whole. There are no allegations that Emmanuel Nelson himself was involved in any illegal activity. No protest at this violence was apparently lodged with the authorities by Western Geophysical or Shell, although the security force presence in the village was directly related to Western Geophysical's request for assistance.

In September 1995, a youth from Elele, Rivers State, where Elf operates several wells, went to speak to Saipem, a contractor for Elf, on behalf of his family on whose land one of Elf's wells was located. The family believed that, since land had been taken for the operation of oil production, they should be compensated in some way for any new activity on the land and the youth was delegated to make representations on their behalf. The public relations representative for Saipem told

[402] Human Rights Watch interviews, July 9, 1997.

[403] Shell International Ltd letter to Human Rights Watch, February 13, 1998.

[404] Shell International Ltd letter to Human Rights Watch, February 13, 1998.

the youth that he should go to speak to Elf; but while the meeting was going on, three soldiers came to the caravan where the meeting was taking place and took the youth to the nearby military cantonment, where he was detained two days and severely beaten. When he was released he spent two weeks in hospital. The family stated that a representative from Elf's offices in Port Harcourt did later come to the site to discuss the company's relationship with the family concerned, but that nothing was done for them and no steps were taken by Elf to intervene with the military in respect of the injuries the youth sustained.[405]

In early 1996, a spillage took place at Uheri, Isoko South local government area, Delta State, for which compensation was agreed. There was a delay in payment—according to Shell, this was because there was a need to "clarify duplicated claims by various groups in the community"—and a number of youths protested at the flow station, telling the workers there to stop production. Federal police came from the divisional police station and arrested six of the dozen youths involved, held them overnight at the police station and released them the next day. According to Shell, the spill was reported to Chief Idu Amadi, chair of the local government authority, who requested the intervention of the police "apparently because he was irritated and embarrassed by the youths' failure to dialogue with SPDC."[406]

Human Rights Watch interviewed a number of youths from Yenezue-Gene, near SPDC's Gbaran oil field in Rivers State, who described how, in March 1996, seven of them went to Mife Construction, a contractor to SPDC, asking for work. According to the youths, the engineer at the site told soldiers posted to provide security to Mife to take the youths to the main construction camp, supposedly to see if employment was available. The soldiers took the youths to the camp, but then told them to strip, forced them to crawl on the road, and beat them with electric cable. They were then taken to the police station in Yenagoa, detained for several hours, until community members came to release them, paying ₦1,500 (U.S.$17) each for their release. They spent two days in hospital recovering from their injuries. Community members stated that the case had been reported to Shell, although no court case had been opened or compensation received as a result of this incident.[407] According to Shell, "soldiers have never been used on this project site," and the company has no knowledge of "incidents of assault, detention and

[405] Human Rights Watch interviews, Elele, July 11, 1997.

[406] Human Rights Watch interviews, July 21, 1997; Shell International Ltd letter to Human Rights Watch, February 13, 1998.

[407] Human Rights Watch interviews, July 5, 1997.

rape," although "due to community hostilities, the contractor asked for the services of Nigeria Police through the Divisional Police at Yenagoa to protect life and property."[408] Human Rights Watch confirmed with local residents interviewed that the security detail present at the site were soldiers and not police. In any event, senior Shell management was apparently unaware of the serious assaults on seven youths.

In Egbema, Rivers State, which neighbors Egbema, Imo State, community members came together in 1996 to demand that Agip, the operator of a flow station close to the village, provide electricity to the village. The delegation was led by Chief COB Aliba, and met with Agip's community relations officer, who stated that it would be too expensive to purchase the necessary transformer. Following the meeting, youths from the village, dissatisfied with the result, began impounding Agip vehicles as they passed through the community. While the matter was still under negotiation, members of the Rivers State Internal Security Task Force, led by Major Umahi, came to Chief Aliba's house and arrested him, with nineteen others, taking them to one of the Task Force's premises in Ogoni. They were held two weeks from June 26, 1996, and released without charge upon petition from other community members. Community members said that they believed that the Task Force, which is usually deployed in Ogoni, several hours drive away, must have been summoned at the request of Agip.[409] Agip did not respond to inquiries about this incident.

On January 4, 1997, Prince Ugo, the secretary of the Umugo youth association in Ogba-Egbema-Ndoni Local Government Authority in Rivers State went looking for work to the Obite gas project construction site, which will collect associated gas from Elf's Obagi oil field to feed into the Nigerian LNG project (a joint venture between NNPC, Shell, Elf and Agip; the site is operated by Elf), where C&C Construction was the main contractor (owned by the Chagoury family, who were close to the former head of state, Gen. Sani Abacha). He was told to leave, but protested, and was then beaten for up to one hour, at his own estimation, by several members of the Mobile Police stationed at the site, and subsequently locked in one of the trailers at the site for several hours. He was released after elders from the community and the chair of the youth association pleaded for him: several other youths from the area had also recently been beaten or detained by

[408] Shell International Ltd letter to Human Rights Watch, February 13, 1998.

[409] Those arrested included Chief COB Aliba, Kennet Aliba, Matt Ajari, Bernard Ojimadu, Maxwell Okunwa, Edwin Aleto, Edwin Egbu, Gozie Nwaribe, Emmanuel Ngbenwa, Jackson Otusu, Chigozie Okwufa, Chukwuemeke Ozinapa, Thankgod Amanya, and Okwudini Osae. Human Rights Watch interviews, July 4, 1997.

Mobile Police stationed at the LNG project. He reported the incident to the police station, but although the police took a statement, he was told that nothing could be done since the Mobile Police were involved. After opening a case for compensation the young man was approached several times by personnel from C&C suggesting that he should settle out of court.[410] Since visiting the location, Human Rights Watch has been told by the youth concerned that, on September 25, 1997, the project manager of C&C threatened him, stating that "if I don't withdraw the case from court, Ken Saro-Wiwa's case should be crystal clear for me to learn lesson." Nevertheless, he still refused to settle. On September 26, 1997, armed men from the State Security Service (SSS) came to his home to look for him. He escaped through the window, slept overnight in the bush, and, on returning to his house and finding that his brother had been detained in his stead, fled several days later to Togo.[411]

In January 1997, over one hundred youths held a demonstration at SPDC's Ahia Flow Station, Omudioga, in Rivers State. The youths demanded that Shell carry out development projects in their village, including tarring the road, completing a water project and providing electricity: a tarred road currently leads to the flow station, but bypasses the village (understandably annoying local residents); a water project has been begun but not completed, and electricity poles have been erected, but no cables are attached.[412] The youths went to the flow station, demanded that the staff there close down production, and occupied the site. About fifteen members of the Rivers State Internal Security Task Force came to the flow station and arrested twelve of the youths. They were taken to Bori camp near Port Harcourt and detained for one month; for the first five days they were beaten every morning, and teargas canisters were fired into their cell on a number of occasions. They were eventually released without charge, with a warning that they should not hold any protests about development projects or they would be detained

[410] Human Rights Watch interview, July 4, 1997.

[411] Letter from the same interviewee, sent from Togo, October 24, 1997.

[412] There was a major demonstration of several thousand people in the village in 1992, as a result of which more than thirty people were detained for up to several months, and a judicial commission of inquiry appointed.

again.[413] SPDC denied knowledge of this incident, stating that "the relationship with the community has been cordial."[414]

In 1978, a serious spillage took place at Opukoshi flow station located next to the village of Obotobo, Delta State. As a consequence the villagers moved away, some to an area on the edge of the ocean facing the Forcados oil field a kilometer or so away from the original site, a community now known as Obotobo I; others further away to a settlement now known as Obotobo II. Obotobo I is a small settlement accessed by a dirt track that leads off a metaled road constructed by SPDC from the jetty where boats moor, bringing personnel and supplies from the mainland to the flow station. A water tank has been installed in the village and a generator donated by SPDC; neither were functioning at the time of Human Rights Watch's visit in July 1997. In late June 1997 the community sent a delegation to the houseboat from which a contractor was currently undertaking work, to demand that Shell tar the section of the road leading to the community. While they were there, two speed boats containing about twenty soldiers came. The soldiers fired into the air, but did not arrest anyone. According to those living there, most of the villagers ran into the bush, until the army had gone.[415] In correspondence with Human Rights Watch, Shell stated that they had no knowledge of this incident, stating that no contractor was working in the area for SPDC at the time; and, in addition, that at the time of writing the generator was working.[416]

In July 1997, ten youths from Edagberi, Rivers State, were detained for a day at Ahoada police station. They had gone to Alcon Engineering, a contractor for SPDC, demanding that Alcon provide diesel for the community, in accordance with an agreement that they understood to have been made with the company as compensation for the disturbance caused by the operations in the community. According to SPDC, no such agreement in fact existed, although there had been an agreement for the provision of an electricity project.[417] Those youths with whom

[413] Those detained were Chinedu Akpelu, Robinson Akpelu, Goodwill Amadi, Movie Amuku, Eric Anokuru, Sylvanus Assor, Amos Chuwume, Stephen Ihuanne, Eziekiel Isaiah, Simeon Ogoda, Sunday Ogoda, and Maxwell Ordu. Human Rights Watch interviews, July 11, 1997.

[414] Shell International Ltd letter to Human Rights Watch, February 13, 1998.

[415] Human Rights Watch interviews, July 15, 1997.

[416] Shell International Ltd letter to Human Rights Watch, February 13, 1998.

[417] Shell provided Human Rights Watch with a copy of a memorandum on the letterhead of Alcon Nigeria Ltd, dated February 28, 1997, which provided for payment of "token homage" (a cash sum of ₦20,000 (U.S.$222), together with a number of

Human Rights Watch spoke reported that the community relations officer for Alcon had said that he would report back to them, but instead they were called to report to the area police commander at Ahoada.[418] They went to the police station, where the commander said that Alcon had laid a complaint against them: Shell confirmed to Human Rights Watch that Alcon had lodged a formal written complaint with the divisional police commander "for the record" as a result of numerous road blockages by community youths and physical threats to Alcon staff. The letter did not make any stipulations that the security forces should exercise restraint or avoid abusing the rights of the communities concerned.[419] The youths were held overnight and for most of the next day, before being released without charge.[420]

In July 1997, a youth by the name of Gidikumo Sule was killed by Mobile Police in Opuama, Delta State in the course of a dispute with a Chevron contractor. Opuama is one of the communities affected by a canal dredged by Chevron which has drastically affected the local hydrology, causing great damage to local fishing grounds. Accounts of the incident given by his colleagues and by Chevron, the oil company involved, differ. According to Chevron, a group of youths stopped a

---

bottles of beer, gin, soft drinks and biscuits); contribution of ₦225,000 (U.S.$2,500) towards purchase of "some electrical items"; employment of local youths on the project and award of minor contracts to community members; and an end-of-contract bonus to be paid to each community worker. Attachment to Shell International Ltd letter to Human Rights Watch, February 13, 1998.

[418] Human Rights Watch interviews, July 5, 1997.

[419] The letter reads, in part, "We hereby report that some members of the above named committee [the "12-man" liaison committee for the project] in Edagberi-Joinkarama yesterday 15.06.97 seized some of our trucks and equipment. The committee members are demanding from us one hundred and fifty bags of cement and sixteen drums of diesel. ... We want to state that we have fulfilled all our obligations to the community. Members of the 12-man committee are principal signatories to all agreements and these two items were not part of any agreement." The letter went on to state that youths had refused Alcon access to the site and "extorted" fifty-five bags of cement and ₦4,000 (U.S.$44) before allowing work to continue, and that one youth had demanded that Alcon refund him ₦8,000 (U.S.$89) incurred to secure his release from an earlier arrest. "Given these circumstances and other unknown plans by the Adibawa people, we appeal for your quick intervention to save us from further harassment, violent threats and attack." Attachment to Shell International Ltd letter to Human Rights Watch, February 13, 1998.

[420] Those arrested were Onis Adolphus, Eshimvie Dimkpa, Chief Kalix Echi, Enoch Eli, Atu Famous, Chief Humphrey Jacob, Joshua Marcy, Chief Akporokpo Orugbani, Owievie Osuolo, and Nwase Wayas. Human Rights Watch interviews, July 5, 1997.

barge owned by Halliburton, a contractor, and blocked the access creek to a Chevron facility, demanding that the barge pay money to them in order to be allowed to pass through community waters. Money was paid, but when the barge attempted to return the same way, the youths again stormed the barge and forced it to return to their village. By this account, two Nigerian police accompanying the barge radioed to their bases, notifying them of the situation. The crew were, however, taken hostage by the youths, relieved of their valuables, and the two policemen, who were armed, had their rifles taken from them.[421] Mobile Police were sent to rescue the hostages in response to the radio call, and Gidikumo Sule was killed in this effort. According to Chevron, their community relations staff immediately went to the community to investigate the incident, and their understanding is that: "A death had resulted while the Nigeria Mobile Police were trying to free their colleagues who had been illegally detained by community youths after an attempt at extortion turned sour. This was, to us, entirely a Police affair. It had to do with the breaking of the law of the land."[422] Chevron say that they were asked for assistance to transport the corpse to Warri for burial and for other expenses, and that "we were at first reluctant, however, on grounds of compassion we yielded." They provided transportation and offered ₦250,000 (U.S.$2,780) to the family of the youth, "on compassionate grounds and nothing more."

According to one of the youths involved, however, the order of events was different. He stated that the barge had been stopped because Chevron had failed to employ any local youths during their operations close to the village, as they understood to have been agreed when the operations began several weeks earlier. While the protest was going on, Mobile Police had shot and killed Gidikumo Sule, and the protesters had then detained and beaten up the other police. The payment of money to the community was believed to be an attempt to silence the chiefs of the area, and the youths had not wanted the money to be accepted. "No amount of intimidation or threats will stop our movement, because we are fighting for our rights: now is not a time for petition writing but for action."[423] Chevron did not report to Human Rights Watch that the company had undertaken any sort of investigation into the methods used by the police, having determined that it was "a police affair," expressed any concern to the authorities about the actions of the

[421] Letter from Chevron Nigeria Ltd to Human Rights Watch, March 11, 1998; Human Rights Watch interviews, Warri, July 15, 1997.

[422] Chevron Nigeria Ltd letter to Human Rights Watch, March 11, 1998.

[423] Human Rights Watch interviews, Warri, July 15, 1997.

Mobile Police that led to the death of the youth, or taken any steps to avoid a similar incident in future.

The major spill from a Mobil pipeline on January 12, 1998 led to protests in a number of affected communities. In Eket, Akwa Ibom State, near to Mobil's Qua Iboe terminal, youths protested in a near-riot on January 19 and 20, demanding that Mobil establish a claims office in Eket itself. According to press reports, the military administrator of Akwa Ibom State, Navy Captain Joseph Adeusi, spent over nine hours negotiating with several thousand demonstrators and at one stage was manhandled by the crowd and had stones thrown at his vehicle. Eventually, following meetings with leaders of the demonstrators, it was agreed that Mobil would establish a claims office in Eket, and Mobil representatives signed a document to this effect. Up to three hundred people were later reported to have been detained in connection with the demonstrations.[424] In July 1998, it was reported that police shot dead eleven people during further demonstrations in Warri, Delta State, over compensation payments resulting from the spill. In August, the Cross River State government stated that Mobil had not yet paid compensation to claimants in communities affected by the spill.[425] Mobil failed to respond to several requests from Human Rights Watch for information about the spill, compensation payments, and the subsequent protests.

In May 1998, a major hostage taking incident took place at Chevron's Parabe Platform, fifteen kilometers offshore from Ilaje/Ese-Eso local government area, Ondo State. Like Opuama, this area is affected by Chevron dredging that has disrupted fresh water supplies and fishing grounds; there have also been a number of oil spills that have caused further damage. On May 25, approximately 120 youths, describing themselves as the "Concerned Ilaje Citizens," occupied the platform, as well as a large construction barge operated by McDermott/EPTM, a company contracted to carry out an equipment upgrade on the platform, and a tugboat, the *Cheryl Anne*, in the service of another contractor. Altogether, 200 employees of Chevron and its contractors were at the facilities, and were prevented from leaving. The leader of the youths, Bola Oyinbo, interviewed by the Nigerian nongovernmental organization Environmental Rights Action, described the occupation as a "peaceful protest ... against the continuing destruction of our environment by Chevron," following the failure of Chevron to participate in

---

[424] Alphonsus Agborh, "How Adeusi charmed a blood-thirsty Eket mob," *Punch* (Lagos), January 28, 1998; Remi Oyo, "Communities Want Compensation for Oil Spill," IPS, February 5, 1998; Reuters, February 2, 1998.

[425] Jude Okwe, "Oil Spillage Victims yet to be Compensated," *Post Express Wired*, August 7, 1998.

negotiations with the group; in particular, the failure of Chevron to come to a meeting arranged by the military administrator of Ondo State on May 7 and a subsequent meeting called by the youths themselves on May 15.[426] Chevron reported that the group demanded employment on the construction barge and a guaranteed annual employment quota of Ilaje residents in Chevron's workforce; more scholarships awarded to local communities; ₦25 million (U.S.$278,000) as reparation for "sea incursion and erosion of their communities caused by Chevron operations over the years"; and ₦10 million (U.S.$111,000) as the expenses incurred to carry out the occupation of the platform.[427] Interestingly, minutes supplied to Human Rights Watch by Chevron of a meeting between Chevron and another group of local residents who "strongly dissociated themselves" from the Concerned Ilaje Citizens, indicate that this group too, while thanking Chevron for certain initiatives "appealed additionally to the company to do something for the plight of their women and elderly people generally whom they claimed could no longer fish in the creeks due to siltation caused by the company's dredging activities in the past, and sea water incursion resulting from the canals opened up to the sea." The group believed that "the company can really not pay for the damage caused by its operation."[428]

Negotiations ensued with Chevron representatives on the platform at Escravos and in Lagos, and Mr. Deji Haastrup came from Chevron's Lagos office to the platform during May 26 and met with the youths. He agreed to go onshore, with the community relations manager, Sola Adebawo, to meet with elders at Ikorigho community; according to Chevron, he also promised an upward review of scholarships by the end of the year, and agreed to give the youths sixteen more jobs on the project to upgrade the Parabe platform, in addition to sixteen Ilaje youths already hired—although they would not in fact be required to work since no further workers were actually needed—and to backdate their employment to March 1998. The youths stated that navy personnel stationed on the platform were present throughout these negotiations. According to Chevron, production at the platform was immediately shut down by the youths when they began their occupation, although the group leader alleged to Environmental Rights Action that production continued through Wednesday May 27.

---

[426] Environmental Rights Action, "Chevron's Commando Raid."

[427] Chevron Nigeria Ltd letter to Human Rights Watch, June 29, 1998.

[428] "Minutes of a Meeting held with the Ilaje Concessional Group at Obe-Sedara Comunity, held on May 14, 1998." Human Rights Watch asked Chevron to comment on these observations, but received no response.

Chevron states that the situation was reported to the Ondo State government and the federal law enforcement agencies on May 27. On Thursday May 28, three helicopters came to the platform. The youth leader alleged that the security force members discharged from the helicopters shot at the youths, even before they landed, killing two people, Jola Ogungbeje and Aroleka Irowaninu, and also fired teargas canisters. Chevron, on the other hand, stated to Human Rights Watch that there was "no shooting at all until one of the youths attempted to disarm the law enforcement officers."[429] In addition to the two men killed, one was seriously injured, and later taken by Chevron for treatment at its Escravos clinic and then to the American Baptist hospital in Warri. According to press reports, Chevron agreed in early July 1998 at a meeting held at the military administrator's office in Akure, the capital of Ondo State, to pay ₦350,000 (U.S.$3,890) in compensation to each of the families of the men killed at the platform, though the company initially refused to negotiate on this point.[430]

Oyinbo alleged that, during radio conversations he had with Deji Haastrup after the soldiers had taken control of the platform, Haastrup responded to the charge that Chevron was responsible for the deaths of the two men by saying "if it means blowing up the platform with you inside, I will not mind doing that."[431] This is denied by Chevron.[432] Eleven youths were eventually detained and taken to the Chevron facility at Escravos and then to the Warri naval base, and, on May 31, to Akure, the capital of Ondo State, where they were questioned by the State Intelligence and Investigation Bureau and detained until June 22, when they were released without charge. Bola Oyinbo, the leader of the group, reported torture while in detention: he said he was hung for several hours by his handcuffed hands from a hook in the ceiling. The other youths left the platform, although, according to Chevron, several continued to occupy the tugboat, *Cheryl Anne*, with five expatriate hostages on board who were taken to villages onshore. Chevron reported this to the Ondo State government "with a strong appeal for government to help in securing the release of the abducted persons."[433] Chevron stated that these final hostages were released on May 31, following negotiations between Chevron, government agencies, and a leading traditional ruler in the area.

---

[429] Chevron Nigeria Ltd letter to Human Rights Watch, June 29, 1998.

[430] "Chevron, Oil Communities, Fail to Agree on Compensation," *Punch* (Lagos), July 16, 1998.

[431] Environmental Rights Action, "Chevron's Commando Raid."

[432] Chevron Nigeria Limited letter to Human Rights Watch, December 11, 1998.

[433] Chevron Nigeria Ltd letter to Human Rights Watch, June 29, 1998.

In an interview broadcast on Pacifica Radio in New York on October 1, 1998, Sola Omole, general manager of public affairs for Chevron in Nigeria, acknowledged that Chevron management had authorized the call for the navy to intervene, and had flown the navy and Mobile Police to the platform. Chevron Nigeria's acting head of security, James Neku, who accompanied the security forces in the helicopters, also confirmed that the youths on the platform had been unarmed. A representative of the contractor EPTM, Bill Spencer, stated that one of those killed was actually attempting to mediate the confrontation. Spencer also alleged that Chevron had paid for this protection, although a spokesperson for Chevron headquarters in San Francisco responded to press inquiries that "we categorically deny we paid a dime to any law enforcement representative."[434] Despite these serious allegations, Chevron did not indicate, in response to inquiries from Human Rights Watch, that any concern had been expressed to the authorities over the incident or any steps taken to avoid future loss of life. Bill Spencer, Chevron's contractor, asked by Pacifica Radio whether he was concerned for those detained by the Nigerian authorities, stated: "I was more concerned about the 200 people who work for me. I couldn't care less about the people from the village quite frankly."[435] Chevron declined to comment on the material in this broadcast, stating that "we do not intend to engage in further correspondence with Human Rights Watch on this issue," though Human Rights Watch should "be assured, however, that Chevron is committed to maintaining its positive long-term relationships with our local communities and will continue our dialogue with the leaders and the people of those communities."[436]

On September 21, 1998, several thousand women from Egi community in Rivers State demonstrated at Elf's nearby Obite gas project, protesting the actions of security officers at the facility, demanding the release of an environmental impact assessment for the project, and calling for social investment in the community. According to information received by Human Rights Watch, a confrontation ensued between youths of the community and Mobile Police based at the site, during which youths destroyed property at the site, while one youth was stabbed and severely wounded, and twenty-one detained. The twenty-one were held without charge until a local human rights organization applied to court, and

---

[434] "Group Prepares to Sue Chevron Over Nigeria Deaths," Reuters, October 12, 1998.

[435] Amy Goodman and Jeremy Scahill, "Drilling and Killing: Chevron and Nigeria's Oil Dictatorship," transcript of broadcast on *Democracy Now* program, Pacifica Radio, October 1, 1998.

[436] Chevron Nigeria Limited letter to Human Rights Watch, December 11, 1998.

they were charged and released on bail. A meeting was subsequently held with representatives of Elf, at which the demands were again presented. On October 11, 1998, Prince Ugo, a youth leader from the community (the same individual who said he was threatened by C&C Construction), was attacked by individuals he believed to be guards employed by Elf at its Obite gas project and by Mobile Police deployed at the facility. He was severely beaten, suffering injuries requiring hospitalization, including a punctured left lung. On November 23, an even larger women's demonstration was held, with the same demands. Following the demonstration, Ponticelli, a contractor to Elf at the site, announced that a particular security officer would be removed from the site, as demanded by the demonstrators.[437] In response to correspondence from Human Rights Watch concerning these incidents, Elf stated that it "neither knows Prince Ugo nor is it aware of any attack on his person," though the company was "aware that some youths were questioned by the police for looting and vandalising EPNL's Obite Gas Project offices on Monday 21 September 1998, following the women's demonstration. The community approached EPNL to intervene on their behalf for the release of the detainees. Since their arrests bordered on crime, EPNL could not tell the law enforcement agencies what to do."[438] Human Rights Watch believes that whatever the reason for security force intervention, oil companies have a responsibility to monitor their behavior and take all steps to ensure that it is not abusive.

On December 30, 1998, Ijaw youths protesting against the oil companies and in support of the "Kaiama Declaration" adopted on December 11, 1998, demonstrated in Yenagoa, the capital of Bayelsa State, and several other locations across the delta, calling on the multinational oil companies to withdraw from Ijaw territories, "pending the resolution of the issue of resource ownership and control."[439] Thousands of troops and navy personnel were brought into the region in response to these protests. In Yenagoa itself, at least seven youths were reported

---

[437] Among the demands listed by the women in a "Charter of Demands" were the removal of Mr. Joseph Wehaibe and Mrs B.D. Adele from the staff of Ponticelli, contractors to Elf; electrification of the Egi community and provision of pipe-borne water; removal of Mr. Bakare, the Elf security manager in Port Harcourt; and the immediate implementation of a 1993 agreement between Elf and the Egi people (described in Human Rights Watch's 1995 report "The Ogoni Crisis"), which, according to the community, had not been fulfilled. Statements from ND-HERO, October 14 and November 24, 1998; telephone interviews with Azibaola Robert, ND-HERO.

[438] Elf Petroleum Nigeria Ltd letter to Human Rights Watch, November 23, 1998.

[439] Kaiama Declaration, December 11, 1998.

to have been shot dead by security forces on December 30, and another sixteen the following day in nearby communities. Twelve youth leaders were detained, including T.K. Ogoriba, the president of MOSIEND; the Bayelsa State police commissioner, Nahum Eli, stated that they were being held in "protective custody" and would be released as soon as the security situation improved. The military administrator of Bayelsa State, Lt.-Col. Paul Obi, declared a state of emergency and a dusk to dawn curfew across the state, which was lifted on the evening of January 3, 1999, although a ban on meetings, processions and other gatherings remained in place.[440] Addressing the situation in the delta in his January 1, 1999, budget speech, head of state Gen. Abdulsalami Abubakar stated:

> This administration is also aware of the dissatisfaction among certain segments of our population arising from certain government actions or inactions in the past. Genuine as such grievances may be, we cannot allow the continued reckless expression of such feelings. The developments in the oil producing areas of Niger Delta region is a case in point. While we appreciate the feelings of the people in the area over their sad condition, this administration notes with great displeasure the disruptions of the activities of oil companies government and private enterprises by rampaging youths. Seizure of oil wells, rigs and platforms as well as hostage-taking and vehicular-hijacking, all in the name of expressing grievances are totally unacceptable to this administration. We are no doubt committed to freedom of expression, the right to dissent, and all other basic freedoms and rights that are the hallmarks of a decent, civilized, open society. The recent activities in the Niger Delta region are a flagrant abuse of our commitment to such rights and freedoms. This administration will not allow lawlessness and anarchy to camouflage as right or freedom. We will not accept brazen challenge to the State authority under threat of violence as recently happened in the Niger Delta region. Government has a responsibility to safeguard the state and the security of life and property of all its citizens and those of foreign nationals on our soil carrying out their legitimate pre-occupations. This administration is resolved to do just that. I will,

[440] Environmental Rights Action, "Unprecedented State of Emergency Declared in Niger Delta," Press Statement, December 31, 1998; Reuters, December 31, 1998; Joseph Ollor Obari, "Govt deploys warships, troops in Bayelsa," *Guardian* (Lagos), January 4, 1999; Reuters, January 2, 1999..

> therefore appeal to all those that have been engaged in the unacceptable excesses of the recent past in the region to stop such actions henceforth, in the interest of peace and decency. This administration is convinced that the Niger Delta region stands to reap tremendous dividend by dissent through dialogue rather than dissent through violence. Such is the path to a civilized and great society which we are all striving to build.[441]

As this report went to press reports reached Human Rights Watch that more than one hundred people had been killed in and around Kaiama, Bayelsa State, a sizeable Ijaw community accessible by road, by soldiers over the new year weekend. Some of these youths had reported been killed in confrontations with the military; some had been summarily executed in searches of vehicles or homes. Ten to twenty houses were reported to have been burnt down, and the community left deserted. Further disturbances took place in Okpoma, near Shell's Forcados terminal on the Atlantic coast.[442]

Other Abuses Resulting from Oil Company Security

The simple presence of the security forces posted to guard oil production facilities causes communities to face additional harassment and extortion, beyond that to which all Nigerians are subjected by the military regimes which have ruled Nigeria for all but ten years since independence. Ordinary community members with the misfortune to have farms or fishing grounds near an oil facility may be subjected to daily harassment from security guards as they go about their work. In September 1995, to take one example, a woman from Yenezue-Gene, near Gbaran oil field, Rivers State, was raped by soldiers posted to guard Mife Construction, a contractor to SPDC. When her husband went to protest he was beaten, forced to eat a lighted cigarette, and locked in a caravan for several hours. On other occasions, soldiers had stolen fish from women of the community at the roadside. Police posted at the camp at the time of Human Rights Watch's visit also regularly threatened the women, who consequently ran into the forest any time they came by, in fear of further harassment or assault.[443]

---

[441] The 1999 Federal Budget address by General Abdulsalami Abubakar.

[442] Human Rights Watch telephone interviews, Azibaola Robert, ND-HERO, January 3 and 4, 1999.

[443] Human Rights Watch interviews, July 5, 1997.

Sometimes there also appears to be a presumption of wrongdoing by the victims of an oil spill, a presumption that the landholders must be responsible if sabotage has occurred. In the case from Obobura, Rivers State, described above in the discussion of the law relating to sabotage, for example, five members of the landholder's family were detained, either on suspicion of sabotage or as a means of intimidation to stop any protests, in early January 1997 following a spill on December 31, 1996, which wiped out their crops. They were released without charge, and there is apparently no evidence to suggest that they were in fact guilty of sabotage. Although the spill was cleaned up, it was done in a shoddy fashion, and no compensation was paid.[444]

On other occasions, abuses occur when locals seek the assistance of security force members at oil installations, in the absence of any other police presence in the riverine areas. In one case reported to Human Rights Watch, a woman from the village of Egbemo Angalabiri, in the Ekeremor local government area in Rivers State, who runs a small store came back to the village on March 31, 1996, from a purchasing expedition, to find that goods had been stolen from her store. She suspected a boy, named Festus Agidi, from the nearby village of Tuomo across the state boundary in Delta State, and went with another woman to the Clough Creek flow station operated by Agip to report the matter to the soldiers stationed there. The soldiers returned with them to the village and arrested the suspect, and beat him severely. He was then taken back to the flow station, together with the two women and the boy's older brother Solomon Agidi, where he was beaten further and eventually made a confession to the theft. The soldiers then returned to the village with the boy to look for the stolen property where he said he had hidden it. They moored their boat and beat the boy again, who fell in the water in front of the village and died. A post mortem was carried out and confirmed that he had been killed by the beating. The relatives of the deceased, on discovering his death, came to demand compensation from Egbemo Angalabiri. The village of Egbemo tried to argue that the death was not their responsibility, but the responsibility of the soldiers, but without success. It was thirty days before negotiations were completed: according to the community chair in Egbemo, the eventual sum paid to the boy's relatives was ₦519,484 (U.S.$5,772) for compensation and to pay their transport and funeral expenses. While representations had been made to Agip, there had been no response.[445] Human Rights Watch wrote to Agip concerning this incident on August 16, 1996, and has also received no response, despite several

[444] Human Rights Watch interviews, July 4, 1997.

[445] Human Rights Watch interviews, June 21, 1996.

reminders. So far as Human Rights Watch is aware, Agip has made no attempt to investigate this incident, to protest unjustified use of force by the security forces, or to ensure that it will not be repeated.

Litigation

A major factor in the cycle of protest and repression in the oil areas is the lack of a properly functioning legal system which could promptly and fairly rule in cases involving compensation, pollution, or contracts. Even if such a system existed, there would remain problems related to the inequality of bargaining power between poverty-stricken delta villages and multinational oil companies, corruption and the lack of genuinely representative political structures at local (or national) level. Nevertheless, the gravity of the situation in the delta is greatly exacerbated by the fact that the Nigerian court system is in crisis. The lack of a properly functioning court system also contributes to conflict between communities and companies because, instead of proper investigation of criminal damage or other offenses, followed by charge and trial, the police instead choose to detain and assault youths and other community members, often on an arbitrary basis as collective punishment for the whole community. Those detained, whether innocent of any crime or not, assume that such assaults and detentions are carried out on the instructions of the oil companies, and ill feeling between communities and the oil industry increases once again.

The quality of judicial appointments has steadily deteriorated over the years, and the level of executive interference in court decisions has increased. Judges, magistrates and other court officers, including prosecutors (and police, who often act as prosecutors), are very poorly paid. Court facilities are hopelessly overcrowded, badly equipped, and underfunded. Interpreters may be nonexistent or badly trained. Court libraries are inadequate. There are no computers, photocopiers, or other modern equipment; and judges may even have to supply their own paper and pens to record their judgments in longhand. If litigants need a transcript of a judgment for the purposes of an appeal, they have to pay for the transcript themselves. There are long delays in bringing both criminal and civil cases to court. This financial crisis encourages the acceptance of bribes, in order to achieve the standard of living regarded as acceptable by someone with a legal qualification. Corruption is a pervasive feature of court cases, whether criminal or civil.

The ability of Nigerian citizens to challenge executive wrongdoing is further curtailed by restrictions placed on the courts. The regular court system in Nigeria has been seriously undermined both by "ouster clauses" in military decrees, which exclude courts from considering executive action taken under such decrees, and by the creation of special tribunals, both to hear politically sensitive cases and to bypass the delays of the court system in the trial of high profile crimes. Among the most notorious of these tribunals is that created under the Civil Disturbances (Special Tribunal) Decree No. 2 of 1987, which tried Ken Saro-Wiwa and the other eight Ogoni activists executed on November 10, 1995. Even when a case is before the regular courts, the Nigerian government itself regularly disregards the court orders made against it.

Delays plague the course of litigation against oil companies. A spill at Peremabiri, Bayelsa State, in January 1987 came to the High Court in 1992, and to the Court of Appeal in 1996;[446] a case heard in the High Court in 1985 in relation to damages suffered on a continuous basis since 1972 was heard in the Court of Appeal in 1994;[447] a case heard in the High Court in 1987, in relation to damages suffered since 1967, was heard in the Court of Appeal in 1990, and in the Supreme Court in 1994;[448] damage caused in 1979 and followed by correspondence leading to a writ of summons in 1984 was first heard in 1987, appealed in 1989, and heard in the Supreme Court in 1994.[449]

The case of *Shell Petroleum Development Company v. Farah*,[450] the leading authority on compensation in oil cases, arose from an oil spill from Shell's Bomu II oil well in Tai/Gokana local government area in Ogoni in 1970. SPDC, the appellant in the case, conceded that the blow out occurred in July 1970, but stated that the company had paid a total of £22,000 to the individual claimants and rehabilitated the land by 1975, and hence that no further obligation was due in respect of the damage caused. The plaintiffs in the case asserted that the land had not in fact been rehabilitated and that an extended period of negotiation had followed over Shell's obligations which terminated in 1988 in refusal by Shell to take any further action. In 1989, the court case was commenced in the High Court. The plaintiffs won their case in the High Court in 1991 and were awarded a total of ₦4,621,307 (U.S.$51,350). SPDC appealed, but lost their case in the Court of Appeal in 1995, and Shell appealed again to the Supreme Court.

Most egregiously of all, in late June 1997, the High Court in Ughelli awarded four communities in Burutu local government authority—Sokebelou, Obotobo,

[446] *SPDC v. HRH Chief GBA Tiebo VII and four others* [1996] 4 NWLR (Part 445), p.657.

[447] *SPDC v. Chief George Uzoaru and three others* [1994] 9 NWLR (part 366), p.51.

[448] *Elf Nigeria Ltd v. Opere Sillo and Daniel Etsemi* [1994] 6 NWLR (Part 350), p.258.

[449] *John Eboigbe v. NNPC* [1994] 5 NWLR (Part 347), p.649.

[450] [1995] 3 NWLR (Part 382) p.148.

Ofogbene and Ekeremor-Zion—₦30 million (U.S.$333,000) compensation in connection with a claim relating to a spill in 1982, brought to court in 1983, that SPDC asserts was caused by sabotage, and for which it was therefore not liable.[451] SPDC announced that it was appealing the decision, which, as the Chikoko Movement pointed out, "might take another 20 years."[452] Furthermore, protests at the appeal were met with at least one arrest and a series of threats. Shortly following the High Court decision, Chief Matthew Saturday Eregbene, head of the Oil Producing Communities Development Organisation and spokesperson for the four communities, announced that SPDC had a deadline of July 8 to pay the sum awarded or cease production pending the appeal, or production would be forcibly closed. On July 7, 1997, Eregbene was detained by members of the SSS in Asaba, capital of Delta State. He was held overnight and released. Later Eregbene and other representatives of the community met with representatives of SPDC and the military administration in Asaba in connection with the case. In addition, as reported in more detail below, contractors working for Shell reported to Human Rights Watch that SPDC had called meetings around the same time at which representatives of Shell had warned those present that the consequences for the communities would be serious if the threat to shut down Shell production were carried out.[453]

[451] Judgment in *Chief Joel Anare and Others v. Shell Petroleum Development Company of Nigeria Ltd*, Suit No. HCB/35/89, Delta State High Court, Ughelli Division, May 27, 1997.

[452] "Enough is Enough," August 1997.

[453] Human Rights Watch interviews, July 1997. See further below, in the section on the role and responsibilities of the oil companies.

IX. THE ROLE AND RESPONSIBILITIES OF THE INTERNATIONAL OIL COMPANIES

The multinational oil companies operating in Nigeria face a difficult political and economic environment, both nationally and at the level of the oil producing communities where their facilities are located. Successive military governments have misspent the oil wealth which the oil companies have helped to unlock, salting it away in foreign bank accounts rather than investing in education, health, and other social investment, and mismanaging the national economy to the point of collapse. At the same time, the government has in the past failed to fund its share of the joint ventures operated by the multinationals, and plays the different oil companies against each other so that it has not been easy—even for Shell, the industry giant—to insist that the government contribute towards the investment needed to keep the industry functioning. The costs of buying political favors are reported to add significantly to the cost of oil production, despite official denials from the oil companies that bribes are paid. While the political environment for the oil companies has improved with the death of General Abacha and succession of General Abubakar, it is unlikely that relations between the multinationals and the Nigerian government, military or civilian, will ever be entirely smooth.

Meanwhile, at community level, the companies are faced by increasing incidents of hostage-taking, closures of flow stations, and other acts which they see in purely criminal terms. While they acknowledge a lack of development in the oil producing areas, the companies see the problems faced by communities as a government responsibility, and no different in the delta from elsewhere in Nigeria: nevertheless, they make substantial investments in development projects for which they believe they should receive gratitude rather than censure. The further demands made of the oil companies by the residents of the oil producing areas are therefore often represented as illegitimate; and when protests resulting from a rejection of these demands are met with repression from the military authorities the oil companies feel that they are unfairly blamed, since they are not in control of this response.

Acknowledging the difficult context of oil operations in Nigeria does not, however, absolve the oil companies from responsibility for the human rights abuses taking place in the Niger Delta: whether by action or omission they play a role.

Most of the cases detailed in this report concern situations in which communities have claimed that operations of oil companies have damaged the material interests of the peoples of the areas in which they operate. The incidents involve disputes over legal obligations to provide compensation for claims of damage, for encroachment on community land or waters, or for access rights, though claims are often couched in terms of community rights to a "fair share" of the oil wealth derived from their land. The evidence in many of the cases suggests that companies benefit from nonenforcement of laws regulating the oil industry, in ways directly prejudicial to the resident population. Alternatively, the oil companies benefit from federal decrees that deprive local communities of rights in relation to the land they treat as theirs. Grievances with the oil companies center on the appropriation or unremunerated use of community or family resources, health problems or damage to fishing, hunting or cultivation attributed to oil spills or gas flares, and other operations leading to a loss of livelihood; as well as on oil company failure to employ sufficient local people in their operations or to generate benefits for local communities from the profits that they make. These cases have come to the attention of Human Rights Watch when companies are shielded by abusive security forces against demands for compensation and against independent verification and arbitration that could fairly establish the merits of opposing claims.

The information from oil companies that is cited in this report comes largely from responses to our correspondence with them concerning particular cases of violations of civil and political rights related to their operations and their general policies in relation to community relations and security provisions: the preparedness of the companies to respond to these questions was in direct proportion to the level of pressure that they have faced about their activities in Nigeria in the countries of their headquarters. The most ample responses were received from Shell, the company that has faced the most adverse publicity in Europe and the U.S. over its role in Nigeria. Shell also provided information concerning operating procedures and the oil industry in general in Nigeria. Responses on several cases were also received from Chevron and general information from Mobil. Both Elf and Agip took months even to acknowledge our correspondence. Elf answered most of our questions, though it avoided some, without giving much detail or taking the opportunity to provide background information on its operations. Agip provided only an uninformative two page general response to our inquiries, and did not address any of the specific incidents we raised.

Corporate Responsibility in Nigeria

International human rights law in general is written by and binding upon states. Nevertheless, in recent years it has been increasingly acknowledged that companies in general, and multinational corporations in particular—which often control budgets larger than those of the states in which they operate and have significant power as a result, have responsibilities with regard to the promotion and protection of human rights as well as the negative obligation not themselves to be the instrument of or contribute to states' violations of human rights.

Human Rights Watch believes that the dominant position of the oil companies in Nigeria gives them responsibilities to monitor and promote respect for human rights by the Nigerian government. Given the overwhelming role of oil in the Nigerian national economy, the policies and practices of the oil companies are important factors in the decision making of the Nigerian government. Because the oil companies are operating joint ventures with the government they have constant opportunities to influence government policy, including with respect to the provision of security for the oil facilities and other issues in the oil producing regions.

The role of Shell in Nigeria has received by far the most attention internationally, for three reasons: first, because it is the biggest oil producer in Nigeria with the longest history, dominating the industry for as long as oil has been produced and in the early days enjoying a monopoly and a privileged relationship with government; secondly, because Shell's facilities are largely in or near inhabited areas and thus exposed to community protests (most of the incidents described in this report concern Shell because of this greater exposure); and thirdly, because it formed the main target of the campaign by MOSOP. While Human Rights Watch believes that Shell has a special responsibility because of its current and historically dominant position in Nigeria, we believe that all the oil companies share this responsibility and that collective action by the oil industry in support of human rights in Nigeria is required.

The oil companies in Nigeria have historically maintained the basic position that to take a stance on human rights issues would be to interfere in the internal politics of the country, something that would not be a legitimate activity for a foreign commercial entity. Human Rights Watch first contacted Shell in connection with its role in Nigeria in January 1995, urging the company to take constructive public steps to end human rights violations in connection with its operations. In its first substantive response to our correspondence, Shell stated "You have called for Shell to become involved in, and to take a public stance on, several issues arising from the current situation—all of which are political. They are clearly issues where we as a commercial organization have neither the right nor the competence to become involved, and they must be addressed by the people of Nigeria and their government."[454] Nevertheless, "SPDC does speak up when it

[454] Shell International Petroleum Company letter to Human Rights Watch, January 13, 1995.

feels that its employees, installations, local communities, or its ability to conduct business safely are threatened."[455] Shell restated this position in its response to our July 1995 report on the Ogoni crisis: "We do support the statement of human rights in Nigeria's constitution and are concerned that all citizens possess such rights. However, as we have said before, we follow a set of business principles endeavoring always to act commercially and operating within the confines of existing national laws in a socially responsible manner. Debate about Nigeria's human rights record is in the political arena and we have neither the right nor the competence to get involved."[456]

Chevron has also stated that "Chevron has an international policy that requires individual Chevron operations to maintain absolute neutrality in matters of the internal politics of the host country in which they are operating." Mobil, on the other hand, states only that "as a corporate citizen, we do dialogue with the government, but this is usually confidential."[457]

Yet companies, multinational or otherwise, regularly attempt to influence governments in relation to their policies on health, safety, and the environment, investment or tax policies, and labor laws; matters which might also be regarded as "political." Human rights abuses in the communities in which the companies operate affect the oil industry in Nigeria as much as any of these other issues, since poor community relations partly caused by such abuses are responsible for the increasingly frequent shut-downs of oil production: it is disingenuous to put questions of respect for human rights in a separate category on which oil companies can have no view.

Shell, at least, has apparently begun to recognize that it cannot any longer maintain that its role in Nigeria is apolitical. In response to international pressure to take action on human rights issues, Shell has pointed to interventions it has made which are in the political arena. For example, as regards the issue of revenue allocation to the oil producing states, the company has stated to Human Rights Watch and others that "The company has made and continues to make representations to the government regarding the distribution of revenues from oil production in the Niger Delta."[458] Similarly, in May 1997, Brian Anderson, outgoing managing director of SPDC, in London for the annual general meeting

[455] Ibid.

[456] SPDC, "Response to Human Rights Watch/Africa publication."

[457] Mobil Producing Nigeria Unlimited letter to Human Rights Watch, February 10, 1998.

[458] Shell International Petroleum Company letter to Prof. John Heath, December 22, 1994.

of Shell Transport and Trading, SPDC's holding company, stated that "it is really essential that the government bring back some more benefit to the Delta."[459]

In addition, under public pressure in Europe and the U.S., Shell took tentative steps towards the condemnation of abuses by the government of General Abacha, especially with respect to detentions of high profile detainees from the oil areas. Shell stated to Human Rights Watch that "SPDC does not have a general policy relating to assistance to be given to communities when there are confrontations with the military. Each case is reviewed on an individual basis. In some cases, this results in public statements being made (e.g. as with the 'Ogoni 19'). In some others, private approaches are made to the authorities."[460] In further correspondence and meetings with Human Rights Watch, Shell indicated that such private approaches had been made on behalf of the detained oil union leaders Frank Kokori and Milton Dabibi (detained in August 1994 and January 1996, respectively, and both released in June 1998, after years in detention without charge, following General Abacha's death), and on behalf of Batom Mitee, detained for several months in early 1998.

Human Rights Watch also asked Mobil, Chevron, Elf and Agip if they had ever made any interventions on behalf of those detained by the Nigerian authorities, including (but not limited to) Dabibi and Kokori. Only Mobil and Chevron addressed the question, but limited their responses to the particular cases of the detained union leaders. Chevron stated that "Chevron has an international policy that requires individual Chevron operations to maintain absolute neutrality in matters of the internal politics of the host country in which they are operating. The present administration in Nigeria, as you well know, is military. It views as politically motivated the involvement of Unions in the 1994 strike that led to the arrest of the two individuals. Given our Company policy, any involvement of CNL in the release of the two gentlemen cannot therefore be overt."[461] In its cursory response to Human Rights Watch's inquiries, Mobil stated only that "We are supportive of NUPENG and PENGASSAN [the oil unions] as many employees are members. The NUPENG and PENGASSAN have made representations for the release of Dabibi and Kokori. As a corporate citizen, we do dialogue with the government, but this is usually confidential."[462] At its annual shareholders meeting in May 1998, Mobil, under pressure from a shareholders' resolution pressing the

[459] Reuters, May 13, 1997.

[460] Shell International Ltd letter to Human Rights Watch, February 13, 1998.

[461] Chevron Nigeria Ltd letter to Human Rights Watch, March 11, 1998.

[462] MPNU letter to Human Rights Watch, February 10, 1998.

company to review its investments in Nigeria in light of the human rights situation, finally undertook to raise the cases of Kokori and Dabibi with the Nigerian government; the death of General Abacha and the subsequent release of detainees, including the unionists, freed them from this commitment.[463]

In addition to the general responsibilities to monitor and promote respect for human rights by the Nigerian government, Human Rights Watch believes that the oil companies operating in Nigeria have specific responsibilities in respect of the human rights violations that take place in connection with their operations. These responsibilities must be seen against the context of oil production in Nigeria and the fact that the security provided to keep the oil flowing benefits both the Nigerian government and the oil companies, since disputes which threaten production affect the revenue of both. Companies have a duty to avoid both complicity in and advantage from human rights abuses.

Many of the cases investigated by Human Rights Watch which have led to security force abuses concern claims that oil companies have not followed environmental standards or provided compensation in accordance with the law for damage resulting from oil exploration and production. Nigerian laws require the oil companies to respect high environmental standards, often explicitly based on international standards, in order to prevent and remedy pollution, to protect inhabited areas from oil flaring and other dangerous aspects of oil production, as well as to provide fair and adequate compensation for buildings, crops, fishing rights, or other property adversely affected by their operations. Nigerian law incorporates the principle of strict liability for damage caused by oil spills, so that it is not necessary to prove negligence on behalf of the operator; though if the oil was deliberately spilled because of sabotage the rule does not apply and negligence must be shown. However, the Federal Environmental Protection Agency and Department of Petroleum Resources, the government bodies with responsibility for enforcing these laws, suffer from a lack of technical expertise and resources, which, coupled with the problems caused by overlapping mandates and corruption, prevent effective policing of environmental standards, and the companies often fall short of their obligations. Other cases concern claims that the oil multinationals have not provided compensation which community members believe to be due to the traditional landholders, though the realities of the Nigerian legal system make it difficult to enforce such an obligation.

---

[463] Christopher Hopson, "Mobil targets Nigeria over rights abuses," *Upstream News* (Oslo), May 22, 1998.

Often, the Nigerian government effectively entrusts the oil companies themselves to provide the facts on such matters as land claims and valuation, environmental impact assessments, agreed terms of compensation for property and labor, assessment of sabotage, and damage claims. Most negotiations for compensation are bilateral, between the community affected and the oil company concerned, although government structures may play a nominal monitoring role. The process of valuation, negotiation, and payment is therefore in practice controlled almost entirely by the company. The affected communities, without effective government support or technical assistance, are in an unequal bargaining position, largely obliged to accept whatever compensation is offered by the companies in such situations. Protests—or even the presentation of claims—are routinely disrupted by violent police actions and arbitrary arrests. Although there are independent lawyers and environmental groups attempting to monitor oil company compliance with the law and assist the oil communities in pressing their claims, their activities have in the past been seriously hindered by security force harassment, office raids, detentions, and other repressive measures.

Although legal action is a theoretical possibility to challenge claimed injustices, the Nigerian court system does not provide an effective remedy, since access to justice is expensive, relevant information is controlled by the oil companies, and final court decisions are indefinitely delayed. In many of the cases investigated by Human Rights Watch the companies have fought vigorously (and benefitted directly by police action, at least in the short term) rather than seek arbitration or independent assessment of claims.

In addition, the oil companies operating in Nigeria have close relations with local elites in the communities where they operate and at state and national level. In part, such relations are required in order for the companies to operate, and are no different from the relations of large companies with government authorities and other powerful figures in any state. The oil companies are obliged to deal with the government of the country at its different levels, whether military or civilian. However, the pervasive corruption that has followed the oil industry profits the national and local power structures as well as adding a cost to the oil companies. Contracts from the oil companies, whether for development projects or for construction or other work needed for oil operations, provide spectacular opportunities for rake-off of percentages both by middle management in the oil companies and by the contractors, who are themselves often associates of state military administrators, other government officials, or traditional leaders (whose status is partly autonomous, but also depends on government recognition). The award of contracts, like the siting of flow stations or other facilities by oil companies, can cause or contribute to conflict between and within communities;

such conflict again invites a repressive response from the authorities. Development programs are largely poorly thought through and fail to incorporate concepts of sustainability or community control. In the absence of independent experts and arbiters, and transparency of information in consultations or negotiations between oil companies and delta communities, relations between the oil companies and local elites can be expected to be flawed by corruption and to fail to satisfy others in the community that their concerns will be addressed.

In recent years, protests targeting oil installations and oil industry workers in the delta have increased. Some of these protests are directed specifically at the behavior of the oil company; some of them are directed rather at the government; many have a mixture of motives. In some cases, protests have been simple attempts to exercise rights to freedom of expression and assembly, and have consisted of peaceful demonstrations at company property. In other cases, company installations have been occupied, especially flow stations, and production closed down, causing significant loss of income to both company and government. In some cases where flow stations or other property have been taken over there has also been damage to the facility concerned. In addition, while the figures are contested, sabotage of pipelines certainly takes place, contributing to the environmental problems caused by oil spills. Incidents of intimidation and hostage-taking of company staff have also increased, and some of these cases have involved attempts to extort money from the oil companies. There are increasing numbers of firearms in circulation in the delta, some of them captured from the security forces, and these have been used in clashes between different communities; but most occupations of flow stations and other protest activities aimed at the oil industry have been by unarmed civilians.

Oil companies are legitimately concerned to prevent damage to their facilities and to the environment and to protect their personnel. The companies also emphasize their commitment to avoid violent confrontations between community members and security forces, while underlining a legal obligation to inform the Nigerian authorities when there is a threat to oil production. Shell, for example, states that "In circumstances where the safety of staff or equipment is threatened, Shell reports the matter to the police, just as citizens or companies would in most countries around the world."[464] Whatever the reason for security force presence at an oil company facility, Human Rights Watch believes that the oil companies have a responsibility to take all possible steps to ensure that arbitrary arrests, detentions,

[464] "Flash Points in the Ogoni Story: What Happened and Lessons Learned," briefing available on the Shell web site (http://www.shellnigeria.com) as of October 1, 1997.

torture or killings do not occur. The cases investigated by Human Rights Watch show repeated incidents in which people are brutalized for attempting to raise grievances with the companies; in some cases security forces threaten, beat, and jail members of community delegations even before they present their cases. Such abuses often occur right next to company property, or in the immediate aftermath of meetings between company officials and individual claimants or community representatives. Many seem to be the object of repression simply for putting forth an interpretation of a compensation agreement, or for seeking effective compensation for land ruined or livelihood lost. There are also cases in which witnesses have reported that company staff have directly threatened, or have been present when security force officers have threatened, communities with retaliation if there is disruption to oil production.

Human Rights Watch is concerned at the level of secrecy that surrounds the arrangements relating to security for oil installations: not one of the oil companies with which we corresponded responded to our requests to be given access to the parts of the Memorandum of Understanding or Joint Operations Agreement with the Nigerian government governing security, nor to internal guidelines relating to protection of their facilities. Given the abuses that have been committed by the Nigerian security forces in protecting oil installations, most notoriously in Ogoni, it is all the more important that there be transparency in these arrangements and clear commitments from the oil companies to monitor security force performance, take steps to prevent abuses, and publicly protest violations that do occur.

None of the oil companies publish regular, comprehensive reports of allegations of environmental damage, sabotage, claims for compensation, protest actions, or police or military action carried out on or near their facilities. Often, based on Human Rights Watch's correspondence, the companies claim to be unaware that arrests, detentions and beatings have taken place in the vicinity of their facilities, despite assertions that they are concerned to maintain good relations with the communities where they operate.

Human Rights Watch believes that the oil companies have responsibilities to monitor security force activity in the oil producing region in detail and to take all possible steps to ensure that human rights violations are not committed. These steps include the following:

- Companies should include in written agreements with the Nigerian government relating to the regulation of the oil industry, especially any agreements relating specifically to security, provisions requiring state security forces operating in the area of company operations to conform to the human rights obligations the government has assumed under the International

Covenant on Civil and Political Rights, the African Charter on Human and Peoples' Rights and other international human rights and humanitarian norms.

- Companies should make public the provisions of their security agreements with state entities and private organizations.
- Companies should insist on screening security force members assigned for their protection, to ensure that no member of the military or police credibly implicated in past human rights abuses is engaged in protecting oil facilities. Companies should similarly screen security staff in their direct employment.
- Companies should investigate abuses that do occur, and make public and private protests to the authorities where excessive force is used, or where arbitrary detentions or other abuses take place. Companies should publish details of such incidents in their annual reports both in Nigeria and in the country of their head office.
- Companies should publicly and privately call on the Nigerian authorities to institute disciplinary or criminal proceedings, as appropriate, against those responsible for abuses and to compensate the victims. Companies should monitor the status of such investigations and press for resolution of the cases, publicly condemning undue delay.
- Companies should adopt internal guidelines surrounding the provision of security for their facilities, emphasizing the need to ensure respect for human rights, and should take disciplinary action against any employee that does not follow such guidelines.

These responsibilities are reinforced when the company has itself called for security force intervention, especially by the military or by notoriously abusive forces such as the Mobile Police, or if the company has made payments to the security forces in return for protection.

The following section considers the incidents described in the chapter on protest and repression in the Niger Delta in terms of the oil multinationals' responsibility for repressive actions by the Nigerian security forces.

The Role of Shell in the Ogoni Crisis

During the height of the Ogoni crisis, allegations of Shell collaboration with the military were regularly made, even after the company ceased production from its flow stations in Ogoni in January 1993.[465] A leaked memorandum, dated May 12, 1994, addressed to the governor of Rivers State and signed by Lt. Col. Paul Okuntimo, head of the Rivers State Internal Security Task Force stated: "Shell operations still impossible unless ruthless military operations are undertaken for smooth economic activities to commence." The strategies proposed include "wasting operations during MOSOP and other gatherings, making constant military presence justifiable"; "wasting targets cutting across communities and leadership cadres, especially vocal individuals in various groups," and "restriction of unauthorized visitors, especially those from Europe, to Ogoni." An "initial disbursement of 50 million naira" and "pressure on oil companies for prompt regular inputs" were requested. The government claimed that this document was a forgery; Shell has stated that "there are reasons for doubting" its authenticity, and that, if it were genuine, the company would regard its contents as "abhorrent."[466] Okuntimo himself stated in June 1994 to three environmental activists in detention that "Shell company has not been fair to him in these operations," and that he had been "risking his life and that of his soldiers to protect Shell installations."[467] Steve Lawson-Jack, head of SPDC's public and government affairs department in its eastern division, was identified by MOSOP as the link to Okuntimo (as well as being named by auditors in 1995 as involved in arranging a ₦1 million (U.S.$11,100) bogus compensation claim against the company).[468] Former Ogoni members of the Shell police, interviewed by Project Underground, have claimed that they were involved in deliberately creating conflict between different groups

[465] See, Human Rights Watch/Africa, "The Ogoni Crisis," for further detail. A case is being brought against Shell in the U.S. District Court (Southern District of New York) on behalf of Ken and Owens Wiwa (son and brother of Ken Saro-Wiwa), Blessing Kpuinen (wife of John Kpuinen, leader of the youth division of MOSOP, also hanged in November 1995), and one other, in relation to the hangings of the "Ogoni Nine," alleging that "Defendants were the employers of and/or working in concert with the Nigerian military regime" and claiming damages. Notice of Motion in Case No. 96 Civ. 8386, *Ken Wiwa and Owens Wiwa v. Royal Dutch Petroleum Company and Shell Transport and Trading Company PLC.*

[466] Complaint submitted to the Broadcasting Complaints Commission, November 1995; reply of Shell International Limited to response of Channel 4, June 10, 1996.

[467] See Human Rights Watch/Africa, "The Ogoni Crisis," p.38.

[468] "Shell axes 'corrupt' Nigeria staff," *Sunday Times* (London), December 17, 1995.

of people, and in intimidating and harassing protesters; Ogoni detainees have also alleged that they were detained and beaten by Shell police.[469]

In January 1995, Shell stated to Human Rights Watch that "our Chief Executive in Nigeria has repeatedly—both publicly and privately—expressed our concerns over the violence and heavy handedness both sides on the Ogoni issue have displayed from time to time, and is doing what he can to counsel the authorities not to do anything which will tend to increase the likelihood of violence either to persons or property."[470] In response to Human Rights Watch's July 1995 report "The Ogoni Crisis: A Case Study of Military Repression in Southeastern Nigeria," Shell followed this up, in the face of evidence that the crackdown in Ogoni was aimed at keeping the oil flowing, by asserting: "it is difficult to conclude that the military presence in Ogoni is anything to do with the oil industry, especially given our many public announcements that we will not return to Ogoniland under military protection and until law and order prevail in the area."[471] Shell also stated that "we play no part in any military activity in Ogoniland and have many times denied any collusion with the authorities."[472]

However, Shell has since admitted having made direct payments to the Nigerian security forces, in the form of "a very small fixed 'field allowance' in cases where members of the security forces have been deployed in connection with the protection of SPDC's facilities or SPDC personnel."[473] More recently, Shell has stated that such payments were made only one time: "The payment of field allowances to Nigerian military personnel happened only once, under duress, at Korokoro [in Ogoni] in 1993. SPDC has made it clear that it will not happen again."[474] Environmental Rights Action, a Nigerian environmental and human rights organization, alleges that SPDC continues to make payments of field allowances to soldiers in Nigeria, elsewhere in the delta, at construction works for

---

[469] Kretzmann and Wright, *Human Rights and Environmental Operations Information on the Royal Dutch/Shell Group of Companies 1996-97*, p.11. Copies of statements referred to in the report on file with Human Rights Watch. Two of the "Ogoni Twenty," Blessing Israel and Kagbara Basseeh, alleged that Shell police had a direct role in their arrest and torture.

[470] Shell International Petroleum Company letter to Human Rights Watch, January 13, 1995.

[471] SPDC, "Response to Human Rights Watch/Africa publication."

[472] Ibid.

[473] Complaint submitted to the Broadcasting Complaints Commission, November 1995; reply of Shell International Limited to response of Channel 4, June 10, 1996.

[474] SPDC, "Response to Environmental Rights Action."

a new airport in Osubi, and at Shell installations on the Atlantic coast at Ogulagha (Forcados), though Shell has denied this.[475] In January 1997, Shell withdrew a complaint to the British Broadcasting Complaints Commission about a Channel 4 documentary on the situation in Ogoni, "Delta Force," broadcast on November 2, 1995, in which allegations were made concerning assistance to the military in Nigeria by SPDC.[476]

Shell came under great public pressure, both inside and outside Nigeria, to intervene on behalf of the accused during the trial and following the conviction of the "Ogoni Nine."[477] Initially, Shell stated that it would be "dangerous and wrong" for Shell to "intervene and use its perceived 'influence' to have the judgement overturned," stating that "a commercial organisation like Shell cannot and must never interfere with the legal processes of any sovereign state."[478] Shell called on "those who currently advocate public condemnation and pressure ... to reflect on the possible results of their actions. ... What is needed from all parties is quiet diplomacy."[479] Nevertheless, as pressure mounted, CAJ Herkströter, the president of the Royal Dutch Petroleum Company, one of the parent companies of the Royal

---

[475] Environmental Rights Action, "Shell in the Niger Delta 1997/98: A Brief Report to Sierra Club USA, from ERA, Benin City, Nigeria," May 1998. Shell stated that "The only time that soldiers have been at the site [Osubi] was during a brief visit of the military administrator of Delta State as part of his escort and conforming to the usual protocol." "Osubi Airport Project: Shell Nigeria's Response to Allegations by ERA," SPDC Press Release, March 23, 1998).

[476] Complaint submitted to the Broadcasting Complaints Commission, November 1995.

[477] Immediately following the November 10, 1995, executions of the Ogoni Nine, SPDC announced, on December 15, 1995, that the construction contract for the Nigerian Liquefied Natural Gas (LNG) project, of which Shell is a 25.6 percent shareholder, had been signed—a diplomatic coup for the Nigerian government. In an advertisement placed in many newspapers, Shell defended this decision: "Some say we should pull out. And we understand why. But if we do so now, the project will collapse. Maybe for ever. So let's be clear about who we'd be hurting. Not the present Nigerian government, if that's the intention. ... the people of the Niger Delta would certainly suffer—the thousands who will work on the project, and thousands more who will benefit in the local economy. ... Whatever you think of the Nigerian situation today, we know you wouldn't want us to hurt the Nigerian people. Or jeopardise their future." "If we're investing in Nigeria you have the right to know why," advertisement on behalf of Shell placed in the *Guardian* (London), November 17, 1995.

[478] "Clear Thinking in Troubled Times," SPDC Press Statement, October 31, 1995.

[479] "Statement by Mr Brian Anderson, Managing Director, The Shell Petroleum Development Company of Nigeria Limited," SPDC Press Release, November 8, 1995.

Dutch/Shell Group of companies that owns SPDC of Nigeria, sent a personal letter to Gen. Abacha on November 9, 1995, pleading for commutation of the death sentences against Ken Saro-Wiwa and his co-accused on humanitarian grounds. At the same time, Shell explicitly denied that this intervention was a "comment on the proceedings of the tribunal," restating that "as a multinational company ... to interfere in such processes, whether political or legal, in any country would be wrong."[480]

Following the trial and execution of the "Ogoni Nine," Shell apparently realized that it had been damaged by statements of this kind, and adjusted its public position, reaffirming on several occasions its commitment to the Universal Declaration of Human Rights, while continuing to state that it could not comment on particular cases.[481] In May 1996, in response to concerns about the trial facing nineteen (later twenty) more Ogonis before the same civil disturbances special tribunal that sentenced Saro-Wiwa, Shell stated: "The Nigerian Government has a duty to investigate the murder of the four Ogoni leaders. And if those investigations lead to the arrest and trial of suspects, then no-one has the right to oppose due legal process. But trials must be fair. And they must be seen to be fair."[482] It did not take the opportunity to state that proceedings before the special tribunal were unfair and in violation of international standards, even though a fact-finding mission sent by the U.N. secretary-general had by that date confirmed the opinion of domestic and international human rights observers that the trial was a travesty of justice.[483]

Shell states that its production in Ogoni has remained closed, although pipelines carrying oil from other Shell oilfields continue to cross the area. The company also claims that it has made attempts over the years to open negotiations with the communities involved in order to resume production. Community members, on the other hand, reported that the Rivers State Internal Security Task

---

[480] "Execution of Ken Saro-Wiwa and his co-defendants," SPDC Press Statement, November 14, 1995.

[481] "Execution of Ken Saro-Wiwa and his co-defendants," Statement by SPDC director Brian Anderson, November 14, 1995; "Shell reaffirms support for Human Rights and Fair Trial," Shell International Limited Press Release, January 30, 1996.

[482] "Fair Trials for the Ogoni 19," Shell International Limited Press Release, May 17, 1996.

[483] "Report of the fact-finding mission of the Secretary-General to Nigeria," Annex I to U.N. Document A/50/960, May 28, 1996.

Force forced individuals to sign statements "inviting" Shell to return.[484] In April 1997, a meeting between Shell and local representatives was arranged by the National Reconciliation Committee, a body created under General Abacha's fraudulent "transition program," which has now been disbanded. In May 1997, SPDC announced the launch of a ten-month "Ogoni Youth Training Scheme," which would train 366 youths in a variety of skills, including carpentry, welding, computer studies, and soap-making.[485] In late 1996, Shell took over the running of the Gokana hospital, and states that it is also involved in rehabilitation of three clinics and the donation of drugs to clinics in Ogoni: these efforts are dismissed by MOSOP as mere window dressing and the quality of the programs challenged. At the same time SPDC stated that "there were no plans to resume oil production in Ogoniland, and the company's priority continued to be to help tackle the problems facing the Ogoni people where it could help."[486] Shell also stated that it opened negotiations with MOSOP representatives (though spokespeople for MOSOP denied this), and in mid-1997 Shell believed that "the process of reconciliation is underway and before the end of the year there will be a breakthrough."[487] MOSOP condemned these remarks as "gravely insensitive and provocative," and repeated its demand that "for dialogue to be useful, basic freedoms must be restored in Ogoni to enable its leadership to freely meet and consult with the people who ultimately decide on these issues."[488]

Shell's statements that its presence in Ogoni is limited to provision of social programs and attempts to arrange a reconciliation with the Ogoni people are challenged by MOSOP. In March 1998, MOSOP issued a press release stating that SPDC had entered Ogoni in order to work on facilities at its flow station at K-Dere. MOSOP reported that a number of Ogonis protesting their activities were arrested by members of the Internal Security Task Force accompanying Shell and their still and video cameras seized, and that they were made to sign statements indicating that they accepted Shell's return to the area.[489] Responding to these charges, Shell

---

[484] Kretzmann and Wright, *Human Rights and Environmental Operations Information on the Royal Dutch/Shell Group of Companies 1996-97*, pp.11-12; Human Rights Watch/Africa, "Permanent Transition," pp.40-41.

[485] SPDC Press Release, May 13, 1997.

[486] Ibid.

[487] Dulue Mbachu, "Shell hopes for deal with Nigeria's Ogonis," Reuters, June 27, 1997.

[488] "MOSOP's Reaction to Shell's Ogoni Re-entry Plan," MOSOP Press Release, June 30, 1997.

[489] MOSOP Press Statement, March 12, 1998.

confirmed that a team of four SPDC staff and three contractors had entered Ogoni on March 5 and 6, as a result of reports from the community of leaks from a disused oil pipeline. Shell stated that, after remedying the situation, the team, which it said was unguarded, left the area, and that at no time did the company witness or hear about any disturbances or arrests. Shell stated that the company had inquired of the authorities, who had denied that anyone had been detained.[490]

The situation in Ogoni has recently improved greatly, as a result of the withdrawal to barracks of the Internal Security Task Force. Nevertheless, the fundamental questions surrounding the consent of the Ogoni people to decisions made on their behalf remain.

Attempts to Import Weapons

During 1996, it was shown that Shell had recently been in negotiation for the import of arms for use by the Nigerian police. In January 1996, in response to allegations relating to the import of weapons, Shell stated that it had in the past imported side arms on behalf of the Nigerian police force, for use by the "supernumerary police" who are on attachment to Shell and guard the company's facilities (and other oil company facilities) against general crime. The last purchase of weapons by Shell was said to be of 107 hand guns for its supernumerary police, fifteen years before.[491] "Although approval for local purchase of arms was given by the police in 1994, SPDC decided that it would be inappropriate to proceed with the purchase. SPDC was sensitive to the possibilities that upgrading weapons purchased for the police on SPDC protection duties could be misconstrued in the prevailing circumstances."[492]

Contrary to this assertion, court papers filed in Lagos in July 1995 and reported in the British press in February 1996 revealed that Shell had as late as February 1995 been negotiating for the purchase of weapons for the Nigerian police. Shell acknowledged to the London *Observer* Sunday newspaper that it had conducted these negotiations but stated that none of the purchases had been

---

[490] Shell International Ltd letter to Human Rights Watch, April 9, 1998, with "Response Statement to MOSOP Press Release of 12 March 1998," attached.

[491] "Firearms—The Shell Position," SPDC Press Release, January 17, 1996; "Shell does not import firearms into Nigeria," SPDC Press Release, January 31, 1996.

[492] "Shell and the Supernumerary Police in Nigeria," SPDC Press Release, February 9, 1996.

concluded.[493] The weapons on order—Beretta semi-automatic rifles, pump-action shotguns and materials such as tear gas clearly designed for crowd control—did not seem appropriate for protection from armed robbers and "general crime." In correspondence with Human Rights Watch, Shell stated that the papers presented to court did not include a final letter in the series that made it clear that the management of SPDC had not at any stage proposed to purchase tear gas or riot control equipment. However, Shell "cannot give an undertaking not to provide weapons in the future, as, due to the deteriorating security situation in Nigeria, we may want to see the weapons currently used by the Police who protect Shell people and property upgraded. This would simply bring them up to the same standard of firearms as those provided to Police protecting other companies within Nigeria."[494]

Threats to Communities

During its investigation of the situation in the delta during July 1997, Human Rights Watch heard disturbing allegations of three separate meetings, two in connection with the same matter, at which eyewitnesses interviewed by Human Rights Watch alleged that SPDC staff, or military authorities in the presence of SPDC staff had directly threatened community members, using the situation in Ogoni as an example. Two of these meetings had occurred only days before Human Rights Watch interviewed the people present; the third dated back two years, to the period of Ken Saro-Wiwa's trial.

---

[493] Polly Ghazi and Cameron Duodu, "How Shell tried to buy Berettas for Nigerians," *Observer* (London) February 11, 1996. The proceedings were brought by XM Federal Limited, a company dealing in arms registered in London, and its Nigerian subsidiary against SPDC for breach of contract. Human Rights Watch has seen copies of the court documents, in which the plaintiffs allege that they had initiated purchases for Shell in reliance on a contract for the supply of weapons and ammunition, when SPDC unexpectedly indicated in a letter to the police that it believed the price too high and that "consequently we may have to suspend all activity on arms procurement until further notice." SPDC had subsequently re-invited tenders from the plaintiffs for the same weaponry. The managing director of the Nigerian subsidiary had obtained the authorization of the Inspector General of Police for the weapons upgrade and purchase of semi-automatic weapons, with which the contract was concerned, only after personal intervention at the behest of Shell. The Nigerian subsidiary noted in correspondence to SPDC that "since the country is under some form of embargo by the Western Nations, we have had to arrange a delivery through a third party." Statement of claim and annexures in *X.M. Federal Limited and Humanitex Nigeria Limited v. SPDC and Mr. V. Oteri*, Case No. FHC/L/CS/849/95.

[494] Shell International Ltd letter to Human Rights Watch, November 6, 1996.

Contractors working for Shell reported to Human Rights Watch that SPDC had called meetings on July 7, 1997, at the Forcados terminal and a day or two later at Shell's premises in Warri, in connection with the threat by members of the four communities (Sokebelou, Ekeremor Zion, Obotobo and Ofogbene) who had won an award of ₦30 million (U.S.$333,000) against SPDC in the Ughelli High Court to close down Shell facilities forcibly unless the award was paid or production suspended. They alleged that representatives of Shell, including SPDC's senior community liaison officer for its Western Division, S.O. Jonny, had warned those present that the consequences for the communities would be serious if the threat to shut down Shell production were carried out. In particular, S.O. Jonny is alleged to have said at both meetings that the communities should "remember what happened in Ogoni," since the same thing could happen to them. Those present who spoke to Human Rights Watch, who did not include the leaders of the court case, said that they took this statement to imply a direct threat of a crackdown from the security forces invoked by SPDC.[495]

In response to questions from Human Rights Watch about these allegations, Shell stated that a "peace-making team" had been sent to talk to the communities when the threat to close down production had been received, and had held meetings in Sokebelou and Obotobo, where the community leaders they met with said they did not know the writers of the letter in which the threat was contained.

> At both meetings, the production superintendent O.J. Agbara who spoke, asked the communities to remain peaceful towards SPDC while the difficulties over the court case were resolved. Noting that the signatories of the letter could not be identified, and were therefore possibly from other communities, he pleaded with them not to be swayed by outside influences, and so should allow production to continue uninterrupted. S.O. Jonny was on the team but he did not speak at either meeting.[496]

The other meeting reported to Human Rights Watch dates from 1995, in relation to the serious disturbances that took place in Egbema, Imo State, in June of that year that were described above. People who attended stated that the meeting took place in Owerri after the disturbances, among representatives of the Imo State government, SPDC, and the community. It was alleged to Human Rights Watch

[495] Human Rights Watch interviews, July 1997.

[496] Letter from Shell International Ltd to Human Rights Watch, February 13, 1998.

that at this meeting, attended by Precious Omukwu, Fidelis Okonkwo, and Egbert Imomoh from SPDC, the director of the SSS for Imo State addressed community members, including both chiefs and youth leaders, making threats that if further protests took place against Shell "they would be treated like the Ogoni" and that there would be a security crackdown.[497] Asked about this meeting, Shell stated to Human Rights Watch that, while there was a meeting convened by the state governor at which the community, supported by SPDC, asked for the Mobile Police to be replaced by regular police, "SPDC was not aware of the presence of an SSS Director at the State Governor's meeting. No threats of a 'security crackdown' or 'treatment like the Ogoni' or any of a similar nature were made at the meeting."[498] Human Rights Watch has no reason to disbelieve its informants, who were present at this meeting, in their account of what was said.[499]

In addition, a wealthy chief from the Egbema area told us that SPDC was "helping" with the creation of a "vigilante group" to provide security in the area. There was a vigilante group operating in the village, which appeared, on the basis of our interviews with other residents, to be intimidating on an arbitrary basis those youths who might be thought to be "troublemakers."[500] Shell stated that "SPDC is not aware of any vigilante group and there is no truth in the allegation that it is assisting in the creation of one."[501]

In another case, described above, a youth from Ogba-Egbema-Ndoni local government area in Rivers State, near Elf's Obite gas project, told Human Rights Watch that he had been assaulted in January 1997 by Mobile Police at the site, and when he brought a case for damages in connection with the assault, threatened in September 1997 by a manager with C&C Construction, a contractor at the site, that he should "learn the lessons" from Ken Saro-Wiwa's case, when he refused to settle a claim.[502]

---

[497] Human Rights Watch interviews, July 19, 1997.

[498] Shell International Ltd letter to Human Rights Watch, February 13, 1998.

[499] A youth from Ogba-Egbema-Ndoni local government area, where the Nigeria LNG project is being built, also told Human Rights Watch that he had been threatened by a manager with C&C construction that he should "learn the lessons" from Ken Saro-Wiwa's case, when he refused to settle a claim against the company for assault. Human Rights Watch interview, July 4, 1997, and letter from the same interviewee to Human Rights Watch, October 24, 1997.

[500] Human Rights Watch interviews, July 19, 1997.

[501] Shell International Ltd letter to Human Rights Watch, February 13, 1998.

[502] Human Rights Watch interview, July 4, 1997, and letter from the same interviewee, sent from Togo, October 24, 1997.

Oil Company Calls for Security Force Assistance

The most serious case in which an oil company is directly implicated in security force abuses continues to be the incident at Umuechem in 1990, where an SPDC manager made a written and explicit request for Mobile Police (a notoriously abusive force) protection, leading to the killing of eighty unarmed civilians and the destruction of hundreds of homes. Shell states that it has learned from the "regrettable and tragic" incident at Umuechem, so that it would now never call for Mobile Police protection and emphasizes the need for restraint to the Nigerian authorities.[503] Nevertheless, there are continuing reports of oil company calls for military and Mobile Police protection in response to protests at oil company facilities. In other cases, companies have called for regular police assistance, but without seeking any guarantees or taking any steps to ensure that such assistance is respectful of human rights, or protesting abuses that have occurred as a result. In none of the following cases had the oil companies made public or protested detentions or other abuses by the security forces, even though requests by the company or a contractor had led to security force intervention.

The youths from Edagberi, Rivers State, for example, were detained overnight following a written complaint to the local police station by Alcon Engineering, a contractor to Shell. While it is claimed by Shell that the youths concerned had been engaged in unwarranted intimidation of its contractor, including "extortion" of cement and diesel that had not been part of the initial agreement with the community, and therefore that security force intervention was appropriate, the letter simply appealed for "quick intervention to save us from further harassment, violent threats and attack," without seeking any safeguards to ensure that such intervention was made in a non-abusive manner. Nor did the company claim any attempt to seek independent mediation of the dispute over compensation.[504]

Similarly, at Yenezue-Gene, Rivers State, Shell stated to Human Rights Watch that its contractors, including Mife and Deutag, had called for police assistance, "due to community hostilities," in order "to protect life and property."[505] No guarantees had been sought for the good behavior of these police; and, according to Human Rights Watch's information, soldiers present at the site had harassed local community members. Shell itself had made a major contribution to hostility from the community by the construction of a causeway to its Gbaran oil

---

[503] SPDC, "Response to Human Rights Watch/Africa publication."

[504] Letter from Alcon Nigeria Ltd to the Divisional Police Officer, Ahoada-West Local Government Area, June 26, 1997.

[505] Shell International Ltd letter to Human Rights Watch, February 13, 1998.

field which had devastated forest of crucial economic importance to local residents; although Shell reported that some compensation payments had been made, these were, apparently, not determined by an independent arbitrator but by SPDC itself.

At Iko, Akwa Ibom State, the Shell contractor Western Geophysical stated that it had requested naval assistance to recover boats taken by youths; following the naval intervention, Mobile Police came to the village and assaulted numerous villagers, beating one to death. Shell has stated to Human Rights Watch that it does not call for military protection, but justified calling the navy in this case due to the terrain; it stated that the Mobile Police had been called by the navy and not by Shell or its contractor. Shell did not report that the company or its contractor had made any attempt to protest the Mobile Police action, simply reporting that "this incident is unrelated to Western's seismic activities."[506]

A spokesman for Chevron acknowledged in a radio interview that the company had called for navy intervention in connection with the May 1998 occupation of its Parabe platform by youths, admitted to be unarmed, and that the company had flown the navy and Mobile Police to the platform. Despite the serious result of this action, including the shooting dead of two protesters, Chevron did not indicate, in response to specific inquiries from Human Rights Watch, that any attempt had been made to prevent loss of life, or that concern had been expressed to the authorities over the incident or that any steps had been taken to avoid repetition of the case in future. Instead, Chevron stated that: "We believe we have fully explained the circumstances surrounding this incident and we do not intend to engage in further correspondence with Human Rights Watch on this issue."[507]

Oil Company Failure to Monitor and Protest Abuses

Even if they have not called for security force intervention, Human Rights Watch believes that oil companies should monitor security force activity in connection with their facilities and protest abuses. In the great majority of cases, however, oil companies have not given any indication that they have protested human rights violations to the Nigerian government. In a handful of high-profile cases of detention, one or two oil companies have, under consumer pressure in Europe and the U.S., made public statements, but the great majority go unremarked. In none of the cases researched by Human Rights Watch which had

---

[506] Shell International Ltd letter to Human Rights Watch, February 13, 1998.

[507] Goodman and Scahill, "Drilling and Killing"; Chevron Nigeria Ltd letter to Human Rights Watch, December 11, 1998.

not reached the international press did any of the oil companies indicate that they had registered concern with the authorities. Only after the behavior of the Nigerian authorities had embarrassed the oil companies on the international stage had oil companies taken action of any kind on behalf of those who had been subject to abuse by the security forces. In other cases, the oil companies maintained they were unaware of incidents reported to Human Rights Watch when we questioned them about interventions they might have made on behalf of individuals detained, even though the incidents related to claims for compensation from the company, or stated that arbitrary detentions and other abuses that had occurred were of no concern because those affected were accused of criminal offenses. Because Agip chose not to respond to Human Rights Watch's inquiries about specific incidents, we have no way of knowing whether the company monitors or acts upon human rights abuses of this type; there is no indication from other sources that it does so.

In several of the cases recorded by Human Rights Watch, the oil companies concerned said they were ignorant of arrests or beatings that had occurred, suggesting either a lack of interest and concern at what goes on at the gates of their facilities or a breakdown of communication between local and national (or international) management. SPDC said it had no knowledge of the incident in January 1997 at Ahia flow station in Omudioga, Rivers State, when twelve youths were detained for one month, stating that "the relationship with the community has been cordial." Shell also denied knowledge of detentions that took place following major disturbances during June and July 1995 at Egbema, Imo State, during which Mobile Police carried out indiscriminate beatings and arrested more than thirty people, who were detained for several weeks and charged with sabotage. Instead, SPDC stated that the issue had been "amicably settled," through negotiations between the community and the military administration. No independent arbitration had been sought. Again, the incident reported to Human Rights Watch at Obotobo, Delta State, in which soldiers threatened the community was said to be unknown to Shell. At Yenezue-Gene, Rivers State, Shell, despite a pattern of harassment noted by Human Rights Watch, stated that "The overall relationship between the community and MIFE [its contractor] had been cordial."

Even when people are killed by the security forces defending oil installations or responding to requests for assistance, it seems that the oil companies do not make public reports of such incidents or protest excesses to the authorities, and at the same time refuse to accept any legal responsibility. Neither Shell nor its contractor Western Geophysical reported making any representations to the authorities surrounding the excessive use of force in respect of the death at Iko, Akwa Ibom State. Chevron, on the other hand, in the case of the youth killed in disputed circumstances at Opuama, Bayelsa State, paid ₦250,000 (U.S.$2,770) to the families concerned "on compassionate grounds" but stated to Human Rights Watch that the responsibility for the death was "entirely a police affair," nothing to do with Chevron, even though the facility involved was a barge contracted to Chevron. Chevron gave no indication to Human Rights Watch that they had expressed concern to the authorities at the death or the conduct of the Mobile Police.[508] Agip, in the case of the youth beaten to death by security guards at the Clough Creek flow station, near Egbemo-Angalabiri, did not respond to community representations (nor to Human Rights Watch), and there is no reason to believe that any protests were made to the authorities about this killing or about the detentions which followed.

In the case from Elele, Rivers State, Elf made no attempt to assist the youth who was detained after he went to Saipem, their contractor, to request compensation for use of family land, a large part of which had been taken for oil production activities. Nor is there any indication that the company protested the abuses with the authorities (whether or not Saipem was responsible for summoning the soldiers who beat the young man). Again, the five members of the landholders family in Obobura, Rivers State, who were detained after an oil leak on their land and threatened with a charge of sabotage, had received no support from Elf. Meanwhile, their claim for compensation for the spill had been rejected on the basis of an assessment by Elf, apparently rubber-stamped by the Department of Petroleum Resources, leaving them without crops to harvest and without financial recompense. Elf denied any knowledge of Prince Ugo, a youth beaten by community "guards" at the Elf Obite gas project in October 1998. While the company was aware of the fact that a number of other youths had been detained, it said that it "could not tell the law enforcement agencies what to do," and hence no intervention to ensure respect for human rights standards had been made.[509] Similarly, SPDC reported no attempt to protest to the government authorities or to the local traditional leader whom they stated had called the security forces, following the overnight detention of youths at Uheri, Delta State, after they protested delays in the payment of compensation at the flow station.

When several hundred people were arrested following demonstrations over the January 12, 1998 spill, Mobil did publicly distance itself from the arrests. However, Mobil did not indicate that any protests had been made to the authorities,

[508] As noted above, Chevron's official policy is that: "Whenever the need to request for help arises, CNL Security insists on exercising reasonable control over those deployed to assist, ensuring that no more than the minimum force required to bring a situation under control is applied."

[509] Elf Petroleum Nigeria Ltd letter to Human Rights Watch, November 23, 1998.

stating to reporters in Lagos: "It is a security issue. It is nothing to do with Mobil at all."[510]

Shell's Internal Review Since 1995

Since the international focus on its Nigerian holdings in 1995, the Royal Dutch/Shell group has undertaken a major review of its attitude toward communities and issues of human rights and sustainable development.[511] As one part of this initiative, the company undertook, over the course of about one year, an internal and external consultation process about the group's Statement of General Business Principles. Following this process, Royal Dutch/Shell adopted in March 1997 a new Statement of General Business Principles, which recognized five "areas of responsibility," to shareholders, to customers, to employees, to those with whom they do business, and to society. As regards their responsibilities to society, Shell companies are now committed: "To conduct business as responsible corporate members of society, to observe the laws of the countries in which they operate, to express support for fundamental human rights in line with the legitimate role of business and to give proper regard to health, safety and the environment consistent with their commitment to contribute to sustainable development." This was the first time that the group had included a general commitment to human rights principles or sustainable development in such a document.[512]

In May 1997, at the annual general meeting of the U.K.-based Shell Transport and Trading Company PLC, one of the parent companies of the Royal Dutch/Shell Group of Companies (the other being the Netherlands-based Royal Dutch Petroleum Company, which holds a 60 percent interest to Shell Transport and Trading's 40 percent) the first shareholder resolution in the U.K. based on environmental and ethical grounds was jointly sponsored by Pensions Investment Research Consultants Ltd (PIRC) and the Ecumenical Centre for Corporate Responsibility (ECCR). The resolution called for Shell to: (i) designate responsibility for the implementation of environmental and corporate responsibility

[510] *Nigeria Today*, February 3, 1998.

[511] Mobil, on the other hand, claims that "We have always had an enviable and unrivaled policy on community relations for many years, and it was not necessary for us to revise it after the Ogoni Crisis." Mobil Producing Nigeria Unlimited letter to Human Rights Watch, February 10, 1998.

[512] The previous version of the Business Principles expressed the responsibilities of Shell companies towards society as: "To conduct business as responsible corporate members of society, observing applicable laws of the countries in which they operate and giving proper regard to health, safety and environmental standards."

policies to a named member of the Committee of Managing Directors; (ii) establish effective internal procedures for the implementation and monitoring of such policies; (iii) establish an independent external review and audit procedure for such policies; (iv) report to shareholders regularly on the implementation of such policies; and (v) publish a report to shareholders on the implementation of such policies in relation to the company's operations in Nigeria by the end of 1997.

Prior to the meeting, Shell took steps to address many of the proposal's recommendations: the group designated a senior director to be responsible for corporate responsibility issues, made a commitment to human rights in its revised Statement of General Business Principles, published a report on the operations of SPDC, its Nigerian subsidiary and its first group-wide report on health, safety, and the environment. At the meeting, the management also said that it agreed in principle with a policy of external verification of environmental information but rejected this approach for the time being.[513] Shell has also taken steps to integrate its commitment to "express support for fundamental human rights" into its internal management procedures, requiring directors of Shell group companies to make annual statements to Shell headquarters indicating that they have complied with the requirements of the Statement of General Business Principles, in the same way that they have to make statements of compliance with financial and other standards. Shell has also produced a "management primer" on human rights issues for distribution throughout the group.

At its 1998 annual shareholders meeting, Shell International published a new report, *Profits and Principles—does there have to be a choice?*, which "describes how we, the people, companies and businesses that make up the Royal Dutch/Shell Group, are striving to live up to our responsibilities—financial, social and environmental."[514] The report examined the company's performance under its new business principles, and considered the case of Nigeria, repeating many of its previous statements. "Shell's approach" to the "issues and dilemmas" surrounding human rights is stated as follows:

> We support the Universal Declaration of Human Rights, and have made specific reference to it in our Business Principles. This is what we have done to ensure we act in the best possible way when confronted with human rights issues.

---

[513] *PIRC Intelligence*, vol.11, issue 5, May 1997.

[514] Shell, *Profits and Principles*, p.2.

- We speak out in defence of human rights when we feel it is justified to do so.
- We included specific references to human rights in our Business Principles when they were updated in 1997. This followed widespread consultation with many different interest groups, including those defending human rights.
- We engage in discussion on human rights issues when making business decisions.
- We have established a regular dialogue with groups which defend human rights. ...
- We are setting up Social Responsibility Management Systems designed to help in the implementation of our Business Principles, and therefore our stated support for human rights.
- We are developing awareness training and management procedures to help resolve human rights dilemmas when they arise. This includes a guide to human rights for managers.[515]

In Nigeria, Shell has engaged in a review of its community assistance projects, and has held its first "stakeholder workshop" on the environment, reportedly attended by over eighty individuals from nongovernmental organizations, government regulatory bodies, industry specialists, academics and community representatives, as well as a "community development listeners' symposium" considering its development programs.[516] However, not all are convinced of the genuineness of this consultative process: Environmental Rights Action, the most vocal environmental group operating in the delta, turned down an invitation to participate in the workshop, stating that "after several meetings and consultations with Shell officials within and outside Nigeria which yielded no concrete results because SPDC would not carry out its promises, the organisation would not be part of another talkshop."[517]

---

[515] Ibid., p.33.

[516] SPDC, *SPDC Community Assistance Projects Review 1992-1997* (Lagos: SPDC, November 1997); SPDC, *Stakeholders' Environmental Workshop (Port Harcourt, April 15 to 17, 1998): Proceedings* (Lagos: SPDC, April 1998); program and papers from "SPDC Community Development Listeners' Symposium: October 21-23, 1998."

[517] Specifically, ERA said it was rejecting Shell's invitation because: "(i) there is no evidence that SPDC has now acquired 'a responsible approach to community relations and community development' as the invitation claimed. Instead Shell still prefers to use

No other oil company operating in Nigeria has, so far as Human Rights Watch is aware, undertaken any similar review of its policies and practices as a result of concern over human rights violations committed in connection with oil company operations. While we welcome this introspection, the test of its effectiveness in changing Shell's practice can only be gauged by its performance on the ground in countries like Nigeria. It is too soon to tell whether this performance will be changed.

---

force in dealing with peaceful requests by the communities for basic necessities of life; (ii) the Managing Director of SPDC according to the consultation agenda has the final say. Meaning that the workshop is just one of Shell's public relations efforts; (iii) the field is not level between SPDC and the principal stakeholders which the oil company wants to meet. While Shell is protected by the military, the people of Nigeria's oil producing areas face death as the Ogoni crisis clearly shows; and (iv) the invitation does not talk about protecting the environmental human rights of the oil communities. Rather, the workshop will focus 'on the ultimate environmental objectives of Shell Nigeria.'" ERA Press Statement, April 15, 1998.

X. INTERNATIONAL LAW

Nigeria is a party to the International Covenant on Civil and Political Rights (ICCPR), the International Covenant on Economic, Social and Cultural Rights (ICESCR), and to a number of other international human rights instruments, including the African Charter on Human and Peoples' Rights.[518] The Nigerian military government is in violation of many if not most of the rights enumerated in these instruments.

Human Rights Watch's research for this report focused on the repressive response by the Nigerian military to protests by members of the oil producing communities to the oil companies, and to attempts to organize the minorities of the delta politically. In the course of this repression, the Nigerian military authorities violate the rights of Nigerian citizens to express their views about the oil industry in Nigeria and to organize protests at injustices resulting from oil industry activities. However, the rights violated include not only the rights to freedom of expression, association and assembly, but also the broader right to live in a democratic society. Ultimately, the Nigerian government must address the rights of the peoples of the Niger Delta to health, education and an adequate standard of living, including food, clothing and housing, and to participate in democratic political structures that enable their voices to be heard in matters concerning the oil industry and the development of their society.

It is clear that a solution to the human rights abuses facing the oil producing communities of the Niger Delta must take into account their relationship with the natural resources with which their region is endowed and ensure that peoples living in the delta are compensated for the damage to their environment and livelihood caused by oil production. Furthermore, it must be ensured that Nigeria's oil wealth is not siphoned off by a small and unaccountable military or civilian elite, but spent by democratically elected and transparent political institutions. Delta minority

---

[518] The African Charter was incorporated into Nigerian domestic law by the African Charter Ratification and Enforcement Act of 1983, although successive military decrees have purported to suspend its operation in particular cases. In the case of *Chief Gani Fawehinmi v. General Sani Abacha and others* ([1996] 9 NWLR p.710), the Lagos division of the Federal Court of Appeal affirmed that "The provisions of the African Charter on Human and Peoples' Rights are in a class of their own and do not fall within the classification of the hierarchy of local legislations in Nigeria in order of superiority. ... The law is in full force and because of its genesis it has an aura of inviolability unlike most municipal laws and may as long as it is in the statute book be clothed with vestment of inviolability."

groups have called for a renegotiation of the relationship between the peoples of the oil producing regions and the federation.[519]

For this to occur, the first requirement is that the government respect the rights to political participation and to freedom of expression and association, and restore the rule of law. Articles 19, 21, and 22 of the ICCPR provide for the rights to freedom of expression, peaceful assembly, and association. These rights may only be restricted in limited circumstances. In the case of freedom of association and assembly, restrictions are only allowed if they are prescribed by law and are "necessary in a democratic society in the interests of national security or public order (*ordre public*), the protection of public health or morals or the protection of the rights and freedoms of others."

While the Nigerian government might attempt to argue that protests in the vicinity of oil installations threaten national security, it is clear that the violent repression of nonviolent protest and of attempts to organize to challenge oil company activity by peaceful means is in violation of the rights to free expression, assembly, and association, and not within any reasonable national security exception.[520] If individuals have allegedly carried out violent acts, damaged property, taken hostages, or other crimes, then they should rather be charged with those offenses and promptly brought before a regular court recognizing international standards of due process.

The ICCPR provides that "No one shall be subjected to torture, or to cruel, inhuman or degrading treatment or punishment" (Article 7); that "No one shall be subjected to arbitrary arrest or detention" (Article 9); and that, "In the determination of any criminal charge against him, or of his rights and obligations in a suit at law, everyone shall be entitled to a fair and public hearing by a

[519] The "Ogoni Bill of Rights" adopted by MOSOP, for example, states that the rights listed are demanded "as equal members of the Nigerian Federation who contribute and have contributed to the growth of the Federation and have a right to expect full returns from that Federation"; the "Kaiama Declaration" agreed by an Ijaw youths conference on December 11, 1998, "agreed to work within Nigeria by to demand and work for self government and resource control for the Ijaw people."

[520] In October 1995, a group of experts in international law, security, and human rights, convened by the free expression organization Article 19 in collaboration with the Centre for Applied Legal Studies of the University of the Witwatersrand, South Africa, adopted the "Johannesburg Principles on National Security, Freedom of Expression and Access to Information," which, while not binding under international law, provide guidelines as to what might be considered a correct interpretation of international law on this subject.

competent, independent and impartial tribunal established by law" (Article 14). Article 14 of the ICCPR covers not only criminal charges, but also cases where an individual wishes to bring a civil action against another individual or company or similar legal entity for compensation for loss suffered as a result of the other party's actions. All of these articles have been regularly violated in Nigeria's oil producing regions.

XI. THE ROLE OF THE INTERNATIONAL COMMUNITY

The activities of MOSOP and the trial and execution of the "Ogoni Nine" in November 1995 brought to the international stage injustices that until then had been largely hidden from international view. The outrage felt at the executions, despite pleas for clemency from around the globe, brought an unprecedented reaction from an international community that had previously paid little attention to the human rights violations associated with the oil industry in Nigeria.[521]

The Commonwealth

The Commonwealth Heads of Government Meeting (CHOGM) which was taking place in Auckland, New Zealand at the time of the executions immediately demonstrated its outrage by suspending Nigeria from the Commonwealth, the first time that this step had been taken. Nigeria was given two years within which to comply with the terms of the Commonwealth Harare Declaration, which commits Commonwealth members to democratic governance.[522] An eight-member Commonwealth Ministerial Action Group (CMAG) was appointed to consider persistent violations of the Harare principles, which has met periodically since 1995 with Nigeria at the top of its agenda.[523] In April 1996, CMAG recommended sanctions to be adopted by the Commonwealth against Nigeria, though these were never adopted.[524]

---

[521] For further detail on this response, see Human Rights Watch/Africa, "Permanent Transition."

[522] On October 20, 1991, the Commonwealth Heads of Government Meeting adopted the Harare Declaration, which committed members of the Commonwealth to "certain fundamental principles," including liberty of the individual, equal rights for all citizens, and "the individual's inalienable right to participate by means of free and democratic political processes in framing the society in which he or she lives."

[523] CMAG examined, in the first instance, the cases of Nigeria, Sierra Leone and the Gambia, the three Commonwealth countries at the time of the CHOGM meeting without elected governments, though Nigeria dominated the discussions even before elected governments were restored in the Gambia and Sierra Leone.

[524] On April 23, 1996, following its second meeting, CMAG recommended various measures to press for change in Nigeria, including visa restrictions on and denial of educational facilities to members of the Nigerian regime and their families, withdrawal of military attachés and cessation of military training, an embargo on the export of arms, a visa-based ban on sporting contacts, and the downgrading of diplomatic and cultural links. It was also recommended that a ban on air links and additional economic measures, including freezing the financial assets and bank accounts in foreign countries

Nigeria remains suspended from the Commonwealth, although the CHOGM meeting in Edinburgh, Scotland, in October 1997, decided not to expel the country, despite lack of progress toward fulfilling the Harare principles. CMAG met for the first time since the death of General Abacha on October 8 and 9, 1998, and adopted a statement welcoming the positive steps taken by General Abubakar, recommending that member states begin to lift bilateral sanctions against Nigeria, and deciding to meet again following the presidential elections scheduled for February 27, 1999, with a view to making recommendations regarding the full return of Nigeria to the Commonwealth.[525]

The United Nations and International Labour Organization

The United Nations General Assembly adopted a resolution on Nigeria on December 22, 1995, in which it condemned the executions of Ken Saro-Wiwa and the others, welcomed the steps taken by the Commonwealth, and expressed "the hope that these actions and other possible actions by other States" would encourage Nigeria to restore democratic rule, thus (unusually) encouraging member states to impose their own sanctions even without Security Council action.[526] The U.N. secretary general sent a fact-finding mission to Nigeria in April 1996, which reported damningly on the trial and execution of the "Ogoni Nine," while also commenting on the general human rights situation in Nigeria. The team recommended, among other things, that the Nigerian government establish "a panel of eminent jurists" to consider financial compensation for the relatives of those hanged, and that a committee chaired by a retired judge and including representatives of the Ogoni and other minority communities make

---

of members of the regime and their families, should be considered in consultation with the E.U., U.S. and other members of the international community. At a further meeting on June 24-25, 1996, however, the imposition of the sanctions agreed in April, which had been delayed to give Nigeria time to engage in dialogue with CMAG about its human rights record, was further postponed, although existing measures consequent on Nigeria's suspension from the Commonwealth remained in place.

[525] Tenth Meeting of the Commonwealth Ministerial Action Group on the Harare Declaration (CMAG), "Joint Statement on Nigeria," London, October 9, 1998. The eight members of CMAG are currently Zimbabwe (chair), New Zealand, United Kingdom, Canada, Ghana, Malaysia, Barbados, and Botswana (in October 1997, Barbados and Botswana replaced Jamaica and South Africa, who had originally been in the group).

[526] General Assembly resolution 50/199 on the Situation of Human Rights in Nigeria, December 22, 1995.

recommendations in connection with the economic and social conditions in those communities.[527]

In 1997, the U.N. Commission on Human Rights voted to appoint a special rapporteur on the situation of human rights in Nigeria, having failed to do so in 1996. The Nigerian government refused to allow the rapporteur, Indian attorney-general Soli Jehangir Sorabjee, entry to Nigeria, and his report to the 1998 session of the commission was therefore based on information gathered outside the country. The report concluded that "widespread violation of human rights occurs in Nigeria," that "the Nigerian legal system does not currently provide effective protection of human rights," and that "the rule of law does not prevail in Nigeria," as well as detailing a range of specific abuses. In addition, "The Government has failed to address the plight of the Ogoni people and to protect their human rights. The recommendation of the Secretary-General's fact-finding mission concerning the appointment of a committee for introducing improvement in the socio-economic conditions of minority communities has been ignored." Moreover, "The Nigerian government is indifferent towards the right to development and to a satisfactory environment. Issues relating to environmental degradation in the Niger Delta region alleged to be caused by the operations of the Shell Petroleum Development Company have received insufficient attention."[528]

In May 1998, the U.N. Committee on Economic, Social and Cultural Rights considered Nigeria's initial report under the Convention on Economic Social and Cultural Rights. The committee "note[d] with alarm the extent of the devastation that oil exploration has done to the environment and quality of life in the areas such as Ogoniland where oil has been discovered and extracted without due regard to the health and well-being of the people and their environment," and recommended that "[t]he rights of minority and ethnic communities—including the Ogoni people—should be respected and full redress should be provided for the violations of the rights set forth in the Covenant that they have suffered."[529] The Commission voted, by revolution 1998/64, to extend the special rapporteur's mandate by another year.

The report of the special rapporteur to the 1998 session of the General Assembly noted improvements in the human rights situation since General

[527] Annex I to U.N. Document A/50/960.

[528] "Situation of human rights in Nigeria: Report submitted by the Special Rapporteur of the Commission on Human Rights, Mr. Soli Jehangir Sorabjee, pursuant to Commission resolution 1997/53," U.N. Document E/CN.4/1998/62.

[529] "Concluding Observations of the Committee on Economic, Social and Cultural Rights: Nigeria," U.N. Document E/C.12/1/Add.23, May 13, 1998.

Abubakar came to power, but also reported that many human rights problems remained essentially unchanged. The report repeated the majority of the recommendations to the Commission on Human Rights, while endorsing the conclusions of the Committee on Economic, Social and Cultural Rights.[530] The rapporteur was finally able to visit Nigeria in November 1998, and traveled to Ogoni, where he urged the appointment of an independent inquiry into environmental and human rights problems in the delta.[531]

In March 1998, in light of the continued detention of union leaders and violations of ILO Convention 87 on freedom of association, the Governing Body of the International Labor Organization voted to establish a commission of inquiry into abuses of labor rights in Nigeria, its strongest expression of disapproval. Following the death of General Abacha, when the new government released detained union leaders and repealed several decrees restricting union activity, the ILO suspended the work of the commission of inquiry and gave the government the opportunity instead of receiving a "direct contacts mission." Such a mission visited Nigeria from August 17 to 21, 1998 and reported to the meeting of the ILO Governing Body held in November 1998, noting the improved situation, including the release of detained trade unionists from the oil sector and the repeal of decrees dissolving the national executives of oil unions, but recommending further steps by the Nigerian government to respect freedom of association.[532]

The African Commission

On December 18 and 19, 1995, at the instance of Nigerian and international nongovernmental organizations, the African Commission on Human and Peoples' Rights (an organ of the Organization of African Unity (OAU)) held its second ever extraordinary session at Kampala, Uganda, in order to consider the human rights situation in Nigeria. The commission resolved to send a fact-finding mission to Nigeria as a result of this session. The mission finally traveled to Nigeria in March 1997, but the commission has not yet made a public report of its findings. In

[530] "Situation of human rights in Nigeria: Interim Report prepared by the Special Rapporteur of the Commission on Human Rights in accordance with General Assembly resolution 52/144 and Economic and Social Council decision 1998/262," U.N. Document A/53/366.

[531] "U.N. Envoy Urges Probe of Damage Caused by Oil Companies in Nigeria," AP, November 30, 1998.

[532] ILO Press Release, "Freedom of Association: ILO Mission Completes its Visit to Nigeria," August 1998; "Report on the Direct Contacts Mission to Nigeria (17 to 21 August 1998)," ILO Document GB.273/15/1, November 1998.

October 1998, the Commission finally decided on communications brought before it in relation to the trial and execution of the Ogoni Nine, alleging violations of articles 4, 7, 9, 16, and 26 of the African Charter on Human and Peoples' Rights.[533]

The European Union and its Member States

Following the executions of Ken Saro-Wiwa and his co-defendants, the European Union imposed sanctions on Nigeria additional to those adopted following the annulment of the 1993 elections and subsequent military coup.[534] Since 1995, no further sanctions have been imposed, although the European Parliament called for an oil embargo on Nigeria under the Abacha government on several occasions, as did the ACP-E.U. Joint Assembly (in which members of the European Parliament meet with representatives of the African, Caribbean, and Pacific (ACP) states every six months).

Following the election of the Labour Party government in May 1997, the U.K. took a much stronger line on Nigeria, though it ruled out a unilateral oil embargo against Nigeria (because of the similarity of Nigerian to Brent crude, the U.K. imports little Nigerian oil in any event). As a form of retaliation for this stance, the European office of NNPC was relocated from London to Paris: even though the great majority of Nigerian crude is traded through London, the Nigerian government cited "commercial reasons" for the move. With the death of Abacha, the NNPC London office has been reopened.[535] The U.K.'s Department for Trade and Industry continued to sponsor trade missions to Nigeria during Abacha's regime, apparently against the wishes of the Foreign and Commonwealth Office;

---

[533] Secretariat of the African Commission on Human and Peoples' Rights letter to Human Rights Watch, December 8, 1998. Decisions of the African Commission are only made public following adoption by the OAU Assembly of Heads of State and Government.

[534] By Common Positions of the Council of the European Union dated November 20, 1995 and December 4, 1995, European Union member states agreed to impose visa restrictions on members (including civilians) of the Nigerian Provisional Ruling Council and the Federal Executive Council and their families (in addition to members of the Nigerian military and security forces and their families, on whom restrictions were imposed in 1993); to expel all military personnel attached to the diplomatic missions of Nigeria in member states and to withdraw all military personnel attached to diplomatic missions of E.U. members in Nigeria; to deny visas to official delegations in the field of sports and to national teams; to introduce a prospective embargo on arms, munitions and military equipment (allowing existing contracts to be fulfilled); and to suspend development cooperation except to projects through NGOs and local civilian authorities.

[535] *Energy Compass*, vol.9, no.35, August 28, 1998.

British trade to Nigeria has nevertheless declined in recent years. France and Germany, Nigeria's other largest trading partners in Europe, consistently advocated a softer line, and both countries repeatedly granted visas for visits by Nigerian officials, in violation of E.U. measures against Nigeria. In the case of France, former petroleum minister Dan Etete visited on several occasions, presumably for discussions about the French role in the oil industry. Elf and Total were prominent in lobbying for increased business with Nigeria, and were rewarded with contracts from the Nigerian government. Both U.K. prime minister Tony Blair and French president Jacques Chirac met with General Abubakar in September 1998.

On October 28, 1998, the Council of Ministers of the European Union voted to remove most of the sanctions applied to the Nigerian government.[536] All measures other than the embargo on arms, munitions and military equipment, the suspension of military cooperation, and the cancellation of training courses for Nigerian military personnel (except for non-combative courses to encourage respect for human rights and prepare the military for democratic control by a civilian government) were repealed, and members of the Nigerian military and government are now able to travel freely to E.U. countries.[537] The assistant chief of defense staff in the U.K., Maj. Gen. Christopher Drewry, traveled to Nigeria shortly after this decision, to discuss the resumption of military cooperation.[538]

[536] The French government succeeded in obtaining a modification to E.U. visa restrictions in November 1997 that would allow the Nigerian team to play in the 1998 soccer world cup and would also allow E.U. member states to grant visas to members of the government on "urgent humanitarian grounds." E.U. Council of Ministers Common Position of November 28, 1997.

[537] In addition, dialogue on development cooperation may be renewed, with a view to re-engagement after the installation of a civilian government; in the meantime, development cooperation may continue only for actions in support of human rights and democracy, and concentrating on poverty alleviation in the context of decentralized cooperation through local civilian authorities and NGOs. E.U. Council of Ministers Common Position of October 28, 1998. The Common Position will be reviewed on or before June 1, 1999.

[538] Lagos NTA Television Network, November 21, 1998, as reported by FBIS, November 21, 1998.

The United States

Following the executions of Ken Saro-Wiwa and his co-defendants, the U.S., like the European Union, imposed additional sanctions on Nigeria.[539] More recently, the Clinton administration's position on Nigeria at times appeared confused and directionless. In March 1998, for example, in advance of President Clinton's trip to Africa, Assistant Secretary of State for African Affairs Susan Rice stated that "electoral victory by any military candidate in the forthcoming presidential election in Nigeria would be unacceptable." In South Africa, however, Clinton himself stated only that "if Abacha stands, we hope he will stand as a civilian."[540]

Some members of the U.S. Congress tried to play a role in strengthening U.S. policy on Nigeria under the Abacha government. In November 1995, Senator Nancy Kassebaum and Congressman Donald Payne introduced bills (S1419 and HR2697) which would have codified existing sanctions in place, as well as prohibiting any new investment in Nigeria, including in the energy sector, and imposing an asset freeze on members of the Nigerian government, a ban on air links and other measures. Payne's bill was reintroduced in June 1997, and in May 1998, Representatives Donald Payne and Ben Gilman introduced a new bill, (HR3890), and Senator Russell Feingold a companion bill (S2102), which set out benchmarks for the lifting of existing sanctions, although neither included the additional economic measures proposed in the 1995 drafts. Various committees of the Senate and House of Representatives also held hearings on U.S. policy towards Nigeria, at which several Nigerian and U.S. human rights and opposition groups argued in favor of a unilateral oil embargo, opposed by representatives of the administration, the Corporate Council on Africa, and Representative William Jefferson and former Senator Carol Moseley-Braun.

---

[539] The United States extended pre-existing restrictions on military links (which included the termination in July 1993 of all military assistance and training) by banning the sale and repair of military goods. It extended a pre-existing ban on the issue of visas to senior military officers and senior government officials and their families to cover "all military officers and civilians who actively formulate, implement or benefit from policies that impede Nigeria's transition to democracy"; and introduced a requirement that Nigerian government officials visiting the U.N. or international financial institutions in the U.S. remain within twenty-five miles of those organizations. It also stated it would begin consultations immediately on appropriate U.N. measures.

[540] James Rupert, "Clinton Sows Some Confusion on Nigeria Policy," *Washington Post*, March 28, 1998.

Several U.S. cities and counties have adopted resolutions forbidding municipal authorities from purchasing products from Nigeria or from companies that do business in Nigeria.[541] There was also an initiative to introduce legislation for similar sanctions in the Maryland state legislature in March 1998, which was defeated: Deputy Assistant Secretary David Marchick gave testimony on behalf of the Clinton administration opposing the bill. U.S.-based oil companies, including Mobil, Chevron, Texaco, and others, invested in lobbying campaigns against unilateral sanctions by U.S. government institutions, through the Corporate Council on Africa, a coalition of U.S. corporations known as USA Engage, and bilaterally.[542]

With the death of Abacha, the U.S. joined other states and multilateral bodies in welcoming the changes brought by General Abubakar, and Under Secretary of State for Political Affairs Thomas Pickering led a delegation to Abuja (in whose presence MKO Abiola collapsed from a heart attack). Assistant Secretary of Defense for International Security Affairs Franklin D. Kramer visited Nigeria in September 1998; the deputy commander of the U.S. European Command, Admiral Charles Abbot, visited in November. On October 30, 1998, the U.S. joined the E.U. in lifting visa restrictions on the Nigerian military and government. Other sanctions consequent on the denial of counter-narcotics certification under Section 481 of the Foreign Assistance Act, including opposition to loans from development institutions, remain in place, as does the ban on direct air flights to the U.S. due to safety concerns. General Abubakar met with President Clinton in September 1998, while visiting the U.S. to attend the U.N. General Assembly; Special Presidential Envoy for the Promotion of Democracy in Africa Jesse Jackson traveled to Nigeria in November.

Codes of Conduct for Business

There have been few serious attempts by governments where the international oil companies have their headquarters to hold those companies to the same standards outside their jurisdictions as they are obliged to follow under national (or, for example, E.U.) regulations. One of the few statements criticizing the oil companies was made in November 1997 by Dutch minister for development cooperation Jan Pronk, who commented at a seminar that Royal Dutch/Shell had

---

[541] They include: Alameda County, California; Berkeley, California; Oakland, California; St Louis, Missouri; Amherst, Massachusetts; Cambridge, Massachusetts; and New Orleans, Louisiana.

[542] See, for example, Ken Silverstein, "Nigeria Deception," *Multinational Monitor*, January/February 1998, vol. 19, nos. 1 and 2.

"on balance" done too little for the Ogoni during its years of operation in that community. Later, under pressure, he partially retracted the statement, saying that Shell had "taken steps to counter the negative effects of its operations."[543]

Efforts to establish binding codes of conduct for multinationals have been, to date, unsuccessful, although there are a number of voluntary codes proposed by nongovernmental and intergovernmental organizations, and by individual governments. Perhaps most significant of these efforts, because the business sector itself played a role in drafting it, is the ILO Tripartite Declaration of Principles Concerning Multinational Enterprises and Social Policy, adopted by the ILO Governing Body in 1977. The declaration states that "all Parties concerned by this Declaration should respect the sovereign rights of States, obey the national laws and regulations, give due consideration to local practices and respect relevant international standards. They should respect the Universal Declaration of Human Rights and the corresponding International Covenants adopted by the General Assembly of the United Nations as well as the Constitution of the International Labour Organization and its principles according to which freedom of expression and association are essential to sustained progress. They should also honour commitments which they have freely entered into, in conformity with the national law and accepted international obligations."[544] The Organization for Economic Cooperation and Development (OECD) also adopted a Declaration and Guidelines on International Investment for Multinational Enterprises in 1976, since revised several times.

The U.N. Commission on Transnational Corporations, established in 1974, developed a draft U.N. Code of Conduct on Transnational Corporations which was submitted to the U.N. Economic and Social Council (ECOSOC) in 1990, though it has not been adopted by the General Assembly. Paragraph 14 of the draft code provides that "Transnational corporations shall respect human rights and fundamental freedoms in the countries in which they operate. In their social and industrial relations, transnational corporations shall not discriminate on the basis of race, colour, sex, religion, language, social, national and ethnic origin or political or other opinion."[545] In 1994, the Commission on Transnational Corporations was

---

[543] *Het Financieele Dagblad* (Netherlands), November 20, 1997.

[544] Paragraph 8, ILO Document OB Vol.LXI, 1978, Series A, No.1. The ILO is a tripartite organization, with representatives of governments, business, and labor having access to its decision-making organs as members of national delegations.

[545] Negotiations on the code ground to a halt in 1992, opposed by the corporations themselves and by governments from the developed world, due to concerns at lack of protection for intellectual property rights, profit repatriation and expropriation of

moved from its position under ECOSOC to become a commission of the Trade and Development Board, and was renamed the Commission on International Investment and Transnational Corporations, reflecting a shift in emphasis from holding companies accountable for their activities to the promotion of foreign direct investment in developing countries.

Various branches of the U.S. government have taken steps to impose obligations on U.S. businesses operating abroad with respect to human rights, as well as, more commonly, with economic objectives in view. The most significant legislative initiative in this regard was the Comprehensive Anti-Apartheid Act (CAAA) of 1986, since repealed, designed to limit investment in South Africa under the apartheid regime. In 1996, the U.S. passed legislation, partially modeled on the CAAA, giving the president authority to prohibit new investment by U.S. citizens or companies in Burma if the Burmese military government physically harmed, rearrested or exiled opposition leader Aung Sang Suu Kyi, or committed large scale oppression against the political opposition. In May 1995, President Clinton announced a set of "model business principles," a voluntary code of ethics to be used by U.S.-based multinational companies, which supports respect for fundamental human and labor rights, though without sufficient detail as to give clear guidance. There have been discussions about the establishment of an E.U. code of conduct for multinationals, prompted by the European Parliament, but these have yet to lead to any concrete steps.

The OECD adopted on November 21, 1997, a Convention on Combating Bribery of Foreign Public Officials in International Business Transactions, which was signed by the twenty-nine members of the OECD and five other governments (Argentina, Brazil, Bulgaria, Chile and the Slovak Republic). When it comes into force, the convention commits OECD members to "take such measures as may be necessary to establish that it is a criminal offence under its law for any person intentionally to offer, promise or give any undue pecuniary or other advantage, whether directly or through intermediaries, to a foreign public official, for that official or for a third party, in order that the official act or refrain from acting in relation to the performance of public duties, in order to obtain or retain business or other improper advantage in the conduct of international business."[546] In the U.S.,

---

property. See, Barbara A. Frey, "The Legal and Ethical Responsibilities of Transnational Corporations in the Protection of International Human Rights," *Minnesota Journal of Global Trade* (Winter 1997) vol.6, pp.153-188.

[546] Article 1(1) Convention on Combating Bribery of Foreign Public Officials in International Business Transactions, adopted by the Negotiating Conference of the OECD, November 21, 1997. The convention enters into force on the sixtieth day

the Foreign Corrupt Practices Act makes it a crime "to make use of the mails or any means or instrumentality of interstate commerce corruptly in furtherance of an offer, payment, promise to pay, or authorization of the payment of any money, or offer, gift, promise to give, or authorization of the giving of anything of value to any foreign official" for the purposes of influencing any act or decision of a foreign government.[547] Within the E.U., the rules vary, but payment of bribes overseas is generally not illegal and is even tax-deductible in some countries. The E.U. Council of Ministers adopted, in October 1997, a Common Position making provision for member states to support the drawing up of international instruments making bribery of foreign officials a criminal offence.[548]

---

following the date on which five of the ten countries with the largest export shares and which represent by themselves at least 60 percent of the total exports of those ten countries have ratified the convention. The members of the OECD are: the U.S., Germany, Japan, France, the U.K., Italy, Canada, Korea, Netherlands, Belgium, Luxembourg (the ten largest; Belgium and Luxembourg are counted together for export figures), Spain, Switzerland, Sweden, Mexico, Australia, Denmark, Austria, Norway, Ireland, Finland, Poland, Portugal, Turkey, Hungary, New Zealand, the Czech Republic, Greece, and Iceland.

[547] Foreign Corrupt Practices Act of 1977, section 30A(a).

[548] In May 1997, the European Council adopted a Convention on the Fight against Corruption Involving Officials of the European Communities or Officials of Member States of the European Union, which establishes a commitment by member states of the E.U. to take necessary measures to make bribery a criminal offence at national level, but the convention does not apply outside the E.U.

XII. CONCLUSION

The oil companies and the communities they operate in occupy two different worlds, geographically overlapping but conceptually light-years apart. The oil companies see themselves as carrying out a legitimate business, which makes a major contribution to the Nigerian economy. They regret, at least officially, the lack of democracy in Nigeria, the abuses carried out against the oil producing communities by the security forces, and the failure of the Nigerian government to spend the oil wealth wisely, in particular in the oil producing communities themselves, but represent these problems as essentially nothing to do with the commercial companies that produce the oil. Nevertheless, as a gesture of goodwill, as they would see it, and in partial recognition of the deficiencies of the Nigerian government, they invest substantial amounts of money in development projects in the communities where they operate. While they admit there are some negative environmental consequences of oil production, the oil companies argue that these are both exaggerated and in any event entirely outweighed by the benefits they bring. Despite this contribution, oil company managers state that they operate in Nigeria in a thankless, even hostile political environment. Although their relations with the federal government have recently improved, they still face difficulties in obtaining payment of the sums due to them under their joint ventures. Furthermore, oil company personnel state that they see no reason why they should answer to the communities in which they work, when they are simply carrying out their normal activities, for which they have received government licenses. They view community protests as unrealistic demands on them to take on responsibilities that are properly the domain of the government, protests which at times amount to simple criminal extortion, sabotage, or intimidation.

For the communities, on the other hand, the oil companies and their contractors are often the most visible manifestation of central government in their areas. They know that the oil companies are operating joint ventures with the government; they see the oil installations guarded by federal police or soldiers, and the rapid response from the federal or state government if there is any threat to oil production. They draw the conclusion that the oil companies and the government are so closely linked as to be effectively the same thing, an idea backed by the government's own comments. They accordingly make their demands for greater revenue allocation to the delta—as well as for compensation for the damage wrought by oil production—of the oil companies as they do of the government, and blame the oil companies as they do the government for the repression with which their demands are met. The communities are well aware that the oil companies are making large profits out of what they see as "their" oil, and believe that these profits bring with them responsibilities towards the traditional landholders. At the same time, they see that a few individuals in their communities, the contractors and traditional rulers, have profited handsomely from oil production—during the same period that land has become less fertile and fish catches declined. Communities want compensation for loss of livelihood caused by land expropriations, oil spills, and other effects of oil production, yet find themselves forced to accept assessments of compensation valued by the oil companies themselves, with no meaningful way of obtaining an independent determination of their loss. The few school blocks and unfinished water schemes do not satisfy their view of what an "oil producing community" should look like. In these circumstances, while most requests for compensation or assistance are settled peacefully, even if not to the satisfaction of all sides, community members do sometimes resort to actions such as shutting down flowstations, taking hostages, or committing criminal damage—actions they regard as political statements of their right to participate in the prosperity currently restricted to a small elite.

In the face of the threat to oil production caused by some of these protests, the Nigerian government has created a number of special task forces handling security in the oil producing areas, of which the most notorious and brutal is the Rivers State Internal Security Task Force, created in response to the Ogoni crisis. While the Internal Security Task Force has been recalled to barracks, the paramilitary Mobile Police remain deployed in the delta, as throughout Nigeria; Operation Flush and Operation Salvage, anti-crime forces created in Rivers and Bayelsa States, are still in operation; and the navy is used to maintain order in the riverine areas. The oil companies operating in Nigeria also hire "supernumerary police," recruited and trained by the Nigerian police force, but paid for by the oil companies; as well as private firms for routine security provision at entrance barriers and other duties at their premises, and local "guards" from among landholders across whose land pipelines run or where other facilities are built.

Nigeria's new head of state, Gen. Abdulsalami Abubakar, has greatly reduced the repression enforced by his predecessor, Gen. Sani Abacha, who died in June 1998, releasing many political prisoners and relaxing restrictions on freedom of expression, assembly and association. Nevertheless, the response of the security forces to threats to oil production continues to be heavy handed, and in the oil regions human and environmental rights activists report little change. As in the past, there continue to be incidents in which the paramilitary Mobile Police, the regular police, or the army, have beaten, detained, or even killed those involved in protests, peaceful or otherwise, or individuals who have called for compensation for oil damage, whether youths, women, children, or traditional leaders. In some cases, members of the community are beaten or detained indiscriminately, irrespective of their role in any protest. The decrees are still in force that allow detention without trial and establish special tribunals to try cases of "civil disturbances" or sabotage without due process protections.

There can be no solution to the simmering conflict in the oil producing areas of the delta until its people gain the right to participate in their own governance and until the protection of the rule of law is extended to their communities. The injustices facing the peoples of the delta are in many ways the same as those facing all Nigerians after decades of rule by successive military regimes, yet in the oil producing regions the suppression of political activity, the lack of legal redress for damage to the environment and the resulting loss of livelihood, and the sheer ubiquity of human rights abuses by the region's security forces have generated greater protest, in turn generating greater repression.

The first responsibility for resolving these injustices lies with the Nigerian government. Yet the multinational oil companies operating in Nigeria cannot avoid their own share of responsibility. It is not enough simply to say that the political environment in Nigeria is as difficult for the oil companies as it is for anyone else, and that the oil industry does not have the power to alter government policy towards the oil regions: the oil companies in many respects contribute towards the discontent in the delta and to conflict within and between communities that results in repressive government responses. Companies have a duty to avoid both complicity and advantage from human rights abuses: the oil companies in Nigeria must take all steps to ensure that oil production does not continue at the cost of their host communities simply because of the threat or actual use of force against those who protest their activities.